Homes at Work

Following the outbreak of the COVID-19 pandemic, working from home became a global phenomenon, yet before 2020, it was a relatively under-studied practice. But in informal settlements, the definition of "home" and "employment" is completely intertwined, which is why there is so much to learn from them. For over half a century, mainstream theoretical approaches to urban informality, dominated by development economics, often fail to see this economic and spatial phenomenon jointly. Labor studies tend to be space-blind and spatial studies often disregard informal employment. Profoundly interdisciplinary, this work connects scholarship in development, public policy, labor studies, and feminist economics, with that in urban studies, planning, housing, architecture, and visual studies.

The book walks the reader behind the closed doors of working homes that make the fabric, both social and economic, of most cities. It applies a visual methodology to reveal their "space-use intensity" and quantify the extent to which houses in informal settlements fill their inner pores with economic activity and community services. The research also revisits urban formalization policies in Latin America and Africa, to uncover a fallacious politics of recognition. It ultimately argues for a recognition continuum: an approach to urban informality that is more practical and fairer.

The book is of interest to development economists, urban scholars, public policy specialists, time-use researchers, and architects working on housing, employment generation, urban livelihoods, gender studies, and related topics.

María Carrizosa is Assistant Director of the Observatory on Latin America at The New School University, New York, and Adjunct Associate Professor of Architecture at City College of New York, USA.

Routledge Advances in Regional Economics, Science and Policy

Urban Change in Central Europe
The Case of Kraków
Jacek Purchla

Clusters and Sustainable Regional Development
A Meta-Organisational Approach
Evgeniya Lupova-Henry and Nicola Francesco Dotti

The Economics of Affordable Housing
Alexander Styhre

The Cultural Sector and Sustainable Economic Development
Innovation and the Creative Economy in European Cities
Biljana Mickov

Evolutionary Urban Development
Lessons from Central and Eastern Europe
Katarzyna Sadowy

The Rural to Urban Transition in Developing Countries
Urbanisation and Peri-Urban Land Markets
Amrutha Mary Varkey

Urban Heritage in Europe
Economic and Social Revival
Edited by Gábor Sonkoly

Homes at Work
Urban Informality and Recognition in Latin America and Africa
María Carrizosa

For more information about this series, please visit: www.routledge.com/
series/RAIRESP

Homes at Work
Urban Informality and Recognition
in Latin America and Africa

María Carrizosa

LONDON AND NEW YORK

First published 2023
by Routledge
4 Park Square, Milton Park, Abingdon, Oxon OX14 4RN

and by Routledge
605 Third Avenue, New York, NY 10158

Routledge is an imprint of the Taylor & Francis Group, an informa business

© 2023 María Carrizosa

The right of María Carrizosa to be identified as author of this work
has been asserted in accordance with sections 77 and 78 of the
Copyright, Designs and Patents Act 1988.

All rights reserved. No part of this book may be reprinted or
reproduced or utilised in any form or by any electronic, mechanical,
or other means, now known or hereafter invented, including
photocopying and recording, or in any information storage or
retrieval system, without permission in writing from the publishers.

Trademark notice: Product or corporate names may be trademarks
or registered trademarks, and are used only for identification and
explanation without intent to infringe.

Every effort has been made to contact copyright-holders to obtain
their permission for the use of copyrighted material. Please advise
the publisher of any errors or omissions, and these will be corrected
in subsequent editions.

British Library Cataloguing-in-Publication Data
A catalogue record for this book is available from the British Library

Library of Congress Cataloging-in-Publication Data
Names: Carrizosa, María, author.
Title: Homes at work : urban informality and recognition in Latin
America and Africa / María Carrizosa.
Description: Abingdon, Oxon ; New York, NY : Routledge, 2023. |
Series: Routledge advances in regional economics, science and policy |
Includes bibliographical references and index.
Identifiers: LCCN 2022056520 (print) | LCCN 2022056521 (ebook) |
ISBN 9781032286235 (hardback) | ISBN 9781032286259 (paperback) |
ISBN 9781003297727 (ebook)
Subjects: LCSH: Informal sector (Economics)—Latin America. |
Informal sector (Economics)—Africa. | Squatter settlements—
Latin America. | Squatter settlements—Africa.
Classification: LCC HD2346.5 .C37 2023 (print) |
LCC HD2346.5 (ebook) | DDC 330—dc23/eng/20221208
LC record available at https://lccn.loc.gov/2022056520
LC ebook record available at https://lccn.loc.gov/2022056521

ISBN: 978-1-032-28623-5 (hbk)
ISBN: 978-1-032-28625-9 (pbk)
ISBN: 978-1-003-29772-7 (ebk)

DOI: 10.4324/9781003297727

Typeset in Bembo
by codeMantra

For well-tempered tentacles

Contents

Acknowledgements	xi
List of figures	xiii
List of tables	xvii

1 Introduction   1
1.1 *Working homes today 3*
1.2 *The meaning of "Homes at Work" 5*
1.3 *Roadmap through the book 6*

**2 Urban informality: mainstream theories and
visible alternatives**   9
2.1 *The history of informality at the International
Labor Organization 10*
    2.1.1 The Comprehensive Employment Mission 11
    2.1.2 The World Employment Program 13
    2.1.3 The Delhi Group on Informal Sector Statistics 16
    2.1.4 Women and Men in the Informal Economy:
        A statistical picture 22
2.2 *Schools of thought on informality 23*
    2.2.1 Dualism 24
    2.2.2 Structuralism 29
    2.2.3 Legalism 34
    2.2.4 Voluntarism 39
    2.2.5 Continuum 44
2.3 *Time-use makes the invisible visible 48*
    2.3.1 Time-use and household economics 48
    2.3.2 Time-use surveying techniques to grasp multitasking 50
2.4 *The place of space in the theories of informality: two examples
from architecture 53*
    2.4.1 Learning from Lagos 53
    2.4.2 Samper's doctrine: standardization for desegregation
        and the wealth of the poor 56

viii   *Contents*

3   Space-use intensity in informal settlements in Bogotá   71

   3.1 Defining space-use intensity 71
      3.1.1 Jacobs' mixed-use 71
      3.1.2 Mixed-use mix-ups 74
      3.1.3 Origin and components of space-use intensity 80
   3.2 Documenting space-use intensity 82
      3.2.1 Getting inside: Access and sampling 82
      3.2.2 What to look for and how: Data collection tools and
         data analysis procedures 87
      3.2.3 Five house-stories: from narratives to diagrams 93
   3.3 Explaining space-use intensity: discreteness and non-porousness 112
      3.3.1 Intensity as the count of discrete uses 112
      3.3.2 Cadastral knowledge 119
      3.3.3 Intensity as the opposite of porosity 120

4   The politics of urban formalization in Bogotá   126

   4.1 Formalization has its origins in the South 126
      4.1.1 Self-help predates Turner 127
      4.1.2 Shelved worldly plans and the unspoken centrality of
         informality 128
      4.1.3 Pirate urbanizers: champions of gray 129
   4.2 From plan-based to code-base planning 132
      4.2.1 Competing with informality 132
      4.2.2 Urban treatments (1979): a second-level zoning 133
      4.2.3 Upgrading is a leaky bucket 136
   4.3 De-politicization and technification of formalization policy 137
      4.3.1 The rise and fall of the housing movement in Colombia 137
      4.3.2 The technical mechanics of formalization in Bogotá 138
      4.3.3 The impossible story of Carmen and the demiurge 141
      4.3.4 After the physical, the economical: business formalization 144
      4.3.5 To subdivide is to formalize 145
      4.3.6 Upgrading, an impossible stair 147
   4.4 The actual purpose of formalization: practical outcomes of recognition 148
      4.4.1 Formalization creates fiscal legibility 148
      4.4.2 Stratification: naturalizations and disincentives 149
      4.4.3 Subdivision, the key from residential to social mobility 151
      4.4.4 The incomplete shift away from code-based planning 152
   4.5 Beyond recognition 153
      4.5.1 Cosmetic upgrading and false recognition 153
      4.5.2 True recognition: remuneration and redistribution 154
      4.5.3 Notes on the philosophy of recognition 156

Contents ix

5 Space-use intensity and urban formalization in African cities 164

5.1 *Background of the study 164*
    5.1.1 Note on the research setup 164
    5.1.2 Note on urban informality in Africa 165
5.2 *House interviews in Kampala, Dar es Salaam, and Dakar 166*
    5.2.1 Agnes's house in Kampala 167
    5.2.2 Neema's house in Dar es Salaam 169
    5.2.3 Traoré's house in Dakar 171
5.3 *Space-use intensity findings across African cities 173*
5.4 *African insights on formalization 178*
    5.4.1 Framing informality 179
    5.4.2 Housing policy needs alternate housing vocabularies: nyumba(ni) and (ma)kazi 186
    5.4.3 Dealing with informality 187
    5.4.4 Can formalization of horizontal property make taxation fair? 190
    5.4.5 Policy should include people's co-production of urban services, goods, and social protections 192

6 Conclusions. Abling intensity: extraction, porosity, and the recognition continuum 197

6.1 *Visual research: data excavation from photographs and conceptual maps 198*
6.2 *Porosity and value creation: counting more than the sum of its parts 206*
6.3 *Imposed disability: the violence of remaining stratified and unrequited 209*
6.4 *Formalization: rather than integration, a recognition continuum 212*

Index 221

Acknowledgements

Research can be so gruesomely lonely that the helping hands along the way are a real treasure. I acknowledge many with gratitude. First, my mentor Michael Cohen who saw this book in my future a decade ago and has since remained a daily inspiration. I thank Victoria Hattam for encouraging me to stay true to myself to the bone and showing me a path to political aesthetics. I thank Georgia Traganou for seeing my project through me and treating me as a colleague when I did not feel like such. I thank Juan John Giraldo for his invaluable friendship and for having taken me by the hand and walked me into the fascinating streets of Patio Bonito and the home of his friends. I thank Lucila Rueda whose delicate tenacity is, like her crystal glass cups, forever engraved in my heart. I thank Marlén López who so generously helped tune in with her reasoning, and whose patience and savviness continue to teach me lessons. I thank Susana Chocontá who by hosting me for a night with unrelenting love, helped me see the unseen. I thank Alex Cedaño who understood so well what I needed to see and rode me in the back of his motorbike to teach me about his world. I thank Martha Bahamón who with boundless generosity, professionalism, and care taught me the intricacies of Bogota's urban regulations. I thank Ximena Samper whose trust, friendship, and encouragement continue to make fruitful so many of my adventures. I thank Angélica Camargo whose down-to-earth clairvoyance I will always admire, and because reading her dissertation helped me find the courage to write mine. I thank Alejandro Florián, my adopted mentor; every conversation and exchange we have is a gift of life that I treasure. I thank Jorge Torres who, because of our conversations, coming from his profound and extensive experience, gave me confidence and reassurance. I thank Lina Maria Botero whose unique expertise I admire and whose upbeat collegiality I treasure. I thank Aureliano Amaya whose research inspired me from the distance. I thank Johnny Tascón whose X-ray view of cadasters helped me close an open arc in my research. I thank Federico Parra with admiration for his brilliance, precision, and unwavering commitment to the service providers he works with. I thank Olga Ceballos who listened to me with such care that she did an unexpected interview for me. I thank Hernando Carvajalino for igniting my lifelong passion with his book *La espacialidad de la periferia*. GIDEST

xii *Acknowledgements*

where I had the most intellectually fascinating year at The New School. I thank Ofronoma Biu who taught me not to make my race invisible; I am proud to have walked this path alongside you. Bastian Schultz for giving me an ideal platform to test my approach in Africa and broaden the scope of this research. I thank Elisabeth Bollrich for giving me the honor of sharing a working space with distinguished Tanzanian housing experts, especially Tatu M. Limbumba, Tumsifu Jonas Nnkya, Albert Nyiti, Felician Komu, and Tim Ndezi. I thank Hafisa Namuli for her intelligence and determination pioneered the replication study. I thank Teddy Kisembo for her professionalism, flexibility, and follow-through. I thank Imma Kapinga because her photos and fieldnotes transport the reader to the core of Dar. I thank Amadou Ndiaye whose journalistic mind connected so well with the approach, dissolving the language barriers. I thank my father, Ricardo Carrizosa, for countless contributions to my process and the many ways in which your spirit is present in my thinking. I thank Amparo González for her loving support in my lone rambles and receiving her admiration is humbling and soul-filling. I also thank all my students who teach me new things every day, pushing me to be my best myself. Finally, I thank my husband and chief editor Juan who earned the doctorate and turned into a feminist alongside me.

Figures

2.1	Conceptual framework for informal employment	19
2.2	Expanded conceptual framework for the informal employment	20
2.3	Conceptual map of ILO's statistical definitions on informality	21
2.4	Overview of the schools of thought on informality	24
2.5	Structuralist definition of informal economy	31
2.6	Formalization steps for housing in Peru	35
2.7	Composition of the Indian informal economy in 2010	44
2.8	Chronological overview of the schools of thought on informality	48
2.9	Images from the first image-supported time-use survey. The wearable camera on adjustable lanyard (left). Sample of participants Autographer images from the pilot study (right)	50
2.10	Visualization comparing activities of each participant ($n = 14$) as recorded in the diary and those in the photographs	51
2.11	Marylin Waring compares gendered time-use data from a village in Pakistan (*Who's Counting? Marilyn Waring on Sex, Lies and Global Economics* (1995))	52
2.12	Tracing and labeling (by author) of a photograph by Koolhaas/OMA (1997) in Michael (2016) showing order in a Lagos informal market	54
2.13	Seven unpublished books finished by Rem Koolhaas and Kunle Adeyemi and Harvard University	55
2.14	Inward and outward research gaze	57
2.15	The social pyramid in Latin America	58
2.16	Bogotá's institutionalized spatial segregation by density in Accord 65 of 1967	59
2.17	Housing supply by explosion (new settlements) and implosion (sublets and tenements)	60
2.18	To quantify space is the link between research and policy: The transformative urban policy of the Minimal Rules	61
3.1	Common problems of land-use mix measures	76
3.2	Coding uses along a primary Live/Work/Visit triangle	77
3.3	Functional Mix in Manhattan (left) and Bogotá (right)	78
3.4	Diagram of the mix of mixes in each hectare	78

xiv *Figures*

3.5	Horizontal mixed-use and vertical mixed-use	79
3.6	Subtypes of informal settlements in Latin America and choice of this research's focus	85
3.7	Localization of house interviews on Bogotá's (2017) stratification map by the author based on SDP (2017)	88
3.8	Sample of notebook jottings with schematic layouts of house #13	89
3.9	Cross-sectional diagram of observed uses in house #6	90
3.10	Photograph of the patio in house #7	91
3.11	Visual record house #15	92
3.12	A corner of the commercial street in Patio Bonito (left) and Aures II (right)	93
3.13	Lucy's houses in Patio Bonito: Current state of former house (left), secondary house (center), and Lucy's home (right)	96
3.14	Lucy's glass engraving table (left), access to rented rooftop (center), and Leo's room and wood workshop	96
3.15	Lucy's home (center) and next-door neighbors (left and right)	97
3.16	Cross-sectional diagrams of cadastral and observed uses Lucy's house (#13)	98
3.17	Susy's apartment in Aures: Outside view (left), room (center), and kitchen (right)	99
3.18	Non-residential uses in Susy's house: Rotisserie (left), insurance office (center), and soapmaking laboratory (right)	100
3.19	Cross-sectional diagrams of cadastral and observed uses in Susy's house (#1)	101
3.20	Ana's catering business: Packing area (left), main kitchen (center), and Ana's room (right)	103
3.21	Ana's home-business: night street view (left), street (center), and produce shop and butchery across the street (right)	104
3.22	Cross-sectional diagrams of cadastral and observed uses in Ana's house (#2)	105
3.23	Rosa's home: inverted ziggurat streetscape (left), entrance (center), and access to second floor (right)	106
3.24	Rosa's social area (left), custom-made cabinet by kitchen (center), and vinyl butterflies' wall decor (right)	107
3.25	Cross-sectional diagrams of cadastral and observed uses in Rosa's house (#16)	108
3.26	Alba's house in Caracoli: façade (left), street (center), and training school for security guards on nearby corner	109
3.27	Alba's room (left), corridor and gym (center), and kitchen (right)	110
3.28	Social cleansing threat in Caracoli circulating on WhatsApp	111
3.29	Cross-sectional diagrams of cadastral and observed uses in Alba's house (#7)	111
3.30	Summary of cross-sectional diagrams of observed uses	113

3.31	First residential use–unit as share of total discrete uses	117
3.32	Count of discrete uses by use types and use-units	117
3.33	Relationship between discrete uses and area-based measures	117
4.1	Wedding of the daughter of Forero Fetecua (far left) attended by President Michelsen (far right)	131
4.2	Map of formalization paths for different types of settlements	133
4.3	Mapping upgrading as one of five types of urban treatments	134
4.4	Dynamics of the conservation treatment from 1900 to 2000	135
4.5	Visual map of urban formalization policy in Bogotá: Steps, phases, and realms	140
4.6	Snapshot of a section of Bogotá's 1990 zoning (left) and its map legend (right)	142
4.7	Map legend to annex of Accord 7 of 1979. Land-use classification by activity areas (left) and Criteria for land-use classification in types and groups (right)	142
4.8	The formalization path from upgrading to recognition does not empower	147
4.9	Cross-subsidization in Bogotá: Contributions and tariff reductions by strata	149
4.10	The Butterfly (La Mariposa) HabitArte upgrading program in Usaquén	153
5.1	Agnes' house in Rubaga, Kampala	167
5.2	Some uses in the front of Agnes's home: vegetable and cooking stoves stall (left), shoe shop (center), and briquettes for sale (right)	168
5.3	Some uses in the back: briquettes machine (left), water tap (center), and toilet stalls (right)	168
5.4	Visual record of observed uses in Agnes' house	169
5.5	Neema's room in Ubungo, Dar es Salaam	170
5.6	Neema making spices next to stored metal (left), shops from tenants (center), sports betting stall (right)	170
5.7	Visual record of observed uses in Neema's house	171
5.8	Traoré's house in Grand Yoff	171
5.9	Traoré's family room of four (left), the corridor/guesthouse (center), and the open-air stairs in the kitchen (right)	172
5.10	Sheep enclosures (left), food containers and drying clothes (center), sheep's waste recycling (right)	172
5.11	Visual record of observed uses in Traoré's house	173
5.12	Visual summary of the 12 house interviews in African cities	174
5.13	Space-use intensity data from house interviews in Kampala, Dar es Salaam, and Dakar	177
5.14	Swahili word for settlement is more closely related to the word work than to the house	186
6.1	Visualization of the continuum between informal and formal	201
6.2	Alternative thinking on urban informality	206

Tables

3.1	List of house interviews and key sample characteristics	87
3.2	Emerging categories summary table	92
3.3	Descriptive statistics of space-use intensity variables	114
4.1	Rough cost estimate of subdividing an informal mixed-used four-story building in Bogotá in 2019	146
5.1	List of space-use intensity variables from house interviews comparing averages across cities	176

1 Introduction

Ideas are products of their time, which is why as time passes and new facts emerge, concepts need reinterpretations and precisions. Time changes ideas. And in the same vein, space shapes ideas. Mine is a story about such changes in the idea of informality. Even if official data lags behind the real world, it is now undeniable that more than half the world is urban, more than half the world works informally, more than half the world lives in countries of the South (even without counting the vast South within the North), and more than half the South's cities grow informally. Urban informality is normal. That urban informality is globally predominant is an uncomfortable fact that poses unavoidable challenges not only in pragmatic terms but, more acutely, in theoretical terms. Deep-seated assumptions guiding policies around the world are called into question. Such a task requires a keen ear to what has already been thought and an open mind to more adventurous cross-disciplinary approaches. It also requires open eyes and an open heart. The work I present here is part of such an attempt.

The "informal" concept was born in the seventies, in African cities, when the world was not urban. But soon after the turn of the century, in 2008 the urban demographic transition took hold and cities became humans' most typical habitat. The half a century since the early days of the concept has been one of intense city-making. Like a wave, urbanization spikes have traversed the globe, and in these 50 years, the equivalent of a new city of a million people got built every week. The urban transition is broadly felt and well discussed. But a far less frequent acknowledgment is the informal transition, which could have been simultaneous to the urban one, and is likely part of the very same phenomenon. Despite all prognoses and efforts, the world has seen an increased informalization of labor. Over 60% of the workers in the world today are informal (ILO, 2018). The calculated estimate from 2018 is consistent with informed guesses by experts declaring that the share of informal built areas in the global South is over 50% (Bredenoord et al., 2014), and that the share of self-built homes in the North is not insignificant and in fact growing (Duncan and Rowe, 1993; Benson and Hamiduddin, 2017). It is no surprise that the notion of urban informality gained traction alongside the urban transition.

DOI: 10.4324/9781003297727-1

2   *Introduction*

Cities house the majority and cities are being made and remade by the majority every day. Urban informality is a city-making way of living for the majority. Yet, the large portion of cities built informally are an eyesore for far too many people. These are hard to look at parts of our cities. Perhaps, it is because these are spaces that do not sit well with our learned definitions. There is nothing wrong with these places even if they are lacking in many respects, it is our ideas of them that are incomplete. It is our inner moral compasses and the eyes of our minds that need to learn to see better what is laying bare all around us.

Keith Hart, the self-described broker between economics and anthropology, who coined the term "informal" and who wanted "to change both disciplines by synthesizing them" (Hart, 2011), has had a rough time grappling with his conceptual creation. Forty years after introducing it, he called it a "monster" responsible for "retarding our understanding of development" (Hart, 2010: 380). Later still, in a candid reflection of his dissertation fieldwork, he admitted that it was only because he started an informal business of his own in a slum in Accra that he was able to understand informality at all (Hart, 2017). Hart's gradual coming to grips with the informal is symptomatic. It is an indication of the way concepts are lenses that help us see—or blur—what we have in front of our eyes, how one's own experience is a spheric horizon of thought, and how time dents into the unseen.

At the onset of my research path, I had a hunch that doctoral work resembled a psychoanalysis, a long process of unearthing unconscious ideas with a luminous therapeutic outcome. In many ways, this early intuition—like a self-fulfilling prophecy—turned out to be correct. As a student I resembled, like so many, a tangled-up bundle of conjoined aesthetical and intellectual passions, striving to conquer the clarity, patience, and stature of an expert. Looking back this lone path is now traversed, and as months pile up into years, it becomes clear how the research lingers after it is "finished," because research is for some of us a way of being in the world. I also realize that indeed a Ph.D., or at least mine, was my earnt psychoanalysis. A personal deep dive into unintentional, unconscious, and forgotten materials, and a slow rise into awareness that brings clarity, strength, and health.

It is not a coincidence that 20 years ago, fresh out of the architecture bachelor and amidst writing my thesis to earn a bachelor's in philosophy, I was also delving into psychoanalysis. At that time the focus was on the need, possibilities, and limitations of extending psychoanalysis to the social realm, following a friendly debate between Hans Georg Gadamer and Jurgen Habermas (master and pupil) on this matter (Carrizosa, 2003). My interest in this philosophical curiosity was motivated by a frustration with the limits of architecture and urbanism dealing with informal settlements. Naïve, insecure, and devoid of enough language tools, I dared only to flesh out the link between my philosophical and urban musings in a set of footnotes. I was most alive in those footnotes. My raw self dared not to occupy the page. I was in the margins like the parts of the city that I wanted to research, wrongly called "marginality." I believed then as I do now that urban development is also determined by neglected city-making events that are brought into conscience. The research into urban informality I present here is nothing different than another attempt to continue this psychoanalytic effort, a conviction that better knowledge and awareness of it will bring clarity, strength, and health.

The reader might have guessed that my relative academic versatility, born out of the uncommon epistemological experiment of being formed in architecture and philosophy simultaneously, did not come without a feeling of disciplinary homelessness. My need to feel at home in some disciplinary realm was paired with a resistance to being fixed to a single one. The tension only began to ease once I gained the courage to build a shack of my own, encroaching the interstices between architecture, planning, development, anthropology, sociology, geography, and economics. This book is about me building my own home. I did it by crafting a conceptual tool (the term space-use intensity) and an innovative visual methodology.

The term space-use intensity transposes to spatial studies some methodological victories gained by time-use studies in macroeconomics. Hence, it fluctuates between the desire to speak the language of those that dominate the narrative, and an ironclad conviction that their relatively space-blind approach is inappropriate. "Space-use intensity" owes much to feminist economists, and their continued battles to rebuild their discipline from within the belly of the beast. On the other hand, with regard to the visuality of my research process, I warn that I deem visualizing complex data and pouring over visual information a high-level task of synthesis, not of stylization. Perhaps I am a frustrated graphic designer, too cerebral to blend into a joyful life only of colors and shapes. However, in this craft I follow quite closely the dogmatic approach of Edward Tufte: "clarity and excellence in thinking is much like clarity in the display of data. When principles of design replicate principles of thought, the act of arranging information becomes an act of insight" (Tufte, 1997:9). In my research, visuals help see urban informality in a new light in such a way, I hope, that the insights gained cannot be undone. Once seen, the city-making of the majority cannot be unseen.

1.1 Working homes today

The pandemic dislocated time and locked us in space. By disrupting our human experience of time-space, it inevitably forced profound reflections about how we live and work, about what we deem necessary, and what should be the new normal. A hinge moment, the pandemic is also a test of sorts. Like the contrast medium in an X-ray that colors tissues so they can be seen, the lockdown exposed what is truly essential for our city-life: food

4   *Introduction*

distribution, waste removal, safe breathing[1] air, and unquestionably, a home. Keeping ourselves healthy and protecting our communities, meant staying inside our houses. This public health mandate strikingly reveals the obvious, that homes are a crucial component of the public health infrastructure. Throughout the pandemic, houses around the world held much more than just residential functions, they absorbed a wide range of activities.

But long before the virus sent the world to work from home, houses were used like this by millions working informally. "Home-based enterprises" is the proper phrase for one of the three occupational subgroups of informal employment (alongside the more visible street vendors and waste pickers), a field of study that passed from understudied to over-experienced as the pandemic stroke. All of a sudden, on March 11, 2020, with the declaration of the World Health Organization, a research area that was far from the spotlight, the economic use of space within homes, became a universally relevant. In lockdown, the relationship between private and public was put on its head, and the home became more public than it ever was, broadcasted in live video feeds on private screens for virtual strangers to see. More importantly, the home became part of the work infrastructure, and its role as a social protection measure became evident: the better the home, the better the social protection, and the higher the chances of dealing better with the crisis at hand.

As an optimist, I would like to believe that the pandemic should be a portal to something new, a marker in history that can shape a before and after. The "after" ought to be grounded in reimaginations of the world we want to live in. Without deep thinking, without better visions and aspirations, a window of opportunity that opened will close again reinforcing previous patterns, "dragging the carcasses of our prejudice and hatred, our avarice, our data banks and dead ideas, our dead rivers and smoky skies" (Roy, 2020). It is not enough to claim radical changes; ambitious alternatives must be detailed if they are ever to become real. The knowledge to rebuild anew is slightly less urgent than the courage to stomach the specific reality of the majorities. More pressing still is the moral imperative "to test out urban policies we have never had the will or the necessity to imagine, much less implement" (Sassen and Ratti, 2021). Sassen, the pioneer scholar of global cities, invites to revisit Lefebvre's now nauseously eminent 1968's "right to the city" principle with its counterpoint: the "duty to the city." The post-pandemic urban imperative is to connect rights to duties, acknowledge that there is no taking without giving, for our duties and rights are connected.

Responsible for 80% of the world's economic health (World Bank, 2020), cities require no less. The duty to the city is defined quite succinctly as the

---

1 Amidst the Severe Acute Respiratory Syndrome (SARS-CoV-2), or as it became called Covid-19, the words "I can't breathe", handwritten on face masks worn by countless Black Lives Matter demonstrators, echoing George Floyd's last words, have forever tinted the verb "breathe".

mandate—for owners and tenants—not to leave any property empty: to use it (Sassen and Ratti, 2021). Intense use of space guards against decaying ghost towns. Boarded shops, empty offices, vacant lots, and unoccupied luxury apartments, draw the life out of neighborhoods. Not letting your property sit empty is a way of respecting the part of the city it stands on, playing a part in its livability. "Of course, the definition of what it means to 'use' a property is not clear cut, especially in an era of remote working, when occupancy is increasingly time-based. To make our policies more adaptable to these variable uses, we could leverage new digital tools. The platforms of the 21st century could help monitor dynamic occupancy, impose fines and implement inclusive housing policies over time" (Sassen and Ratti, 2021). Without embracing this novel proposal too swiftly, I second that it places the right and the duty to the city along a continuum, where the role of progressive policies is to define the break line between giving and taking, fine tune the gradients in between and update it regularly. Policy analysts know how extraordinary and how potent policy windows are. Whenever they open, it is imperative to take advantage of them. The pandemic's out-of-joint opportunity is to—as Sassen and many others aptly call for—rewrite the urban social contract.

1.2 The meaning of "Homes at Work"

The title of the book "Homes at Work" not only refers to people that work from home in the sense that the house becomes the workplace. More than about working from home, this book is about homes that play functions of work, it is about houses that are put to work. To explore this difference, it is useful to consider at least four different connotations of working homes that account for the interconnectedness between "home" and "work." The first and most obvious is to "work at home," that is, people perform their work at the place where they live. Here, the domestic space is the site of economic production, much like what so many experienced during the pandemic, and also much like the craftspeople's cottages were in the pre-industrial economy.

The second conception can be referred to as "working on home," or simply making home, highlighting the labor of making homes work. In this connotation the home is the center of all care work and reproductive labor, nurturing or not. In this sense, homes are not only the *place* of work but the *object* of work. Functioning homes require permanent work to actually perform as homes instead of being just houses, empty receptacles of activities. The domestic is not passive nor actionless, but a constant activity and effort, to home is to work. Feminist efforts tackle the contradictory fact that despite its importance, this type of homework goes unnoticed and unpaid, and remains largely undervalued. In both these notions: "working at home" and "working on home," the home is the workplace. That residential spaces are at the same time places of economic production and social reproduction is significant, but it is only part of the story that I tell here.

6   *Introduction*

There is another connotation of "homes at work" that emphasizes how houses perform economic and social functions themselves. In these cases, the phrase "homes at work" refers to the fact that the home is itself doing work, is being put to work, or in other words "homes *do* work." Here, the connection between "home" and "work" is more structural, and the roles of the noun, adjective, and (participle) are more blurred still. In this third connotation, houses are not just things or commodities themselves, but also capital goods. Homes are assets utilized to manufacture and transform other goods to be sold in the market (Dolinga and Arundel, 2022). This way in which homes are at work is particularly relevant for self-build houses that are built incrementally and expand. These houses, like land itself, are the utmost urban factor of production. Houses of progressive development are capital assets that render revenue and can be put to work again and again.

Finally, the fourth connotation of "homes at work" is the least explored, yet it is perhaps more promising.

Here, by virtue of the ways in which people use houses (especially informal ones), homes offer not only income but also benefits and protections akin to those of formal employment: pension, unemployment, severance, and the like. In this notion of "homes at work," "homes *are* work." The house gives its dwellers what a full employment would: income, plus fringe protections and benefits. A home at work, like the (often missing) employer, gives salary and other compensations to its residents, and in this sense, it is a physical expression of employment. Understanding that housing plays social protection roles is for many a simple fact of life. But homes at work with more intense uses, especially economic uses, offer more protections to their residents in times of need, acting exactly as social insurance: as a source of life insurance in times of death, severance or unemployment payments, and the like.

It does take some degree of intellectual flexibility to understand that social protections can take many forms and that some of those forms can be spatialized, even photographed, if one dares to look close enough. But at the same time, using their spaces as social protection is just a natural way of getting by in the city, and in fact, the notion that housing is used as a pension, and old-age security and fundamental patrimony to leave one's offspring, is connatural to urban development, a widespread practice across the social spectrum.

The research in this book reveals how, in informal settlements, the definitions of what a house is and what employment is, are so intimately connected, that in fact they cannot be separated. This book will make the case a house is not a house, any more than work is not (formal) work. Working *at* home, working *on* home, *a* working home, and a home that *is* work, are all notions that point to the fact that, today, home and work are inseparable.

1.3 Roadmap through the book

This book is about the indivisibility of employment from domesticity. It will also show how visual research can effectively fill methodological and conceptual gaps between feminist economics and visual studies and how self-built architecture offers urban services and plays social protection roles. This book also offers a critical assessment of upgrading policies and a renewed perspective on the contribution of sites and services programs. It also suggests a framework to understand how informality has been thought of throughout the years, situating leading thinkers and noting key missing ones. It covers a large arc across several disciplines. I do not claim to have successfully woven these threads into a single story. Some disciplinary narratives are more prominent in some chapters and then move away from the center of the stage. For instance, at the beginning development is in the spotlight, at the middle the text becomes more ethnographic, and by the end it moves into policy analysis. In this sense, the book resembles an arching set of building blocks across a gap more than an ebbing flow through a continuous landscape.

Chapter 2 faces the literature on urban informality. It begins diving into the institutional history and then moves to a thorough but distilled summary of the main views between 1972 and 2018. Finding these dominant views too ingrained in development discourses and also relatively spatially blind, I turn to time-use studies, the strategic instrument of feminist economics: I see it as a promising alternative that places the home at the center and that uses time as a unit of measurement of the economy. The chapter ends with two examples of spatial approaches to informality, a personal homage to two architect-thinkers who shaped my particular way of looking.

Chapter 3 walks the reader deep into a set of houses in consolidated informal settlements in Bogotá. Systematically and also vividly, it presents the visual-laden methodology I developed around my term space-use intensity. This includes the house interviews (that interrogate space rather than the residents) and use space-use diagrams (that are both analytic and communicative pieces). The chapter ends with the prompt that intensity is a feature of space that can be visualized conceptually as the opposite of porosity.

Chapter 4 is an archeology of the bureaucratic procedures of formalization in Bogotá. I unearth an undeclared theory of formalization from the local urban plans, codes, and regulations and present it in a synthesized visual form. What emerges from this is a theory of urban landscape where the vformal and informal are blurred by design from the beginning and yet, they are carefully stratified. This is a story of the fallacious politics of recognition: it shows formalization is compulsory but at the same time unattainable. The chapter ends by repudiating pretended inclusion and pleading instead for redistributive recognition.

Chapter 5 illustrates the "space-use intensity" concept and the "house interview" methodology used to document it, through a replication study done in three African cities: Kampala in Uganda, Dar es Salaam in Tanzania, and Dakar in Senegal. This text also shares insights of local experts' insights about formalization policies in their respective cities, extending and detailing some of the findings exposed in Chapters 3 and 4. This two-pronged empirical study confirms the cross-regional applicability of space-use intensity beyond the specific case in point of the original study in Bogotá, Colombia,

8 *Introduction*

and offers a South-South perspective where Latin America and Africa engage in direct theoretical conversation based on their concrete realities.

The conclusion in Chapter 6 weaves together the major probing lines that were thrown in the earlier chapters. First, it revisits the analytic role of the different visual rituals in my research, how visuals are not escorting aids but rather raw and distilled data in itself. Continuing with the visuality, I return to porosity, an analogy that serves as a rudimentary explanation for the source of economic intensity. Finally, the chapter includes a speculative proposal to the violent state of affairs of formalization policy: a recognition continuum enabled by the notion of space-use intensity.

References

Benson, Michaela and Hamiduddin, Iqbal. eds. (2017). *Self-Build Homes: Social Discourse, Experiences and Directions*, UCL Press, London. https://doi.org/10.2307/j.ctt1xhr521

Bredenoord, Jan, Lindert, Paul Van, and Smets, Peer. (2014). *Affordable Housing in the Urban Global South*, Routledge, New York.

Carrizosa, Maria. (2003). *La analítica del tú ante la pseudo-comunicación en el debate Gadamer – Habermas*. Centro de Estudios Socioculturales CESO, Universidad de Los Andes, Bogotá.

Dolinga, John and Arundel, Rowan. (2022). "The Home as Workplace: A Challenge for Housing Research", *Housing, Theory and Society*, 39:1, pp. 1–20. https://doi.org/10.1080/14036096.2020.1846611

Duncan, Simon, and Rowe, Andy. (1993). "Self-provided Housing: The First World's Hidden Housing Arm", *Urban Studies*, 30:8, pp. 1331-1354. https://doi.org/10.1080/00420989320081291

Hart, Keith. (2010). "Africa's Urban Revolution and the Informal Economy", In Padayachee, V. (ed) *The Political Economy of Africa*, pp. 372–387. Routledge, London.

Hart, Keith. (2011). "The Informal Economy: A Story of Ethnography Untold", *The Memory Bank*, Blog entry January 8, 2011.

Hart, Keith. (2017). "Greybacks", In Mauer, B., and Swartz, L. (eds) *Paid: Tales of Dongles, Checks, and Other Money Stuff*, MIT Press, Cambridge, MA.

Sassen, Saskia and Ratti, Carlo. (2012). "The Case for a Duty to the City", *Bloomberg CityLab*, March 1, 2021.

Roy, Arundhati. (2020). "The Pandemic Is a Portal", *Financial Times*, April 2, 2020.

Tufte, Edward. (1997). *Visual Explanations: Images and Quantities, Evidence and Narrative*, Graphics Press, Cheshire, Connecticut.

World Bank. (2020). *Urban Development Overview*, April 20, 2020, www.worldbank.org/ens/topic/urbandevelopment/overview

2 Urban informality

Mainstream theories and visible alternatives

This chapter is a literature review written in first person. Not in the sense that I am the protagonist, but in the sense that there is no effort to remove who I am from the way I critically understand the topic. This narrative point of view is the result of a long, lonely, and hard-fought maturation process to realize that one can only go deepest by ceasing to ignore one's own *mode* of thinking, of working, of engaging with the unknown. This review comes after dwelling in many pages of books, articles, policy reports, economic studies, working papers, presentations, speeches, syllabuses, other literature reviews, and colleagues' dissertations. It is also shaped the gradual process of hearing my own voice as a maturing teacher and an emergent researcher. As I grow more confident inside this complex and fragmented field, I see why other researchers have shied away from such a Sisyphean task. Empirical and theoretical discoveries happen, and then are disregarded with unfair prejudices. The conceptual clarity reached in some subfields is rarely transferred to other circles, so much gets forgotten. This chapter offers the reader a personal pathway across this half fascinating, half discouraging, and invariably prejudiced, Babel Tower.

I begin with a humble attitude of reviewing a largely untold history, the history of the concept within the international organization closest to embracing this issue as its mission statement, the International Labor Organization. Next comes the centerpiece of the chapter: a literature review presenting the key authors, definitions, causal theories, methods, policy suggestions, and critiques of the main schools of thought on the informal economy from 1972 to 2018. This literature gravitates around development economics. Its protagonists and audience have benefited from the fruitful overlap and interaction between two main disciplines: economics and anthropology (development anthropology, economic sociology, and urban economy, among others).

The rest of the chapter delves into alternative approaches that have remained relatively disconnected from the central discussions on informality. I argue that such alternatives if adequately brought to the forefront, hold much promise contributing to future theories. In this context, the third section presents a fringe school of thought centered on time-use data and particularly concerned with making visible the contribution of household production as the

DOI: 10.4324/9781003297727-2

10 *Urban informality: mainstream theories and visible alternatives*

future of the postindustrial economy. In the last section, I come to terms with my background as an architect. By means of two paradigmatic examples, I put forth some sort of revindication of spatial thinking, in particular, visual research methods, and by the same token, critique the spatial blindness of the mainstream accounts on informality. Overlooked as unscientific while envied for their communicative power, visual methodological approaches like the ones regularly deployed by architects are more than repositories of spatial information, they remind us that what counts as real is usually what is seen.

2.1 The history of informality at the International Labor Organization

The story I am about to tell reveals that informality is a topic without a home, devoid of a committed institutional platform, the concept itself is somehow disenfranchised. Everyone knows about it, but no one dares to embrace it in full and dare to call it its own, informality is always an elephant in the room. Despite this, the birth and development of the informal economy concept have had an intimate relationship with the International Labour Organization (ILO) over the last half century. Shortly after its—now famous—coinage in 1971 by the anthropologist Keith Hart, the ILO adopted it almost instantly, becoming "responsible for transforming it into an important development policy issue" (Rodgers, 2009:206). In fact, "[t]he ILO has been the largest single contributor [to the informal economy literature], both year by year and also commutatively" (Bangasser, 2000:16), a trend that still continues. Despite this, and very telling of informality's puzzling fate, an official ILO history written on the occasion of the organization's centenary, does not devote a single chapter to the informal economy. The book's conclusions admit that failing to address informality more directly was disastrous in terms of policy efficacy: "achieving universality is the ILO's Achilles' heel. In every chapter of this book, we ultimately find that a limiting factor on the ILO's influence lies in the difficulty of reaching what we characterize as the informal economy or the informal sector" (Rodgers, 2009:253). Therefore, some historical notes on the relationship between the concept and the organization shed light on old, new, and also "new" ideas on informality.

The ILO is one of the oldest international development organizations, predating the United Nations (UN) itself. It was created in 1919 as a subsidiary organization to the League of Nations, with the treaty that ended World War I. Peace, or more exactly "the importance of social justice in securing peace" has been ILO's grand institutional objective. While it has remained the UN work-related agency, its efforts toward peace were acknowledged with a Nobel Peace Prize in 1969. Employment and peace are in fact built in into its configuration, giving shape to what is ILO's single most defining characteristic: is its tripartite structure. Despite predating most other international organizations, the ILO is the only UN body where not only member states (national governments) but also employer (private sector) and worker representatives (citizens), have both equal voice and decision power. Experts highlight among the positive outcomes of ILO's tripartism: "a connection with economic reality that cannot be reproduced in an organization where governments are the only spokespersons ... [as well as] a notion of society built around collaboration among structured interests rather than individual actors" (Rodgers, 2009:15). Thanks to the tripartite structure some members remain longer than government delegates, thus accumulating know-how and power base (Rodgers, 2009:16). This also extends the institutional memory and encourages long-term thinking. In addition, tripartism breeds an unusual operational dynamism: workers often align with the Office of the Director, while the employers' block often acts as breaks. ILO's first director Albert Thomas explained this system like 'having both a straitjacket and a lifejacket' (Rodgers, 2009:16) pushing the organization into the future with its eyes open. Despite these virtues, no other international agency has copied this democratic political architecture (a trait notably missing from UN Habitat [UN General Assembly, 2017]).

The "informal" concept was developed under three ILO programs: the Comprehensive Employment Mission, the World Employment Program, and the Delhi Group on Informal Sector Statistics. Revisiting these programs helps understand informality's paradoxical fate, that is, the hiatus between the theoretical understanding of the concept and the actions implemented to deal with it.

2.1.1 The Comprehensive Employment Mission

The concept first appeared in ILO's history with the *Comprehensive Employment Mission* to Kenya in 1972. These Missions were innovative in their approach to development assistance. Designed as field trips where a large group of experts (up to 30) with diverse backgrounds concentrated their analytic efforts for up to two months on a specific country. The comprehensive missions were not only multidisciplinary (economists still dominated but they dared to enter in conversation with others), but they were also cross sectoral: "made up of experts from many institutions, not just the ILO. Considerable effort went into making these teams not just technically but also culturally and institutionally heterogeneous" (Bangasser, 2000:6). The group's composition was designed to produce a broad and balanced mix of perspectives. In this Kenya Mission, 9 UN agencies participated, 10 universities, 8 Kenyan ministries, 11 representatives from employers, and 10 representatives from unions, among others (Singer et al., 1972:xii–xix). Looked at from today's perspective, they were not balanced enough: men were overrepresented, the final version of the report done in Geneva, with no input from national team

12 Urban informality: mainstream theories and visible alternatives

members. Plus it lacked spatial data and maps. Still, the care and depth of the effort is undeniable. These Missions were a highly visible endeavor in the international sphere, they nurtured a community of inquisitive experts that was prolific for many years to come.

These Missions, more descriptive than interventionist, were quite unusual at the time, though not really unprecedented. Like the 19th-century geographic expeditions, they were scientific area-based field observations, only that ILO's describe the economic ecosystem rather than the biophysical. The emphasis "went into analysis and diagnosis rather than remedial activities ... The whole thrust of a comprehensive employment mission was to analyze and recommend rather than to implement" (Bangasser, 2000:6). This lack of teeth did not sit well in development circles. Moser was particularly vocal stating that ILO's Missions put forward "politically utopian recommendations" (Moser, 1978:1045) that sideline the political dimension where its policy recommendations had to be situated (Moser, 1978:1046). This does not mean that the Missions were fruitless. Their "output would be a comprehensive national employment plan, parallel or tandem to the national development plan, usually embodied in a general report" (Bangasser, 2000:6). What was absent was a direct link to further bureaucratic or budgetary efforts from ILO (Bangasser, 2000:6). Moreover, ILO did not formally endorse its recommendations to the government, nor committed funding for future actions. In fact, the Kenya Mission was not even paid by ILO but by the United Nations Development Program (UNDP). The disconnectedness between descriptive analysis and an action agenda proved problematic, "[i]n short, the missions tended to raise expectations for subsequent assistance which later proved financially impossible to satisfy" (Bangasser, 2000:6). An inconvenient hard fact hindering much interdisciplinary endeavors: a job too thorough is likely to be programmatically bulky or even inoperative.

Not surprisingly, the Kenya Mission report is unmistakably positive in the way it describes informality: "Informal economic activity is often *efficient, productive, and creative*" (Singer et al., 1972:51). This is not an isolated comment but a recurrent conclusion the team derived from evidence. A few examples are relevant. "The evidence presented in Chapter 13 of the report suggests that *the bulk of employment in the informal sector*, far from being only marginally productive, *is economically efficient and profit-making*" (Singer et al., 1972:5). Later, the report explains: "We give evidence later to show that the small-scale producer in *the informal sector is more efficient economically and achieves higher outputs from scarce inputs than the large-scale producers*" (Singer et al., 1972:108). Furthermore, when talking about the advantages of Kenyan innovation, the report adds: "First, *informal-sector artisans utilize capital much more efficiently*. This constitutes an important *saving* as well. Secondly, there is *greater re-use* of spare parts in the informal sector" (Singer et al., 1972:219) (*emphasis added*). The Mission's report insists unambiguously on this positive account and blames the routinely disproving statements about the failure of informality to be

Urban informality: mainstream theories and visible alternatives   13

productive to unimaginative academics that are blind to piling evidence. Allow me to cite in extenso:

> Often people fail to realize the extent of economically efficient production in the informal sector because of the low incomes received by most workers in the sector. A common interpretation of the cause of these low incomes (in comparison to average wage levels in the formal sector) [sic] has been to presume that the problem lies within the informal sector; that it is stagnant, nondynamic, and a net for the unemployed and for the thinly veiled idleness into which those who cannot find formal wage jobs must fall. It is hardly surprising that this view should be widespread, for *academic analysts have often encouraged and fostered such an interpretation*. Further, from the vantage point of central Nairobi, with its gleaming skyscrapers, the dwellings and commercial structures of the informal sector look indeed like hovels. For observers surrounded by imported steel, glass and concrete, it requires a leap of the imagination and considerable openness of mind to perceive the informal sector as a sector of thriving economic activity and a source of Kenya's future wealth. But throughout the report we shall argue that such *an imaginative leap and openness of mind* **is** not only necessary to solve Kenya's employment problem, but is entirely *called for by the evidence* about the informal sector. There exists, for instance, considerable evidence of technical change in the urban informal sector, as well as of regular employment at incomes above the average level attainable in smallholder agriculture. The informal sector, particularly in Nairobi but to varying degrees in all areas, has been operating under extremely debilitating restrictions as a consequence of a pejorative view of its nature. Thus there exists an imminent danger that this view could become a self-fulfilling prophecy.
>
> (Singer et al., 1972:9)

Even as interdisciplinary groups encountered evidence of economically efficient production in the informal sector, ingrained judgmental prejudices in mainstream narrow definitions of productivity created a "self-fulfilling prophecy" around informality (Singer et al., 1972:5). There is no doubt today, half a century later, that such prophecy prevails. Optimistic accounts of informality have not gone far outside of economics either. In the social sciences, positive accounts of informality are perceived as romantic, branded as disguised modes of exploitation, and unfair celebrations of naturalized entrepreneurialism, as will be discussed later.

2.1.2 The World Employment Program

Parallel to—rather than intersecting—the work of the Comprehensive Missions, the ILO deployed the World Employment Program on Urban Unemployment. Initiated in 1968 by the famous economic historian Paul

14   Urban informality: mainstream theories and visible alternatives

Bairoch and later joined by Lubell and Seruthaman, this program had a distinct city-level approach. Its first phase carried out studies in six cities: Bogotá, Calcutta, Jakarta, Lagos, Abidjan, and Sao Paulo, followed by other developing world cities in the second phase. The program soon became ILO's hub for the "urban informal sector," a concept that gradually replaced "urban unemployment" or awkward phrasings like "disguised unemployment" (Bangasser, 2000:12). The urban informal sector literature and data thrived under this program for six years. It produced an important amount of studies (almost 80) which altogether contributed "to demonstrate the importance of the urban informal sector in employment and income generation," as stated by a report on the progress of ILO's cooperation. Further still, the "World Employment Programme was the leading source of ideas and new thinking and expertise on employment issues in developing countries throughout the 1970s... the programme offered a promising alternative to the failures of the development strategies of the 1950s and 1960s" (Rodgers, 2009:209).

Soon after, a couple of events backtracked these efforts. First, decisions taken at two major employment conferences in 1976 subsumed the topic under a rural rubric, halving its institutional visibility and budget (Bangasser, 2000:12). Though the rural and urban informal economies have strikingly similar structural manifestations,[1] the range and type of policy alternatives are drastically different. Merging urban and rural informality programmatically in the ILO structure, meant disregarding conceptual advances and embracing loose definitions, which ended up being detrimental to development to both accounts (Bangasser, 2000:18). Moreover, budget to the urban informal sector plunged after the United States, ILO's biggest contributor, withdrew—albeit temporarily—from the organization.

During the 1980s, the informal sector re-gained institutional attention: it was designated one of the five major global themes in the ILO Medium Term Plan (Bangasser, 2000:13), and it also gained more budgetary lines, although scattered across many different programs (a tendency that continued into the 1990s). This fragmentation had negative effects for both, the conceptual evolution of the topic and also its operational accountability. "With no specific organizational unit responsible for the informal sector as such, everybody got into the game; but no one took overall responsibility" (Bangasser, 2000:15). What was worse still, attention on the subject raised, but the emphasis of ILO's work in the urban informal sector, and even on the informal sector in general, shifted from analysis to "remedial" actions, which proved to be extremely detrimental.

---

1 I have elaborated elsewhere on the similarities between urban informality's strategies and the ones described in Chayanov's *Theory of the Peasant Economy* (1925): flexibility, heterogeneity, autonomy (self-exploitation), which received a renewed interest in the Anglo literature with its first translation 1966.

Urban informality: mainstream theories and visible alternatives   15

It was much safer to "help" those suffering from informality than to confront those benefiting from it. The portfolio of actions drifted gradually away from measuring and analyzing the informal sector and its causes, over towards taking actions to "help" those caught in it. While these remedial efforts were certainly worthwhile, they drew attention away from *why* the informal sector existed. So it continued to grow!

(Bangasser, 2000:15) (emphasis from the original)

This remedial turn had budgetary, organizational, and political reasons that took shape as the World Employment Program ended but lingered on.

The avoidance of looking into the causes of the informal sector had a political payoff for various interest groups within the ILO community. In the short run at least, *it gave the appearance of "doing something"* about this social problem … The institution could also *avoid risking the conclusion that some traditional ILO programmes and procedures were either irrelevant to the informal sector, or possibly even exacerbating it.* By concentrating attention on "helping" those suffering from informality (that is, by concentrating on remedying the symptoms rather than correcting the causes of the informal sector), we have been able for three decades to claim that we were responding to an increasingly virulent social disease without having to change our own modus operandi nor risk making any of the technical capacities the Office has built up over the years obsolete.

(Bangasser, 2000:15)

Going from symptoms to causes led to a more vigorous ILO action, but it simultaneously bred a "miserabilist" vision of the informal sector, which was completely absent from the Kenya Mission and the World Employment Program. The "positive vision of the informal sector atrophied. [Instead,] this "miserabilist" vision fitted well with an orientation to "helping the victims" rather than analyzing the causes" (Bangasser, 2000:16). Actions were often copy-pasted from site to site, bypassing and even forgetting conceptual clarity that had been achieved before. Operation was divorced from analysis. In other words, the shift to a pessimistic view on the informal sector meant trading efficacy for effectiveness. The remedial turn proved to be unfortunate and counterproductive, as the sector seemed to be impervious to this "help." Informality did not curb but continued to grow. Persistent informalization, even in contexts of economic prosperity presents a logical challenge for the development paradigm. The proactive but blind miserabilist approach is a questionable development strategy, it needs to see poverty in order to maintain its own relevance, overlooking new ideas and alternatives. Against all predictions, economic growth and urbanization did not bring "modernization" but rather "informalization." The arc of this argument will be explored later in the next section when discussing well-known critiques to neoliberalism linking informalization and deregularization (Sassen, 2000).

2.1.3 The Delhi Group on Informal Sector Statistics

Informality is so often labeled as so overly complex, elusive, and unmeasurable, that it is hard to believe that for three decades now there are available agreed definitions, shared survey methodologies, and comparable statistics across rich and poor countries. The main driving force in these developments has been the Delhi Group on Informal Sector Statistics. The Delhi Group from the Statistical Commission of United Nations Statistics Division (UNSD) was set up in 1997 as a collection of experts primarily from national statistical agencies but also including research centers and NGOs, who exchange experience about the measurement of informality to "improve and speed up the international standards development process" (UNSD, 2015: Web). Put shortly, the group is a data innovation hub. Participation in the groups is voluntary, representatives self-fund their participation in the meetings, and they set their own agenda. Since much of the work of these groups results in international standards, the UNSD ensures the work integrates the views of all countries, not just those wealthy enough to participate (UNSD, 2015: Web). This institutional arrangement assures their work remains agile and flexible enough, detached from political swings. The Delhi Group authored ILO statistical manuals used worldwide. Its work ended in 2013, with the publication of a detailed manual titled "Measuring Informality."

The most relevant contribution of the ILO to the knowledge of informality is the international official statistical definitions for informal sector in 1993 and of informal employment in 2003. The concept was first born into anthropology and development studies in the 1970s, and then, after a two-decade hiatus, the term "informal sector" was reborn into labor statistics, making its way into the system of national accounts. This definition literally brought to light a phenomenon that was wrongfully referred to as "black," "hidden," "shadow," or "underground" (ILO, 1993:2). Unfortunately, the 20-year delay did much harm, it barred informality as an ill-fated field of research, mushroomed misunderstandings about it, blurring non-statistical conceptual advances. A paradigmatic example is the fact that 30 years after Keith Hart coined the term, he regretted his contribution to the field: "I have often wondered if it has advanced or retarded our understanding of development" (Hart, 2010:380). It is more likely that the term required developments in different fields of knowledge to evolve further, rather than it was an unsound concept to begin with.

There are two key interconnected aspects of the statistical definition of informal sector, as defined by the concluding resolution of the 15th International Conference of Labour Statisticians (ICLS) in 1993. First, the informal sector refers to unregistered enterprises, which means it sees it as production units or firms, rather than persons or types of activity. Second, being firms, their activity should be added to the UN System of National Accounts (SNA), as household enterprises are part of the household sector

(ILO, 1993:2). The link to the SNA allows reflecting the informal sector in the Gross Domestic Product (GDP) calculations (Hussmanns, 2003:2), recognizing that the informal sector creates jobs and reduces poverty. So, not only did the concept come to light, but its size, behavior, and relative contribution to the national economies were exposed. Evidencing the contribution of the informal sector to the economic strength of a country helps justify proportional public expenditures. Statistical clarity on informality opened the door for the formulation, monitoring, and evaluation of economic and social policies and programs in all countries to be more exhaustive (Hussmanns, 2003:3), more real (Feldstein, 2017), and fairer. The full range of advocacy effects brought about by this definition is to this date yet to be fully explored.

In 2003, a decade after the statistical definition of the informal sector, came a new breakthrough: the official international definition of informal employment, part of the guidelines issued after the 17th ICLS. This new definition focused on jobs (both de jure and de facto) is even more important to the field (Hussmanns, 2004; Routh, 2011; Vanek, 2014, among others). The 2003 ICLS defined informal employment as: "total number of informal jobs, whether carried out in formal sector enterprises, informal sector enterprises, or households" (ILO, 2003). Put shortly, informal employment means unprotected employment. A remarkable feature of this definition is the acknowledgment that informal employment exists both inside and outside of the informal sector, and both within and outside household jobs. The Delhi Group statisticians nudged governments to admitting officially and internationally that there are a variety of informal and formal employment statuses across diverse types of production units, that data must be compiled accordingly, and that policy approaches must be differentiated.

These conceptual developments gradually impacted worldwide data collection. Before the 2003 definition of "informal employment," ILO reported a statistical picture using direct measures of only 25 countries and on the rest, it used an indirect residual approach. In 2008, the ILO expanded this account by incorporating a proxy of informal employment for developed countries: "non-standard work" (i.e., jobs that are not regular, not full-time, nor year-round wage employment). This proxy proved controversial but very helpful, enabling a new world dataset with direct measures from 40 countries and indirect measures from other 81 countries. The data on informal employment and non-standard work was harmonized, yet it did not allow change-over-time comparisons (Vanek, 2014:7). As the "informal employment" definition ages, more and more data points from enough countries across development stages and geographies are gathered. ILO's 2018 landmark Statistical Picture report used "a common set of criteria to measure informal work has been applied to more than 100 countries, both developed and developing" (ILO, 2018) concluding that 61.2% of the world's employed population have an informal employment.

18 *Urban informality: mainstream theories and visible alternatives*

These statistical developments are monumental, yet they have not been as influential as they could and should be. For some reason, the breakthroughs of the Delhi Group remain relatively disconnected from core academic discussions in urban informality. The Delhi Group experts are very vocal about this problem, vigorously claiming the urgency to recognize these official international definitions (Hussmanns, 2004; Vanek, 2014:32), among others. At stake are the results of a long-fought consensus across countries and sectors (employers, employees, and governments); but numbers alone do little if researchers and national and local policymakers do not use the concepts. Unless these concepts and numbers are shared and used, they will have no impact. Worse still, not using them can render inconsistent results: "the use of unofficial definitions and proxy measures will not generate the coherent set of data that is badly needed for research and policy purposes" (Vanek, 2014:3). Breaking the life cycle of these statistics prevents knowledge on urban informality from building up, integrating evidence, and clearing out hypothesis, cursing it to incessantly repeat itself. Concepts will be cyclically "discovered" and forgotten unless analytical clarity is appropriated and disseminated. This chapter not only shows that urban informality research has suffered from this fate, but it puts forth schematic visual synthesis that hopefully contributes to its conceptual appropriation.

The official 2003 ICLS document annexed a visual model enthusiastically designed by Hussmanns to summarize and disseminate these conceptual developments (see Figure 2.1). The diagram was a much-needed piece of information aiming to synthesize the landmark consensus on this topic, displacing once and for all the conceptual confusion and imprecision lingering in the field for so long. Unfortunately, the visual fell short of this purpose. It did not become a communication tool to clarify the concepts and stimulate their use beyond a community of experts, but more of an aide for statisticians themselves to check the conceptual reach of labor force surveys. A visual can certainly be broadly useful bridging over rather than scaring new users. In fact, effective visual interfaces help to transfer key insights from data overloads by "surfacing knowledge" (Bevington, 2007:1), rendering clear a set of complex concepts, quantities, and relationships. But Hussmanns' visualization has design flaws and conceptual weaknesses that make it unsuccessful. It is not helpful in hinting the relative size of the informal sector and the informal employment. It also violates several precepts of a good communicative piece: it has a counter-intuitive color coding, it gravitates toward non-possibilities, it superimposes redundant codes (color and number), and it overburdens the reader with an exacting level of detail as well as with long redundant scripts and instructions.

The table in Figure 2.1 lays out the components of the 1993 informal sector definition in the vertical axis and the 2003 informal employment ones in the horizontal one. Total employment is spread out in two dimensions: the first column lists the type of firms (sector), and the first row is the type of jobs (employment). This clarifies the two concepts are never interchangeable.

ANNEX
<u>Conceptual Framework: Informal Employment</u>
(Seventeenth International Conference of Labour Statisticians)

Production units by type	Jobs by status in employment								
	Own-account workers		Employers		Contributing family workers	Employees		Members of producers' cooperatives	
	Informal	Formal	Informal	Formal	Informal	Informal	Formal	Informal	Formal
Formal sector enterprises					1	2			
Informal sector enterprises[a]	3		4		5	6	7	8	
Households[b]	9					10			

(a) As defined by the Fifteenth International Conference of Labour Statisticians (excluding households employing paid domestic workers).

(b) Households producing goods exclusively for their own final use and households employing paid domestic workers.

Dark grey cells refer to jobs that, by definition, do not exist in the type of production unit in question. Light grey cells refer to formal jobs. Un-shaded cells represent the various types of informal jobs.

Cells 1 and 5: Contributing family workers: no contract of employment and no legal or social protection arising from the job, in formal sector enterprises (Cell 1) or informal sector enterprises (Cell 5). The informal nature of their jobs follows directly from the status in employment.

Cells 2, 6 and 10: Employees holding informal jobs, whether employed by formal sector enterprises (Cell 2), informal sector enterprises (Cell 6) or as paid domestic workers by households (Cell 10).

Cells 3 and 4: Own-account workers (Cell 3) and employers (Cell 4) employed in their own informal sector enterprises. The informal nature of their jobs follows directly from the characteristics of the enterprise, which they own.

Cell 7: Employees holding formal jobs in informal sector enterprises.

Cell 8: Members of informal producers' cooperatives. The informal nature of their jobs follows directly from the characteristics of the producers' cooperative of which they are member.

Cell 9: Own-account workers engaged in the production of goods exclusively for own final use by their household (e.g. subsistence farming).

Employment in the informal sector: Cells 3 to 8.
Informal employment: Cells 1 to 6 and 8 to 10.
Informal employment outside the informal sector: Cells 1, 2, 9 and 10.

Figure 2.1 Conceptual framework for informal employment (Hussmanns, 2003).

"One of the two concepts cannot replace the other, they are concepts that complement each other" (Hussmanns, 2004, ppt). The first row is qualified by the following line, where formal and informal are displayed in tandem columns, always considering both plausible kinds of employment statuses. The resulting grid of 27 boxes multiplies the intricacy of the analysis. Curiously, this wealth of options is not completely necessary, as almost half the possibilities, the 12 boxes in dark gray, are "inexistent," meaning they map statuses that are "impossible by definition." Analogously, this matrix fails to illustrate the fact that formality is an exceptional category. Formal employees in the formal sector represent only one of 10 possible employment statuses. Dealing with an overload of inexistent statuses makes it harder to deliver its messages effectively. Furthermore, it does not communicate which is a broader concept, informal sector of informal employment, and in this sense can be quantitatively misleading (Negrete, 2002:9).

Likely unsatisfied, a year later Hussmanns (head of the Methodology and Analysis Unit of the Bureau of Statistics at International Labour Office) redesigned his visualization (Figure 2.2). Though apparently simpler, it almost doubles the problem of having a surplus of inexistent alternatives. "The result is a three-dimensional cube composed of (…) 45 smaller cubes. Each of the smaller blocks stands for a specific combination of type of production unit, type of activity and type of job" (Hussmanns, 2004:10). Optimistically, he saw this issue as a plan for a future research agenda. But none of these models

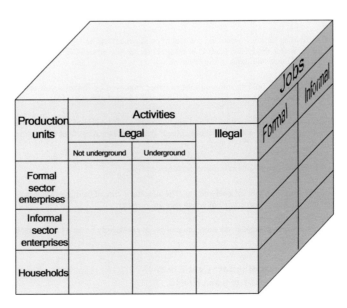

Figure 2.2 Expanded conceptual framework for the informal employment (Hussmanns, 2004).

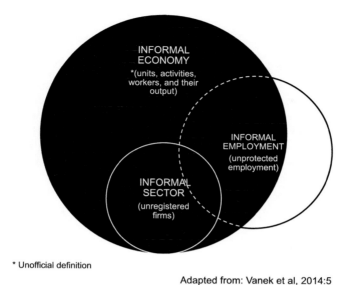

Figure 2.3 Conceptual map of ILO's statistical definitions on informality (by the author).

became widely used or referenced beyond overspecialized circles, and the broader conceptual confusion was far from being dissolved.

In closing this critique, I present my own visualization synthesizing the conceptual evolution described so far in this chapter. The Venn diagram in Figure 2.3 makes evident that informal economy, informal sector, and informal employment are far from interchangeable terms. What was inaugurated with the Kenya Mission was not the "informal sector" concept, but the broader "informal economy" which includes not only firms but units, activities, workers, and their output. Within the formal economy, the formal sector (which includes all registered firms) is larger than the formal employment, but in informality, firms are less frequent than informal employment. As the visual shows, the "informal sector" limits itself to firms within the informal economy (as per the ICLS definition), while the latter term "informal employment" notably makes clear that unprotected employment exists both inside and outside of the informal economy and can happen both within and outside of informal firms. Put differently, this 2003 definition allowed to acknowledge that formal firms informalize. What is most interesting about the diagram below is the fact that it helps understand that as more statistical data becomes available, there is proof that the informal employment circle enlarges and that it moves to the right, making more room for diverse types and intensities of informalization.

22 *Urban informality: mainstream theories and visible alternatives*

2.1.4 *Women and Men in the Informal Economy[2]:*
A statistical picture

This worldwide statistical consensus is slowly proving to be more than ground-breaking, a world changer. In 2018 ILO published the report: *Women and Men in the Informal Economy: A statistical picture*, demonstrating that the world as a whole is already predominantly informal. The report uses "a harmonized definition of informal employment and employment in the informal sector to micro data for more than 100 countries representing more than 90 per cent of the world's employed population" (ILO, 2018:67). Of particular importance is the fact that informality is being officially measured (allowing for some national flexibility) in both poor and rich countries, something unthinkable a few decades ago. The publication makes available for the first time cross-country and cross-region estimates that make it possible to confidently say that, since the 2000s, informality is the rule globally: 61.2 percent of the world's workers, that is, two billion people, are informally employed (ILO, 2018). The implications of this sole fact are so deep that it may change forever how employment is thought of.

This 2018 *Statistical Picture*, much like previous statistical breakthroughs from ILO, remains somehow a hidden treasure. The WIEGO (Women in Informal Employment: Globalizing and Organizing) network has done important contributions to bring it out in the open, through a user-friendly summary of the report (Bonnet et al., 2019), a one-pager pamphlet, and a few social media pieces. Made in close collaboration with ILO, WIEGO's work of reaching to wider audiences is fundamental. For instance, Bonnet, Vanek, and Chen's publication simplifies the tables of the original report by removing some variables, and it also presents data in four main groups of countries: "world, developed (high-income), emerging (middle-income) and developing countries (low-income)" (Idem:7). To further enhance the intelligibility and comparability of the data, selected "dimensions of employment are compared across all of the geographic regions rather than presented by individual regions as in the full report" (Idem). The cleaning the of data for advocacy purposes is a laudable endeavor, but the work of unpacking its theoretical implications is a different one and one that is still pending.

Before ending this section, a brief mention of data on informal housing and settlements is necessary. Perhaps a similar effort to the one done above within ILO's history can be done within the United Nations Human Settlements Program, UN Habitat. However, while there has been notable progress in

---

2 This chapter was written before the 2020 publication of WIEGO's landmark book: *The Informal Economy Revisited*, edited by Martha Chen and Françoise Carré, with contributions from three dozen experts. That volume matures many of the threads discussed in this section. Some its recommendations will be discussed in Chapter 6. For the moment, I note that it acknowledges the stature of theories of informality in urban studies since the 1970s (Chen and Carré, 2020:1), and insists interdisciplinary is unavoidable this topic (Idem, 258).

the technical definitions of "slums," "informal settlement," and "inadequate housing"[3] especially as part of the metadata for indicator 11.1.1. of the 2015 Sustainable Development Goals (UN Habitat, 2018:5); the rigor and consistency of these efforts is pale in comparison to the developments in the landscape of the informal economy.

One might argue that to claim the urgency of acknowledging the official definitions contradicts the whole exercise of doing a literature review. Why care about different ways of thinking about this issue, if an official understanding exists, has been developed via a multistakeholder consensus, has supporting data, and is yet to be fully appropriated by academics and policy makers? Is this official understanding one of many—equally valid—alternatives? Is the knowledge about urban informality splintered into irreconcilable subfields? Or is the profusion of schools of thought something that emerges when a field is nascent? I hope to bring clarity to these questions after delving into the different schools of thought in urban informality, each of them depicting a different foundational myth for how the informal comes into being, and each presenting a recipe for what must be done about it.

2.2 Schools of thought on informality

Informality has long had an aura of impenetrability. Never left unacknowledged, yet always intractable. Of the countless approaches to structure a literature review on this topic, I opted to follow closest the view of Martha Chen and the WIEGO network (Chen, 2012; Chen et al., 2016), and then extend it. Chen highlights four main schools of thought: dualist, structuralist, legalist and voluntarist. These schools of thought belong to the economic development literature and to a large extent have an emphasis on labor economics. Contrary to what she argues, I find that the urban studies literature does not complement this framework but actually reinforces it. Nevertheless, I do find it necessary to expand Chen's framework with a fifth school of thought, the continuum approach, that represents the leading theoretical atmosphere up to 2020.

Strikingly different narrative styles often give the impression of ideas belonging to opposing paradigms. However, the fluidity of some narrative registries in radical urban studies and their overt political affiliations (most notably the work of Ananya Roy), are not enough to set apart truly different approaches to informality. Instead of differentiating between development studies and urban studies arguing that the latter is politized while the former

---

3 The technical definition of slums or informal settlements promoted by UN Habitat has these five points: access to water, access to sanitation, structural quality and location, security of tenure, and overcrowding. The term "inadequate housing" is a recent effort to include developed countries (who shy away from the words "slums" and "informal"). It adds to the 5-points these: affordability, accessibility, and cultural adequacy (UN Habitat, 2018:15).

24 *Urban informality: mainstream theories and visible alternatives*

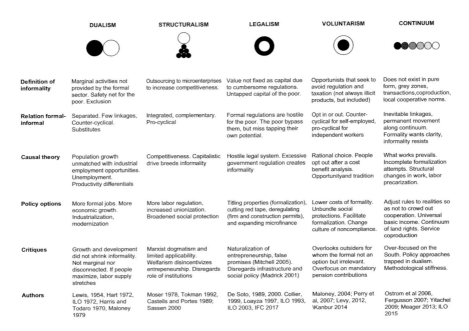

Figure 2.4 Overview of the schools of thought on informality (by the author).

is not (Chen et al., 2016:8), I suggest that a more profound division exists between labor studies and spatial research. The arc they cover together is wider: they are more complementary. This is not a mere choice of wording or emphasis but can prove instrumental when defining what is really new about emerging approaches. As I hope to show below, under a labor studies lens, radical approaches seem less new.

In other words, my review is not multidisciplinary (where disciplines are *added*) but rather interdisciplinary (knowledge is woven *across* disciplines). This interdisciplinary lens takes advantage of a framework from economics with its methodological rigor and its tendency to stylization but is not patient with its arrogant jargon nor its alleged political neutrality. A relentless visual thinker, I read through the main schools of thought and distill their underlying composition in a set of icons that strip to the bones the essential structure of each view. These simple visual aids, together with the summary table (Figure 2.4) help transverse spurious disciplinary siloes and facilitate a broad comparative perspective.

2.2.1 Dualism

The dualist school of thought of the informal economy is as prevailing as it is vilified. One can argue that all schools of thought are by definition dualist.

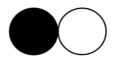

Dualism is engraved into our conventional understanding of informality, fixed in the very word "informal" which establishes a contraposition between what is formal, official, according to the norms, correct; and what is not. In development economics, dualism is a construct with an extensive lineage tracing back to the classical economists (Smith, 1776; Malthus, 1798; Ricardo, 1817), or at least dating a century (Boeke, 1942; Lewis, 1954, among others). Dual models of the economy operate on the distinction between two juxtaposed systems of organization: capitalistic versus peasant (focused on the production types as in Chayanov [1924]), or firm-based versus bazar-type (centered on the organization [Geertz, 1978]), or 'upper' versus 'lower' circuits of Santos (1977), or modern versus traditional (emphasizing on the technologies used) (Sethuraman, 1976:70). Dualism implies the existence of parallel universes. Using the formal-informal axis to determine duality was a contribution from the aforementioned cross-pollination between Hart's ethnography and ILO's institutional efforts from the 1970s and onwards. As Sethuraman explains, the formal-informal distinction is better than the modern-traditional dichotomy because it does not imply tradition is detrimental to development, but instead, it is a "neutral distinction" (Sethuraman, 1976:72). Such "neutrality," however, has been the root of much confusion and debate, as will be explained.

2.2.1.1 Definition of informality and causal theory

For dualists, the informal sector is for those who cannot afford to stay in the formal. Informality, then, is the universe of suboptimal and marginal activities that remain in the shadow of formal regulations and are also withdrawn from its benefits (Harris and Todaro, 1970; Hart, 1972; ILO, 1972; and others). From this perspective, the informal is the realm of the disadvantaged, a hostile environment comprised of marginalized enterprises with: "low entry barriers in terms of skills, capital, and organization … low levels of productivity; and low levels of capacity for accumulation" (Flórez, 2002:10). Singer (1970) described dualism in labor markets as dangerous: "high levels of casual and intermittent employment, as well as disguised or open unemployment … an employment crisis due to an acute land shortage in overcrowded farming communities and an acute job shortage in overcrowded urban communities" (Chen, 2012:2). Dualism rests in the idea that absence of economic growth and reduced employment opportunities or "the mismatch between people's skills and the structure of modern economic opportunities" (Chen, 2012:5), give rise to informality and assumes that workers would invariably prefer a formal job if they had the opportunity (Bangasser, 2000). The logic is always one of exclusion. People working informally, bypassed by the opportunities of modern industrialization, are miserable. As mentioned before, this causal theory of informality substantiates the need for development. Hence, by painting a bleak picture the dualist perspective is optimistic: with the right mix of development interventions, the formal sector will expand, thus shrinking informality (Navarrete, 2007:34). Dualism reinforces the link between informality

26 *Urban informality: mainstream theories and visible alternatives*

and poverty (Flórez, 2002:5), which is challenged by subsequent schools of thought.

2.2.1.2 *Relation formal-informal*

The dualist perspective adheres to a dichotomic view of the economy that distinctively separates the labor market between what is regulated and protected, and everything else. Two sides, two parallel universes that do not intersect. Instead, the formal and informal are substitutes (Edgcomb et al., 2002:11). Most thinkers "subscribe to the notion that informal units and activities have few (if any) linkages to the formal economy but, rather, operate as a distinct separate sector of the economy and that the informal workforce—assumed to be largely self-employed—comprise the less advantaged sector of a dualistic or segmented labour market" (Chen, 2012:5). The word "sector" reaffirms the idea that the two types of economies (or labor, or cities) are in different areas isolated from each other. As Hart asserts, dualism is reinforced in the term "informal sector," which "gives the impression that the two are located in different places" (Hart, 2010:379), rather than parts of a single whole. Consequently, these two—for the most part—disconnected sectors of the economy, react differently to the economic cycles. Dualists agree that the informal sector is counter cyclical (Lubell et al., 1991; Biles, 2009; Navarrete, 2017:32). Because the informal economy serves as the poor's safety net that absorbs whatever the formal sector cannot, "during economic downturns, informality grows, but the earnings of those in it decrease" (Flórez, 2002:9). Most schools of thought on informality agree that the informal economy has countercyclical character. However, in the dualist view, the fact that informality grows as unemployment increases gives reason to see the informal sector as "disguised unemployment," a type of unemployment that does not affect aggregate output, that is literally unaccounted for.

2.2.1.3 *Evidence and methods*

Economists have developed different methods to measure or estimate the size of informality, each with varying comparability across countries, and with generally narrow time series. Unfortunately, one cannot say that these methods map perfectly the different schools of thought under review here. Indeed, some thinkers have argued that the schools of thought are dependent on the methods: "in the case of the informal sector, methods often construct the concept, which has contributed to the plurality of its meanings" (Sindzingre et al., 2006:6). Other experts argue the contrary, asserting that in fact, methodologies are often lacking "adequate theoretical support, and that they are applied indiscriminately to countries in which the underlying assumptions do not hold" (Perry et al., 2007:1). Estimates under different methodologies are often incongruent with evidence from alternative sources or methods. Garcia-Verdú presents a typology of measurement methods to make sense of this cacophony: direct (voluntary surveys, tax audits), indirect (aggregate income vs. expenditure, total labor force vs. formal, monetary methods), and the model approach based on electricity consumption data (Perry et al., 2007:28). The most common is the Multiple Indicators Multiple Causes—MIMIC—but experts confess it has a rather large black box of causal assumptions (Perry et al., 2007:33). Without a doubt, and as discussed previously, the informal employment measure is superior to many others and has already gained prevalence. It is beyond the objective of this literature review to describe and discuss the different econometric nuts and bolts of the methodologies applied. What is worthwhile mentioning is that conceptually, the dualist school of thought aligns with indirect residual methods.

2.2.1.4 Policy options and interventions

Navarrete (2017) distinguishes two distinct periods in dualist policy attitudes toward the informal sector. An initial phase in the 1950 and 1960s where the reigning mindset was one in which not much was needed, but to wait until state-led development (Navarrete, 2017:34), social protection policies, public housing, and economic growth would push informal workers, businesses, and neighborhoods out of existence. The initial hands-off approach believed that the modernization of the economy with its expanded offerings of formal jobs, as well as a steady provision of enough low-cost social housing alternatives, would suffice to curtail informality. By the 1970 and 1980s, it was clear that the informal economy was not easily curbed, thus shifting policy attitudes toward repressive measures. Hence, under later dualist policies, the parallel between informal and illegal became discursively relevant. Prescriptions for public action mandated more control and supervision over unregulated realms. For example, in the case of street vending, the generalized idea is police eviction of illegal occupations of the public space, as food street vending is depicted unequivocally as unsanitary and dangerous and their transactions fraudulent (Bromley, 2000:16). In the case of home-based enterprises, the two policy attitudes seem to coexist. On the one hand, small businesses inside residential spaces are rendered a marginal phenomenon and hence routinely ignored. Household economic units are secluded in what is thought to be a non-economic realm, hidden or invisible to mainstream micro and macroeconomic analysis. On the other hand, when home-based enterprises are recognized, for instance, by policies in the built environment, urban policy highlights the nuisances that businesses pose to residential areas: unstable building materials, toxic fumes, improper disposal systems, and noise pollution (Nohn, 2011).

2.2.1.5 Limitations and critiques

Soon after the debut of the "informal sector" term, and alongside its appeal and rapid dissemination made effective by ILO and others, it sparked strong criticism. One of the most salient early critiques is that of Bromley (1978),

28   *Urban informality: mainstream theories and visible alternatives*

which in turn triggered an interesting vindication penned by Lipton (1984). Lipton's defense of dualism illuminates why this school of thought continues to speak some truth today. He argued that the confusion around the concept was creative and that the whole vibrancy of the debate was proof of the term's usefulness. As Ostrom et al. recount:

> The informal sector concept has become discredited on account of three alleged deficiencies: *misplaced dualism, misplaced isolation,* and *confusion.* He then goes on to specify each critique and to mount a defense against it. Misplaced dualism refers to the fact that in practice there is no clear split between formal and informal; rather, there is a continuum. The defense is that a dichotomy can nevertheless prove useful in analytical terms. Misplaced isolation is the neglect of the fact that the relationships of the informal sector to the rest of the economy are not investigated. While this is a valid critique of some of the literature, as Lipton also notes, we agree with Lipton that this is not an inherent weakness of the dichotomy, but rather of the uses to which it is put. Under the third critique, that of confusion, is the idea that the characteristics of this sector are not well spelt out. Nor, relatedly, are the entities that would fall into this sector.
>
> (Lipton, 1984:196) in (Ostrom et al., 2006:4) (*emphasis* added)

"Misplaced dualism" is a structural critique. It points out that the idea of two distinct economies or types of city, one formal and modern, and the other informal and 'backward,' is spurious because there is a continuum of gradients between the two extremes. This critique is the basis for today's current theoretical environment, which I will describe later. Interestingly, Lipton argued that in a continuum the contrasting terms continue to be useful analytically. The continued usage of the term (even if only to disprove it) across so many disciplines demonstrates its usefulness. The "misplaced isolation" critique to dualism highlights the false impression that the formal and the informal are disconnected, when in fact they are functionally linked. Lipton repeats the same argument in this case and explains that the pretense of isolation does not come from the concept itself, but from a weakness in its usage. An unexplored rebuke then was that the tendency to view the formal and informal realms as isolated comes from the fact that they are defined as nouns (sector, economy, city) instead of verbs (practices). If "informal" refers to an action, a tactic, a strategy, rather than a condition or quality, then the two terms would be understood as being at play, only existing when enacted. Anyhow, the false disconnect between formal and informal is the fundamental argument of the structuralist school of thought explained below.

It is commonplace for many scholars to point out the now draining circularity in the theoretical discussions on informality. Some celebrate the movement away from dualism into a continuum view, while others call the "blur[ing] boundaries as the irony of success" (Meager, 2013:5). This critique echoes the one raised by Gilbert about the inappropriateness of the resurgence of the term "slum" in Western scholarly literature and in UN jargon, for it disregards years of theoretical progress (like the concept Social Production of Habitat [Ortiz, 1996]). In any case, the "resurrection of old definitional debates tends to draw on literature from the 1970s and 1980s, glossing over the conceptual clarity that has emerged since then or confusing conceptual with operational debates" (Meager, 2013:4). In sum, the critique to dualism presented here is stronger with regard to its derived policy implications than in its theoretical underpinnings.

2.2.2 Structuralism

2.2.2.1 Definition of informality and causal theory

In opposition to the marginalist perspective of the standard dualism, the structuralist understanding sees the informal as being essentially linked to the formal and necessary for a more successful performance. Moser (1978) is one of the most outspoken early advocates of this school of thought, which was later developed further—among others—by Castells and Portes (1989) and was later complemented by Sassen (2000, 2002). For structuralists, informal practices are not only closely related to the modern capitalist society but in fact support it. Moser talked about informality in Marxian terms, as simple (or petty) commodity production. "Petty commodity production performs a number of important functions within the capitalist mode of production" (Moser, 1978:1057). The informal is necessary to the formal: "the underdevelopment and backwardness of the informal sector are necessary conditions for the development and advancement of the organized, formal" (Moser, 1978:1058). The emphasis shifts away from how to define, classify, and measure the two distinct sectors operating in isolation from each other; and focuses on the relation between them.

> [T]he dependent linkages between 'small-scale enterprises' and the 'capitalist sector' are numerous and diverse. These include direct incorporation through subcontracting and outworkers as well as more complicated procedures such as the utilization in retail distribution of 'agents'

30 *Urban informality: mainstream theories and visible alternatives*

who put up their own deposits thereby relieving the mother company of many of the risks involved.

(Moser, 1978:1056)

For structuralists the informal economy gives support to the formal economy, not in vain did Portes and Castells referred to informality as "the world underneath."

Authors aligned with this view stress the fact that the divide between formal and informal sectors is fictitious. Sectors are not clearly delimited, firms and people engage in formal and informal activities at the same time, and often within the same day.

> There is strong evidence of the systematic linkage between formal and informal sectors, following the requirement of profitability [...] Individual workers may switch between the two sectors even during the same workday [...] In fact, it is because there is a formal economy that we can speak of an "informal" one and vice-versa.
>
> (Portes and Castells, 1989:13)

A very crucial contribution of structuralism is its effort to disconnect informality from illegality. The informal economy may produce and distribute its products via unregulated channels, but its products are not different from those in the formal sector. For details, see Figure 2.5 with the definitions and relationships in the three realms: formal—informal—criminal.

Departing from the dualist developmentalism, structuralists understand the informal economy is not a Third World phenomenon. "Informality is universal [...] 'is not a marginal phenomenon for charitable social research, but a fundamental political and economic process at the core of many societies'" (Portes and Castells, 1989:17). It took another 20 years for this argument to amass enough evidence, both qualitative and quantitative. Sassen provided empirical evidence and theoretically compelling arguments highlighting the fact that informality exists in the North, and not only as an import of immigrant communities. She insisted that informality is a structural feature of advanced capitalism (Sassen, 1994:2290). For Sassen, expanding informalization in the industrialized countries is caused by macroeconomic changes derived from the shift to a service, information economy (Sassen, 1994:2304). Informalization in the North is driven by the pursuit of efficiency and productivity pressured by economic globalization, to the extent that the world economy is informalizing as much as it globalizes (Sassen, 2004) as supply chains get longer (Carré, Negrete, and Vanek, 2015:3). Moreover, informalization is essentially tied to weakened unions and labor precarization (Standing 2011), to the point that flexibilization in the bottom and deregularization in the top are part of the same phenomenon (Sassen, 2010:85). The work of Sassen is unique among the structuralists, not only as an effective North-South bridge (her being a native Spanish speaker certainly helped) but

Types of economic activity, definitions, and relationships

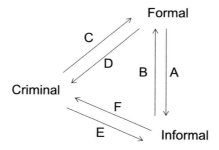

A State interference, competition from large firms, sources of capital and technology
B Cheaper consumer goods and industrial inputs, flexible reserves of labor
C State interference and disruption, supplies of certain controlled goods
D Corruption, gatekeepers rents for selected officials
E Capital, demand for goods, new income-earning opportunities
F Cheaper goods, flexible reserves of labor

Type of economy	Production and distribution	Final product
Formal	licit	licit
Informal	illicit	licit
Criminal	illicit	illicit

(Portes and Castells, 1989:14)

Figure 2.5 Structuralist definition of informal economy (Portes, Alejandro, Manuel Castells, and Lauren A. Benton, eds. *The Informal Economy: Studies in Advanced and Less Developed Countries.* pp. 14, Fig. 1.1. © 1989 Johns Hopkins University Press. Reprinted with permission of Johns Hopkins University Press).

also for being spatial (explaining the new urban world geography and even gentrification [Sassen, 2004]).

2.2.2.2 Relation formal-informal

In a nutshell, structuralism sees the relationship between the formal and the informal as subcontracting and outsourcing. Management flexibilization strategies reduce costs and improve the competitiveness of formal firms. Big firms and in particular large multinational corporations, striving for a competitive advantage, fuel informality. Companies outsource to save the costs associated with social protection, labor, environmental, and other regulations. Hence, for structuralists, it is the formal that creates the informal realm. "If informal is defined as non-salaried, there will always be an informal sector

32 *Urban informality: mainstream theories and visible alternatives*

and, moreover, it will contribute to maximize productivity" (Levy et al., 2012: 32). To better succeed in the formal sector, firms tap into smaller firms in the shadow economy[4].

The two types of economies are intimately integrated, inseparable. In fact, this is the only school of thought that sees the relationship between the two economies as being pro-cyclical with regard to the economic expansion and contraction cycles (Biles, 2009:224, Jütting et al., 2008, Navarrete, 2017:37). Whereas dualist predictions assumed informality would shrink with economic growth, structuralism assumed it would expand en par with GDP growth, as it indeed happened: "Following structural adjustment and the liberalization of markets reforms in the first half of the 1980s, the informal economy expanded along with the worldwide economy in the 1990s and early 2000s" (Perry et al. 2007; Drechsler et al. 2008; Navarrete, 2017:38). Hart, the father of dualism, also acknowledged this dualist shortcoming: "What happened next could never have been anticipated around 1970: in the name of the free market, deregulation of national capitalism led to the radical informalization of world economy" (Hart, 2010:377). Deregularization drives informalization, not only in "petty production," but also in global value chains where multinational corporations, via offshoring, outsourcing, and subcontracting stimulate informal working arrangements, production, and distribution of goods and services.

2.2.2.3 Evidence and methods

As explained earlier, it cannot be said that the schools of thought on the informal economy map perfectly with methods to measure its size, its growth, or contraction trends. Authors aligning with structuralist ideas have recurred to estimates and surveys of the number of very small businesses (Portes and Castells, 1989), city case-studies, in-depth interviews (Flórez, 2002:12), and global value chain studies, much more than on labor surveys or employment statistics from national censuses. When it comes to global value chains and offshoring, empirical evidence and detailed studies have tended to focus more on East and South Asia (Humphrey and Schmitz, 2000; Gereffi et al., 2005; Lund and Navdi, 2010; others), as well as in India and South Africa (Meager, 2013:7). Structuralist economists would prefer direct measurement methods

---

4 An interesting variant of structuralism can be found in the analysis of Claudia Goldin, who explains that women undergo a u-shaped labor force participation across the process of economic development: high participation in home-based informal economies, low for the middle classes, and high again for those highly educated in the upper income levels (Goldin, 1995). In this case, the policy prescription is for working hours flexibilization. For instance, in her optimistic view, the pandemic will encourage this and also more fairer workloads at home (Goldin, 2021). I am grateful to Robert Buckley for introducing me to the work of Goldin.

to gauge the size of the informal economy, rather than residual, indirect methods championed by dualists.

2.2.2.4 Policy options and interventions

Those ascribing to the structuralist perspective agree that there is a direct inverse relationship between the two types of economy, making what is favorable for big firms, generally detrimental to informal workers. While this is the traditional structuralist perception, in rigor, labor flexibilization can have winners and losers on both sides. In her seminal paper, Moser argued: "Clarification as to whether the linkages are benign or exploitative is essential to assess whether petty commodity production is tolerated by or functional to, the capitalist system" (Moser, 1978:1041). A decade later, other core structuralist authors stated: "The informal economy simultaneously encompasses flexibility and exploitation, productivity and abuse, aggressive entrepreneurs and defenseless workers, libertarianism and greediness" (Portes and Castells, 1989:11). In any case, traditional structuralism stresses the exploitative practices, where the more firms benefit from deregularization and flexibilization, the more informal workers suffer its burdens, and in this sense, just like dualism, it falls into miserabilism. But interventions advocated by structuralists differ from those of dualists in that they reject criminalizing informal workers. "[F]rom an economic perspective, criminalization makes no sense" (Sassen, 1994:2301). Instead, structuralism strives to "reduce the tensions between these informal economic units and the government structures" (Sassen, 1994:2301). On the contrary, the purpose is to defend workers, broaden social security schemes, foster unionization, and associations of disenfranchised and spread-out workers. Structuralists champion right-based approaches to welfare and social protection. More welfare is the structuralist prescription, not more growth.

2.2.2.5 Limitations and critiques

The neomarxist underpinning of the structuralist school of thought, antagonizing workers and owners of the means of production, is likely to have played against it, particularly as neoliberal approaches became more and more dominant. Theoretically speaking, structuralism was not displaced, rather it became cornered (in practice not in scholarship) by the persuasiveness of legalism.

> In reality, development theory policy proposals take place, not in a vacuum, but within orientations of particular political and ideological frameworks and to varying degrees for the benefit of particular groups and class interests. Thus the analytical tools used in policy formation are not value free, and include some political biases.
>
> (Moser, 1978:1041)

34 *Urban informality: mainstream theories and visible alternatives*

The class-based clash, where the powerful win and the disenfranchised loose in the face of globalization and deregulated vertical integration, found a disfavorable environment amidst a broader neoliberal consensus. A both interesting and highly contested approach that can be ascribed as structuralist is the "Bottom of the Pyramid" (Prahalad and Stuart, 2001) which explores the linkage between big multinational corporations and informal businesses from a business management perspective. Here, the idea is that informality represents a new market frontier that corporations can "colonize" aided by community groups and non-governmental organizations (Elyachar, 2012).

Roy's notion of "informalization from above" is regularly seen—even by Chen—as a sweepingly novel idea, even though it is no different than a structuralist view. Coated in a magnetic rhetoric power, what is certainly refreshing is the analytical emphasis on those in power. Roy's informality from above describes how the state suspends or bends the rules, and declares exceptions deliberately informalizing, as a mode of doing urban planning. Such "misrule of law" (Roy, 2009:80) works through "geobribes," that is, "spatial instruments of neoliberal development: eminent domain, special economic zones, land acquisition" (Roy, 2009:79) decrees, and selective eviction mandates. These tools of governance operate by "deregulation, ambiguity, and exception" (Roy, 2009:76), to allocate exceptional benefits to capture profits for those more powerful.

2.2.3 Legalism

2.2.3.1 *Definition of informality and causal theory*

Hernando de Soto, a Peruvian economist educated in Switzerland, stands seemingly solo as the leading advocate of the legalist school of thought in the informal economy. In his two of two grand bestsellers: *The Other Path* (1989), and *The Mystery of Capital* (2000), and through his Institute for Liberty Democracy (ILD) (deemed the world's second most influential think tank), he expounds and implements a theory of pro deregulation, debureaucratization, and privatization, as a means to prosper out of poverty. This is why, unlike his critics, he was heard loud and clear in Washington (particularly by right-leaning circles but also at the International Monetary Fund and the World Bank) and has extensively influenced policymaking worldwide. The first page of *The Mystery of Capital* states: "Capitalism stands alone as the only feasible way rationally to organize a modern economy" (Soto: 2000:1). Pragmatic and optimistic, this school of thought is habitually referred to as neoliberal, his approach was celebrated and his books were endorsed by influential conservatives like Hayek, Thatcher, Friedman, Bush, and Nixon (Mitchell, 2005:308). Within legalism's many advocates, de Soto's rhetoric stands out because being Peruvian, his argument was more credible (Mitchell, 2005:306), and also because unlike many others, it successfully bridges from economics to the spatial realm.

De Soto sees informality as a creative response to cumbersome and irrelevant regulations. Those that operate informally do so because formal proceedings are hostile and costly. Figure 2.6 portrays the 207 steps in the first of five stages of bureaucratic procedures that a homeowner in Peru must go through to acquire a formal deed for a legally obtained home. De Soto presents similar studies in Philippines, Egypt, and Haiti (De Soto, 2000:19–24).

Unnerving red-tape procedures are the cause of informality. For de Soto, taxes, byzantine permits, and other Kafkian regulations fuel informality. The stiffer the norms, the bigger this sector. According to this view, all informal entrepreneurs need in order to prosper out of poverty, is to have easy access to property rights, which would—in de Soto's fantasy—be followed with

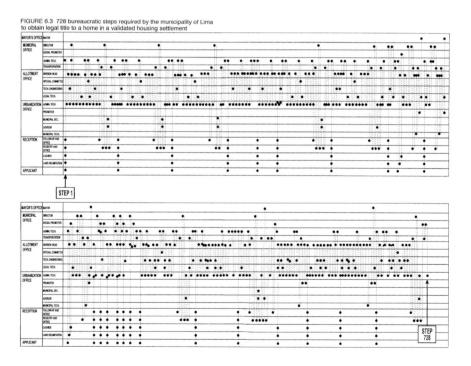

Figure 2.6 Formalization steps for housing in Peru (From *The Mystery of Capital* by Hernando De Soto, copyright © 2003. Reprinted by permission of Basic Books, an imprint of Hachette Book Group, Inc.).

36 *Urban informality: mainstream theories and visible alternatives*

game changing mortgages and microcredits. The argument is that redundant, strict, and overly complex legal systems create informality, so the solution to the informal economy is theoretically straightforward: deregulation to encourage formalization. Giving property rights and cutting red-tape will guarantee that those dwelling in the informal sector can be integrated into the formal.

2.2.3.2 Relation formal-informal

As explained, for legalists it is the formal sector that drives informality by raising high entry barriers. Thus, the relation between formality and informality is not positive and fluid, but rather one of restriction and exclusion. Micro-entrepreneurs and slum dwellers have no option but to revert to informality to survive. "For him [de Soto], the informal entrepreneur was an economic hero who manages to prosper and survive despite the state's controlling measures" (Alsayyad, 2004:13). Since government regulations create the divide, the government is seen as an enemy, standing in the way of a *natural* entrepreneurial spirit that all poor people have. Indeed, this neoliberal narrative requires all poor to be entrepreneur heroes. "Legalists ... acknowledge that formal firms—what de Soto calls "mercantilist" interests—collude with government to set the bureaucratic "rules of the game" (de Soto, 1989). They argue that governments should introduce simplified bureaucratic procedures to encourage informal enterprises to register and extend legal property rights for the assets held by informal operators to *unleash* their productive potential and convert their assets into real capital" (Chen, 2012: 6) (*emphasis* added). De Soto argued that "what creates capital in the West is an implicit process buried in the intricacies of its formal property systems" (De Soto, 2000:46). All developing countries have to do, according to the legalist view, is facilitate access to property titles, thus *unleashing the dead capital* in the poor's own assets. *The Mystery of Capital* affirms, there are 9.3 trillion dollars of this dormant capital (De Soto, 2000:32), waiting to be released via titling.

2.2.3.3 Evidence and methods

De Soto estimates the size of the informal economy as the number of untitled real estate properties (De Soto, 2000:33), and puts forward aggregate numbers not only for the share of the sector but of its total worth (9.3 trillion dollars), based on calculations on Egypt, Peru, the Philippines, and Haiti (De Soto, 2000:243–246). Scholars across the board disavow these calculations. As mentioned earlier, economists prefer macroeconomic measurements and statistics tied to labor surveys, rather than on examination of legal proceedings. "This [i.e. the legalist] is a difficult to measure perspective, thus it has largely remained unoperationalized" (Flórez, 2002:14). However, one could argue that de Soto's approach is perhaps the most operationalized. Favored by many developing countries and especially by international finance institutions, de

Urban informality: mainstream theories and visible alternatives 37

Soto's legalism has inspired a cadre of titling and deregulation programs, convinced of the promise that by formalizing property tiles, property values would double as people would improve them by using the title as collateral for credits. Notably, the ILD-designed massive property registration program in Peru argued increases of 23 times the investment: "By spending only $66 million, the government would create $1.74 billion in economic benefits. (World Bank, 1998:9)" (Mitchell, 2005:299). Time showed titling was indeed widespread and successful, but its associated rise in credits simply did not happen (Gilbert, 2004; Mitchell 2005; Payne et al., 2009).

Probably the most notorious measurement of red-tape deterrents to entrepreneurialism is the Doing Business (DB) indicator developed by World Bank's International Finance Corporation (IFC) in 2002. Both extremely influential and highly controversial, the DB index measures and ranks the procurement and regulatory environment across 190 economies and selected cities. Via secondary sources IFC collects "quantitative indicators on regulation for starting a business, dealing with construction permits, getting electricity, registering property, getting credit, protecting minority investors, paying taxes, trading across borders, enforcing contracts, and resolving insolvency" (IFC, 2017). In this sense, by default, IFC's ease of DB index is a watered down, measurable benchmark that ranks countries or localities according to their prone-ness to informality. Critiques to DB's methodological flaws were pointed out by the World Bank Chief Economist himself, Paul Romer, costing him his resignation in 2018, and causing further ripple effects at the highest rungs in management. The controversy was centered around Chile's politically motivated sway in the ranking, which was adjusted down by the Bank during Bachelet's socialist terms in office. But an even deeper critique points out that simplifying excessive formalities jeopardizes formalization policies by producing reforms that render valueless results faster, instead of promoting the benefits of formalization (Arruñada, 2008).

2.2.3.3 Policy options and interventions

Transmutation of dead into liquid capital proved not to be as automatic as De Soto's narrative implied. But curiously, this has not dwindled its charm. By openly declaring informality "is not the problem but the solution" (De Soto, 2000:34) (a phrase thinkers across all schools of thought have at some point defended), legalism is in and of itself a prompt into action. Legalist policy interventions advocate legalization of informal activities through three interconnected components: property titling, deregulation (specifically easing firm and building permits), and microfinance. This three-pronged approach, simultaneously spatial, legal, and economic; became a prominent development strategy.

The use of market approaches to "solve" informality and poverty (because indeed "De Soto conflates informality and poverty" [Roy, 2004:315]), came as a silver bullet into the hands of development agencies. "[T]he legalist

38 *Urban informality: mainstream theories and visible alternatives*

approach had a significant impact in a number of contexts, particularly micro level professional interventions by non-governmental organizations, international donor agencies, and private entrepreneurs... The goal of their work was poverty alleviation... primarily through credit programs" (Alsayyad: 2004:13). Moreover, "legalization of urbanization was exactly the kind of pragmatic, cost-effective approach to the urban crisis that McNamara favored" (Davis, 2006:71). Local governments with tight fiscal bases liked the fact that they could transform dead capital into wealth by mere strike of the pen. "The neoliberalist, legalist approach of de Soto and the microenterprise NGOs has garnered great political support in the last decade and a half in much of the Third World. This has occurred simultaneously with the introduction of new possibilities for development based on market mechanism" (Alsayad: 2004:13). De Soto's premises and promises aligned in the 1990s with structural adjustment programs and in the 2000s with public-private partnership models, advocated by the multilateral banking corporations. The fact that the recipe was "politically placid" (Gilbert, 2004; Varley, 2012; Davis, 2006:81) has boosted its popularity for decades.

2.2.3.4 Limitations and critiques

No single author in this field has received more critique than Hernando de Soto. Rebukes grow in parallel to the grandiloquence of his statements and their impact on policymaking. The three main strands of critiques go back to the spurious statistics backing De Soto's analysis, the overstatement of the impact titling has in the mortgage market (Gilbert, 2002), and the unfair assumption that the poor are naturally entrepreneurial. On his supporting data, Bromley explains that the global statistics are based on a cursory analysis conducted in Cairo, Mexico, Lima, Mumbai, and Port-Au-Prince. "The data on the five cities are apparently extrapolated to cover five-sixths of the world" (Bromley, 2004:282). This a serious flaw that surprisingly, did little to prevent its broad policy diffusion.

The second brand of critiques note that having a formal title actually makes little difference in practice. Gilbert's research in Bogotá (where—as in Lima—the land-titling program has been applied consistently for four decades) compares titled properties with untitled ones and concludes: "In Bogotá's self-help settlements, property titles seem to have brought neither a healthy housing market nor a regular supply of formal credit. The uncomfortable truth is that in practice, granting legal title has made very little difference" (Gilbert, 2002:18). Many authors share this view: "Land prices indisputably affect housing prices, what is still to be settled is if titling matters as much as De Soto assured... Titling matters, but is not sufficient" (Buckley, 2006:29). Buckley and others insist on the myriad implementation problems that come along with titling programs. These might include: high adjudication costs (because claims of ownership can be contradictory), new encroachments encouraged by titling, properties cannot be used against a mortgage collateral because people lack a steady income stream, or that the formal title means little in communities where verbal contracts are more respected (Buckley, 2006:30), or where other tenure categories have more legibility. These arguments have connected with legal pluralism[5], rendering very fertile studies (Guyer, 2004), and policy initiatives (UN Habitat, 2006), with particular emphasis on Africa.

The third strand of critiques focuses on the naturalization of the poor's entrepreneurial talent. Akin to the 'culture of poverty', the 'culture of entrepreneurialism' "allows the Third World poor to bear responsibility for their destinies. (…) It presents capitalism as a benign trade of assets, and thereby presents informality and poverty neither as exploited nor exploitative" (Roy, 2004:304). As critical scholarship highlights, assuming that the poor will join the credit market once they have a title in their hand, hides exploitative economic configurations, disregards colonial histories, and gendered practices. Optimism in the entrepreneurial power of the poor is ciphered in the fact that—especially women—are capable of saving and paying back loans (Roy, 2010). But the women's discipline to debt is more a form of exploitation (Davis, 2006:158), than a real springboard out of poverty. Where progressives see a sea of exploited market victims, de Soto prefers to see an ocean of eager business-minded subjects.

De Soto's optimism and assumptions continue to be influential. As Mitchell brilliantly explains, his ideas were a laboratory for mainstream economics. "It organize[d] the world in ways that provided economists with the opportunity to produce its facts" (Mitchell, 2005:309). Seen this way, it is clear this school of thought will linger unless more structural theoretical transformations take place.

2.2.4 Voluntarism

2.2.4.1 Definition of informality and causal theory

Not much different from a standard rational choice theory, the voluntarist school of thought on the informal economy comes mostly from literature and evidence from Latin America, where, however, measured, informality

---

5 De Soto allegedly endorsed legal pluralism. As Varley (2010) explains, the concept flourished in Africa and bypassed Latin America, likely because by opposing titles to social embeddedness, it remains somehow trapped in a colonializing dualism, that ignores that people in informal settlements are also rent capitalists.

40   *Urban informality: mainstream theories and visible alternatives*

remains high. The main idea of this theory is that rather than people being excluded or marginalized out of the formal sector, they opt out of formality following a rational decision. Arguing that workers are voluntarily informal does not […] imply that they are not living in poverty or that they are content with this status, only that "they would not obviously be better off in a formal job for which they are qualified. Being in the informal sector is often the optimal decision given their preferences, the constraints they face regarding their level of human capital, and the level of formal sector labor productivity in the country" (Maloney, 2004:1160). That workers prefer to be informal even if they have the chance of joining the formal sector, is very meaningful. It means that the working conditions within the formal sector are not as good, and that those within the informal sector are not as adverse. Either way, the decision to prefer and remain in informality denounces in and of itself narrow market benefits, inefficacy of formal social protection and, more broadly, makes evident a lack of trust in the government. People exit and they opt out of formality. Voting with their feet, they voice their distrust of government by taking their business elsewhere (Hirschman in [Perry et al., 2007:1]).

The seminal study in the voluntarist school of thought is titled *Exit and Exclusion* in direct reference to Hirschman's "voice and exit" theory, which ties economic theory (exit) and political science (voice) (Hirschman, 1992[1970]:77). Finding a foothold in Hirschman is no coincidence. Hirschman was a student of "economics in the wild," especially during the time he spent in Latin America: "during his stay in Colombia [almost five years] … he participated in government missions across the country, [that] enabled him to design a research method based on factual observations of what people *actually* did, contrary to the views raised by orthodox standards based on what people *ought* to do" (Adelman, 2008:1). Hirschman had explorative conversations with people of all kinds. This experience funneled his "analytical observation" method that defined his theoretical approach (Adelman, 2008:3). Voluntarism, then, is more closely based on describing real-life strategies than with economic modeling.

2.2.4.2 Relation formal-informal

Voluntarism is founded on the movement in and out of formality. For these thinkers (Maloney, Perry, Kanbur, Levy, and others), there is a fluid opt-in, opt-out relationship between the two sectors, people are constantly balancing out the pros and cons that producing, consuming, or dwelling in each sector has. "Earnings and welfare assessments support the view that the majority of independent workers are largely voluntary and attach significant value to the non pecuniary benefits of autonomous work" (Perry et al., 2007:79). This fluidity is exacerbated in the case of small firms. "Informal workers and firms don't always earn less. Hence, some choose to stay informal even if given the chance to be formal, even if they could afford to. This is starker in the case of smaller firms" (Flórez, 2002:27). A rational cost-benefit analysis evidences the opportunities of remaining in the informal sector which might include more income, and more flexibility, and more autonomy to use both time and space at one's discretion. "The large majority of micro-firms remain too small to benefit sufficiently from formality to overcome its various costs" (Perry et al., 2007:27). Since small-sized firms constitute 90% of total firms across world geographies, it is safe to say that this is a majoritarian phenomenon.

> Many informal workers enter the sector voluntarily and are able to remain largely outside the formal regulatory structures. Presumably, aspiring entrepreneurs wait for an auspicious business climate before leaving a protected job to launch their enterprise because they are more likely to fail during a downturn, which explains pro-cyclical patterns of entry and exit predicted by the dualistic view.
>
> (Maloney, 1997 in Flórez, 2002:12)

Altogether, the relationship between the formal and the informal realms in the voluntarist school of thought can be portrayed as a revolving door.

2.2.4.3 Evidence and methods

Voluntarists study the flows from between sectors by using different types of methods. For instance, the seminal World Bank report cited earlier uses ILO's informal employment measures of non-pensioned labor force (residual), as well as direct labor surveys from selected countries. Detailed accounts contradict what dualists believed: people are more likely to join the informal sector later in life, pointing out that informality's pension substitutes are more efficient: "the evidence is consistent with a life cycle model in which many workers enter formal employment to accumulate both human and financial capital, and then become self-employed or open a small business" (Perry et al., 2007:58). The most recent global statistical picture also suggests strong gender effects: rates of informal employment for women are higher in 56% of countries, the difference is larger still in lower income countries (Vanek et al., 2019).

Even though aggregate econometric evidence on the balance of flows is patchy on historical data and inconclusive across political tendencies, early voluntarists have suggested movement is strong in both directions: "flows from formal salaried to informal salaried are not so different from the reverse—or, put differently, if an informal salaried worker has a comparative advantage in formal salaried work, the reverse is also likely to be true. Further, the symmetry of the flows also suggests that, overall, there is not a one-way flow from informality into formality, with some exceptions" (Perry et al., 2007:56). However, data seems to consistently point that the exiting movements are stronger than those entering formality.

42 *Urban informality: mainstream theories and visible alternatives*

For example: "In Colombia, over 70 percent of independent workers are voluntary, in the sense that they would rather be independent if they were able to choose their job… [similarly,] more than two thirds of the Brazilian informal self-employed in the early 1990s reported that they would not take a formal salaried job, and less than 20 percent in Mexico reported involuntary reasons" (Perry et al., 2007:64). More recent studies readily suggest that informality is more of a one-way street. Navarrete concludes from ample empirical evidence from street vendors, home-based workers, and waste pickers in Chile, that: "As seen across subsectors, regardless of the multiple reasons for initially undertaking informal self-employment, once in the activity, people tend to decide to stay informal. This is generally because the majority of people obtain higher monetary and non-monetary benefits than they would in the type of employment available to them in the formal economy" (Navarrete, 2017:240). As measurements advance and evidence amounts, it becomes clearer that the balance between informalization and formalization movements is not even.

2.2.4.4 Policy options and interventions

Since the size of the urban informal sector depends on voluntary decisions, this perspective is particularly susceptible to policy mediations that change the terms of the alternatives available. "Policy is able to affect the cost-benefit analysis underlying this choice to move towards or away from informality and impacts the informal sector's size and salaries accordingly" (Maloney, 2004:1173). For instance, a reduction in the minimum wage would encourage business to hire formally, but at the same time, it encourages informally employed workers to remain in informality. Similarly, universal social protection packages like the ones advocated by dualists would, of course, increase social welfare, but at the same time, they increase the appeal of firms to remain in the informal sector. Because of this, "voluntarists advocate 'revisited' dualist recommendations of carrot (pro-growth) and stick (repression) policies" (Navarrete, 2017: 44). Hence, voluntarism favors a mix of policy options, as well as training to diversify skills and to build human capital, something all other schools of thought support too.

It is under the voluntarist perspective that more positive attitudes toward the informal economy appear. For instance, in 2007 the Food and Agricultural Organization (FAO) started to advocate forcefully in favor of supportive policies toward the "informal food sector," with the understanding that their increased market coverage represents a crucial contribution to food security in many localities (FAO, 2007:2). Supporting the ability of informal economies in their task of covering difficult to reach market rungs, opens the need to add supporting measures to ease informality's negative externalities like health and hygiene standards and improvements in infrastructure.

Interestingly, because voluntarists render labor market fluidity positive, that is, naturally crowding in the formal economy, they also favor flexible arrangements in social security programs, that consider different types of risks and autonomy (Carré et al., 2015:12). For them, a broad, overly generous, or universal social protection system is a mistake. Perry and Maloney insist that high informality rates in Latin America are due to an overbundling of social protections. They see as a key design weaknesses of social security programs the high payroll contributions that disincentivize formal employment. Excessive bundling in one-size-fits-all multibenefit packages (with health care, risk, life insurance, pensions, housing, childcare, severance, and sports and recreation), become "pure taxes" rather than contributions (Perry et al., 2007:44). More sensible approaches, in Perry and Maloney's view are social security programs that account for workers' mobility into and out of the formal sector during their careers and throughout their life cycles. Voluntarists hint the need for a more transparent tax policy where contributions are seen as a service to payers, one from which everyone benefits. Perhaps the most developed voluntarist policies available are those that follow the Danish flexicurity model (Wilthagen and Tros, 2005).

2.2.4.5 Limitations and critiques

Voluntarists generally assume that the balance of the flow between the formal and the informal ultimately favors formality. They assume formalization policies are stronger than their countering informalization. But this is simply not true. The informal economy is majoritarian. Worse still, as neomarxists and structuralists would argue, the flexibilization of social protections contributes not to formalization but to precarization and further informalization. Reconciling with the fact that informality is prevalent has not been easy for any discipline, least of all for urban planning and for development economics.

An interesting proof of concept that informality is majoritarian came from the empirical and theoretical work of Kanbur who demonstrates not only that those outside the formal economy are the majority, but that the largest share of those living and working informally do so inadvertently. In 2014 he gauged the size of India's informal economy in terms of firms and employment (Figure 2.7), as composed of four types of attitudes toward regulations: evaders, avoiders, and outsiders. *Evaders* are those covered by regulation and not complying (illegal). The weaker the state's compliance mechanisms, the bigger this category will be. The 'evaders' category maps well with the dualistic school of thought. *Avoiders* are those who conveniently adjust themselves out of the regulation. This category denounces badly designed norms and is consistent with the voluntarist school of thought. Those formal, or *insiders*, are both within the purview and complying with regulations. However, they are a clear minority. Finally, the *outsiders* are those not covered by the regulation, for whom rules are simply irrelevant.

This statistical portrait reflects that "avoiders" (what voluntarists call "informal," and what Kanbur later called "ghosts" [Kanbur, 2020]) are a

44 *Urban informality: mainstream theories and visible alternatives*

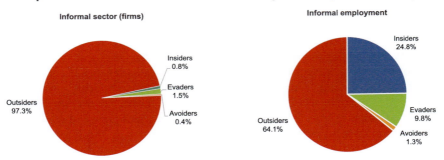

Figure 2.7 Composition of the Indian informal economy in 2010. Adapted from: Kanbur (2014).

minuscule slither compared to an ocean of outsiders. The sheer size of the phenomenon is an inconvenient truth, hidden in plain sight, that challenges informality scholars to rethink definitions, assumptions, and prescriptions, of the voluntarist school of thought and beyond.

2.2.5 Continuum

2.2.5.1 Definition of informality and causal theory

Recently, urban informality literature underwent a shift from frozen to fluid categories akin to the one experienced in gender studies in the last half of the 20th century. A hundred years ago, it would have been difficult to imagine that the binary taxonomy male-female would be as fluid as it is today. And yet, non-conforming identity types have exploded (L.G.B.T.Q.I.A.+ Lesbian, Gay, Bisexual, Transexual, Queer, Intersex, Asexual or Allied, and many others). Similarly, informality's outdated taxonomies are currently in flux. Today all approaches to the informal economy, and to informality in general, share a disregard for the formal/informal discreet binary, and prefer to focus on the middle ground, the in-between realm. Authors talk about co-production (Joshi and Moore 2004), continuum (Ostrom et al., 2006), gray zones (Yiftachel, 2009), coral reefs (Fergusson, 2007), linkages (Meager, 2010), fractures or hinges (Simone, 2010:45), rhizomes (Dovey, 2011), constellations (Barry, 2015), and moving fractals, to name just a few of the most recognized metaphors. Allegoric narratives are more inviting to audiences from architecture and the arts, which has revived interest in the field. However, by

Urban informality: mainstream theories and visible alternatives 45

emphasizing the aesthetical over the functional in their rhetoric power, this language is often blamed of glossing the conceptual clarity that emerged since the early debates of the 70s (Meager, 2013:4).

My review deliberately embraces the perspective of Elinor Ostrom, as presented in the book *Linking the Formal and the Informal Economy* (2006). Ostrom's work advances old economic sociology debates[6] on the social embeddedness of economic practices and thus manages to influence economics from outside of economics, as her 2009 Economics Nobel attests. Plying to her view, I render transparent a preference for an optimistic transdisciplinary effort that finds beauty in the world as is. Ostrom et al. are razor-sharp asserting that the informal is not unstructured nor chaotic. "Such an association is conceptually unsound, empirically weak, and has led to policy disasters" (Ostrom et al., 2006:16). Further still, Ostrom's break with dualism goes beyond and concludes that the formal-informal terms are only useful concepts within a continuum, and under the understanding that good and bad do not rest at either end of the spectrum (Idem:16). Simply put, informal is not bad, and formal is not good. This is a radically new definition. What we are used to refer to as informal, are simply practices that exist because they work, and because they do, they must be learned from. Labeling informality as bad blocks our understanding of what is really happening and hinders our capacity to help them thrive.

2.2.5.2 Policy options and interventions

Derived from this view of informality, Ostrom et al. are particularly wary of policy interventions. They confess that all too often "abstinence of the government is indeed a blessing in disguise" (Idem, 2006:5), and strongly guard against "counterproductive formalizations" (Idem:2) that do more harm than good by crowding out functional rules in place. When recognizing institutional arrangements along a continuum, more or less regulation is not necessarily good or bad. Rather, the point of policy is to find "the right reach of government" (Idem:6), so as not to destroy functioning collaborations, but

---

6 I refer to the debate between formalists and substantivists first exposed by Polanyi when he made the distinction between a formal economy (the economy of economists where self-interested actors operate) and a de facto one (an economy of collaboration, redistribution, and householding (Polanyi, 1944:57–59)). Four decades later, Granovetter returned to this debate offering not "downward" ethnographies of distant backward cultures, but "upward" ethnographies of the world of business and high finance. Granovetter's neo-substantivism revisits Polyani's embeddedness promising an approach that is neither under-socialized nor over-socialized (Granovetter, 1985:483–487). Later, Callon revamped this view once more arguing "there is nothing non-social about the economy" (Callon and Kalliskan, 2009:392) and calling attention to the relationship between economics and the economy. My research reverses Callon's view asserting that: there is nothing non-economical about embeddedness. Is also explains that embeddedness is not over-socialized nor under-socialized, but rather spatially determined (as per Chapter 3).

46 *Urban informality: mainstream theories and visible alternatives*

instead fine tune them so they work better. This approach also highlights that the difference between a good policy and a bad one is the implementation capacity. Good measures, then, are those that "tailor intervention to the capacity of the structure" (Idem:13), rather than offer blanket solutions (like de Soto's property rights [Idem:14]). Among the principles, Ostrom et al. offer for policy actions are: subsidiarity (going as closer to the problem as possible), offering bundles of complementary interventions, and using "voting with feet" as an evaluation criteria for efficacy (Idem:15).

A recent and remarkable policy breakthrough that embraces the continuum approach is ILO's 2015 Recommendation 204 (R204) on the transition from the informal to the formal economy. This recommendation was voted for by all but one of the 169 countries (a historical record) and was also adopted by the Sustainable Development Goals (indicator to target 8.3.1). R204 reflects a hard-fought consensus on the longstanding debate about whether and how to formalize the informal economy (Roever and Rogan, 2017:6). The importance of this recommendation goes beyond acknowledging the high incidence of informality worldwide. Only until R204 did ILO part away from the idea of repressing informality and began forcefully advocating that the informal economy should be supported. With this shift, it broke a glass ceiling in public funding restrictions, like "the right to access public resources" (Bonner, 2017:98), and shattered dilemmas that advised that supporting those working informally would encourage the sector to grow. In fact, this is "the first ILO standard to cover all informal workers" (Bonner, 2017:96), thus closing taxonomic loopholes opened by Hussmanns' matrix (Figure 2.1). R204 also makes an effort to harmonize this policy with other UN instruments (the 1948 Universal Declaration of Human Rights, the Social Protection Minimum Standards Convention of 1952, the Migrant Workers Convention of 1975, and the Home-Work Convention of 1996, and the Sustainable Development Goals for 2030).

2.2.5.3 *Evidence and methods*

The recently uncovered fact that informality is a majoritarian phenomenon across the world (i.e., 61% of the globally employed work informally [ILO, 2018]) fits most comfortably within the continuum school of thought. The continuum approach rejects the factual existence of purely formal and informal statuses, thus making all the shades of informality (with their movements of both formalization and informalization) unexceptional and normal. This variegated reality does not need to be tamed, funneled into a better, preestablished, more formal state. Hence, methodologically speaking, the continuum school of thought relegates prescriptive approaches and embracing descriptive tasks. The challenge becomes to suitably specify and measure functioning arrangements in each context (Ostrom et al., 2006:11). The continuum brings back to the table ethnographic methods that systematically observe and illustrate how things *are* rather than how things *ought* to be. Descriptive

Urban informality: mainstream theories and visible alternatives   47

examinations are more colorful and less evaluative. Description does not need to express the approval or disproval that prescriptive accounts regularly succumb to whether overtly or inadvertently.

2.2.5.4 Limitations and critiques

Displacing fixed normative notions, the current continuum approach is more conciliatory, more sensible, and arguably, it has a more promising future than the previous approaches. However, this is an emerging view, not fully fledged yet. Its level of penetration across all related disciplines is uneven and its methodological tools are underdeveloped. This school of thought is a work in progress at this moment.

Ideas deployed around informality and especially policies geared to dealing with it are still trapped in latent forms of judgmental dualism where formalization is unequivocally desired. For example, even minding the due praise to R204, it is clear that it remains constrained by traditional understandings of informality when it assumes that "most people enter the informal economy not by choice but as a consequence of a lack of opportunities in the formal economy and in absence of other means of livelihood" (ILO, 2015). Contradicting its own progressive overtone, statements like these overlook voluntarist and structuralist critiques and bounce back to the miserabilism of the earlier dualism. So, despite its intention, the continuum approach often blurs the distinction between informality and poverty, which has taken much effort to build. For instance, the R204 calls for "policies and institutions to help low-income households to escape poverty" (ILO, 2015), gravitating to arguments of "liberty deprivation" that contradict the continuum's spirit. Even Ostrom falls prey to similar tendencies. Despite the fact that she forcefully rejects the notion that informality is chaotic, disorganized, and wrong, her approach is far too concerned with South-bound developmentalism, and it is overfocused on the poor (Ostrom et al., 2006:7). All in all, I argue that these undertones should be regarded more as stubborn ideological debris that will slowly but surely fade away as the continuum school of thought matures.

My research sees in the limitations of the continuum approach opportunities to contribute to its methodological and theoretical construction. Chapter 3 presents my own methodological approach to observe, describe, and communicate the multiplicity of colorful statuses as they array in what seem to be residential spaces. My approach sits within the continuum school of thought but intends to move further by making sense of the shades of grade as colored arrangements organized in three-dimensional space, rather than tightly ordered along a one-dimensional formal-informal axis. The remaining chapters further elaborate on the continuum structure connecting it with the notion of recognition both in regulatory terms and also philosophical. I will show how recognition policies operate on the ground and then explain why incomplete recognition processes are those that are not bidirectional.

48 *Urban informality: mainstream theories and visible alternatives*

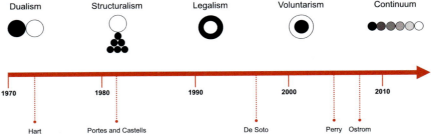

Figure 2.8 Chronological overview of the schools of thought on informality (by the author).

In recognition, two parts come into mutual cognition. I argue that for recognition policies to be effective they must operate in two directions. Not only should they address formalization of informal practices, but also informalization of formal ones. Further still, policies that recognize informal housing or businesses, should acknowledge not only informal infractions, but also make an inventory of their contributions. In order to get there, it becomes necessary to *count* and account practices that are usually unseen.

2.3 Time-use makes the invisible visible

2.3.1 *Time-use and household economics*

In parallel to the development of the schools of thought reviewed, there is an alternative view that does not restrict informality to the poor in less developed countries, but instead sees it as the worldwide intensification of work within the household. In this rather marginal view, informality is productive in economic terms, its contribution is believed to increase as society moves to a postindustrial phase. Gershuny's research trajectory is an excellent exponent of this view. In his early work, he predicted that "our jobs will be displaced not by automation but by export to the informal economy" (Gershuny and Pahl, 1981:77). In this approach, the informal economy is not a complement but a supplement to the formal one. Informal household production and services are the practical response to the shrinkage of employment opportunities and of the welfare state. Hence, informality is a privatization of social services. Informality represents a turn not to a service economy, but toward a self-service economy and it is encouraged by capitalism in rich countries for the exact same reasons it emerged in the South (Henry and Sills, 2006:50). The empirical evidence confirming the strength and magnitude of the informalization of the economy was only found as time-use studies matured.

Time-use research analyzes the way people spend their time on a regular day doing activities like working, sleeping, and in leisure time. Measurements are captured via detailed time-surveys or time diaries, that record a person's activities along the 1,440 minutes of the day. Under the direction of Gershuny, the Multinational Time-Use Survey (MTUS) has been consistently collecting, standardizing, and harmonizing data from more than 30 countries for over 55 years. Time-use information is instrumental in understanding a range of policy issues in transportation planning, public health, penetration of digital technologies, childcare, and most saliently, the impact of non-market work on gender inequality and economic well-being. In fact, time-use research is a highly gendered field of study since its beginnings. Early in the period under study, in 1974, Joan Vanek's ground-breaking article in *Scientific American* demonstrated that compared to the 1920s, despite the time-saving technologies like the dishwasher and washing machine, women were not saving housework time. Vanek's study revealed that expectations about home cleanliness and parenting have also risen. As time-use research continues to gain visibility in national statistic departments and as datasets become increasingly available, there is mounting evidence showing that time budgets are quite different for men and women. Women engage in a wider range of activities, their time-use is more fragmented, and they multitask more. In fact, time-use surveys are the major instrument to account for the extent of participation of women in productive but unreported or "non-economic" activities. Hence, time-use is the cornerstone tactic of feminist economics.

Ever since *The Wealth of Nations* (1776), specialization of work activities is associated with time savings and increased productivity. At Smith's pin factory, each worker does 1/18th of the tasks needed to produce a single pin, 20 times as quickly (Smith, 2000[1776]:4). The industrial paradigm believes people get the job done better and faster if they specialize in doing only part of the job, and conversely, if they do more than one task, energy is dissipated and leads to inefficiencies. But recent studies on multitasking present counterevidence. There is evidence of the "restart effect," where workers who alternate tasks improve their output, their job satisfaction, and their permanence in the firm (Staats and Gino, 2012:1). There is also evidence of increases in productivity derived from rest, termed "productive consumption" (Jackson and Palmer, 1998:iii), concurrent with ideas of "positive contamination" between different activities done concurrently. New business management models are incorporating a positive approach to multitasking, one that sees it as correlated with increases in productivity, fewer occupational hazards, and more job satisfaction. But apart from valuing multitasking as positive or negative, what is clear is that it happens and that its magnitude is not negligible.

In fact, multitasking is a central topic within time-use research, first of all, because it is so prevalent. "Around 95% of the population report multitasking each day, and that people report multitasking at least one third of each day... [Moreover,] multitasked activities are not trivial activities, but are those that impact upon quality of life and life chances" (Kenyon, 2010:44). However, multitasking has been a hard to conquer frontier for time-use surveys. Confounded by the fact that adding up simultaneous activities leads to days with more than 24 hours, some surveys (notably the American Time Survey) refuse to record multitasking. But this problem can be avoided by recording primary and secondary activities. Without this distinction, time devoted to secondary activities (which regularly include childcare, exercising, or socializing) is vastly underestimated. Unpaid childcare is a main concern: taking average MTUS data for 2001, Gershuny shows that time devoted to childcare as a primary activity is merely one-eighth of the total (Gershuny, 2009:198). Relying exclusively on primary activities implies that if new activities are added, others are substituted. Instead, if multitasking is taken into account, what experts see happening is that the "total activity participation is *increased*, as time-use is *intensified*" (Kenyon, 2010, 45). That time is used more intensely means that people actually do more within the same amount of time when multitasking.

2.3.2 Time-use surveying techniques to grasp multitasking

Furthermore, tests with new surveying techniques reveal that the notion of depth of time-use intensity is quite sensitive to the data collection methods. For instance, results from "the first non-memory-based study to use images as a prompt for participants to recall their activities" (Gershuny et al., 2017), revealed that conventional day-after time-use surveys grasp only a fraction of multitasked activities in a regular day. Participants in this experimental study wore a camera on a lanyard that takes three photos per minute from the "wearer's perspective" (Figure 2.9). The next day the interviewee participates in a "reconstruction interview" to answer the time-use survey while reviewing the 4,000 photographs. The experiment surfaced that people tend to "underestimate the number of discrete events on any given day" (Idem),

Figure 2.9 Images from the first image-supported time-use survey. The wearable camera on adjustable lanyard (left). Sample of participants Autographer images from the pilot study (right) (Gershuny et al., 2015).

and it further measured just how much the images help remember yesterday's activities. In every case, people do more in a normal day than what they think they do. We all multitask inadvertently. The extent of underreporting of conventional surveys versus image-prompted ones is of 46.7% (Idem). This has led time-use researchers to conceptualize multitasking as a "broadening" of time (Kenyon, 2008:887). Taking this notion from time-use studies into space-use, Chapter 3 will explain how spatial multitasking can be thought of as a deepening of space.

To be honest, I stumbled upon feminist economics a bit reluctantly. But as my research evolved, I discovered I had already entered it through my interest in time-use methodologies, and also because of my earnest conviction in the policy urgency of making visible the activities performed within the home that are productive but are not accounted as such. As a visual thinker, I was initially captivated by the potent representations of time-use surveys (Figure 2.10) and inspired by the efficient way in which they demonstrate, so often by comparison, the magnitude of the unseen. Work is equally invisible in poor and rich countries but "it is the *magnitude* of what is invisible what is concerning" (Waring in: Nash, 1995:50'20") says Marylin Waring, author of the seminal book in feminist economics *If Women Counted: A New Feminist Economics* (1988). Her work eloquently explains the politics of what is invisibilized in the economy and claims that the magnitude of what is invisible (revealed through time-use surveys like those in Figure 2.11) puts a high onus on policy. Waring's personal trajectory is in fact crucial to this story. At a young age she became the only woman parliamentarian in New Zealand and the chairperson of the Public Expenditure Committee, representing her

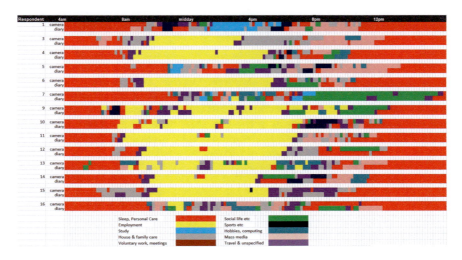

Figure 2.10 Visualization comparing activities of each participant (*n* = 14) as recorded in the diary and those in the photographs (Gershuny et al., 2017).

Figure 2.11 Marylin Waring compares gendered time-use data from a village in Pakistan (*Who's Counting? Marilyn Waring on Sex, Lies and Global Economics* (1995). National Film Board of Canada. 23'50", reproduced with permission of copyright owner and Waring's).

constituency of sheep farmers. "Developing the art of the dumb question" (Idem: 19"18) in her role as watchdog of the national budget, she discovered the extent of non-sensical values and premises hidden in economics jargon, a language those in power use to justify the unjustifiable. But once you learn that "the emperor has no clothes, tactics [to make visible a more real economy] are endless" (Idem: 1'28'30).

Spearheading Waring's argument is her critique to the flaws in the United Nations System of National Accounts (UNSNA), the accounting framework for measuring GDP. The system, designed in 1953 by Keynes and other white Western men, sets the rules for defining what contributes and what does not to a country's economic growth. By questioning the parameters of productive boundary, Waring brought forth the politics of counting. Going back to the original UNSNA documents, she denounced their obtuse claim that home production is "of little or no importance" and that people working at home are "inactive or unoccupied" (Waring, 2018:3). She exposed the neocolonial and patriarchal ingrained biases of the UNSNA, its ecological blindness, and the perversity of the fact that it has "no debit side, no place to record the costs and damages of economic growth" (Waring, 2018:1). Moreover, Waring showed the baselessness of the original arguments: The reason mentioned in the supporting documents of the UNSNA for not including the household's productive contributions to the economy is "convenience and practicality," nothing else. The document mentions the inconvenience of "increase survey operations and costs" (Waring, 2018:14). Waring exposed that a fundamental reason for erasing unpaid work from GDP was surveying difficulties.

Of course, this erasure is more complex and has other causes. As the 1993 revision of the UNSNA argued, if household production were accounted, self-employment would expand "making unemployment virtually impossible by definition" (UNSNA, 1993:6), thus heavily disrupting the mechanics of macroeconomic theory. This is not the place to get further into this discussion. What is relevant to note is that as evidence from time-use surveys piles up, it becomes increasingly difficult to ignore or to continue to invisibilize the value of unaccounted work done within the households, which emerges from time-use data as the "economy's biggest sector[7]" (Waring, 2018:36). Awareness of GDPs flaws has grown steadily over the last half a century, but despite the handful of alternatives no other indicator has taken over. Learning about the efforts of Jacinda Arden's government to replace GDP with a well-being indicator as a measure of economic success, Waring concluded that sadly: "the economist grandsons of the GDP architects are stuck [despite the new robes] in the old paradigm" (Waring, 2018:iv).

My research places itself within the efforts of survey experiments that intend to make visible the economic activities within the homes. Taking inspiration in the now mainstream time-use studies, my effort is one of imagining what the correlate of time-use research could be for space. How could space-use surveys look like? This is what Chapter 3 initiates.

2.4 The place of space in the theories of informality: two examples from architecture

2.4.1 Learning from Lagos

In 1995, as a first-year student of architecture, a thick shiny silver book that was just hitting the shelves was quickly becoming our self-adopted bible: *S, M, L,* and *XL* by Rem Koolhaas. Getting your hands on one was difficult yet crucial, for riffling through its pages guaranteed you were caught under its spell. Privileged enough, this is where I first encountered Koolhaas' research on informality, alongside his famed buildings, and infused with a critical reflection on the popular culture of the time. This book seemed to be coming from the future, especially for us sitting in a cold and isolated Bogotá, which was just beginning to turn the deadly tide of violence, having one of the highest homicide rates in the world.

Koolhaas began his involvement with Lagos in the 1990s, conducted a prolific Harvard design studio there, and went on designing and researching the city for more than three decades. For Koolhaas, Lagos was a window into a fundamentally different approach to architecture, infrastructure, and city-making. His research innovated different ways to document the form of

---

7 Measuring the Gross Household Production of Australia, Ironmonger (1995) proved this sector was ten times larger than manufacturing and three times that of all mining extraction (Waring, 2018:39). A 1998 national survey in New Zealand found it equivalent to two million full-time jobs, more than half the total population of the country (Warring, 2018:14).

the informal, the form of what allegedly has no form. Further, its reflections hinted a reconceptualization of what is meant by a city, a new ontology of the urban, one where urban informality is radically anti-modern (rather than premodern), and more importantly, it represents a viable future that displaces traditional Western notions. Koolhaas' unpublished Lagos Charter (an alternative to the Athens Charter, the quintessential CIAM manifesto of the modern city [Mumford, 2000]) states: "We refuse the idea that Lagos is on its way of becoming modern (...) Lagos is not catching up with us. Rather we may be catching up with Lagos" (Koolhaas et al., 2002:138). The manifesto continues: "The informal is an understanding that the largest effects can be gathered from operating at the smallest scale, that the humblest means can achieve the greatest ends, that liminal spaces hold endless possibilities for program and that time is a source of wealth" (Koolhaas et al., 2002:319).

The strength of Koolhaas' argument is heavily derived from visuals: images are not accompanying ideas, but literally fleshing them out. His photographic and film-led research into the urban landscape is inseparable from his writing. For instance, the bird-view photograph of an open-air informal market (Figure 2.12), invites the eye to unlearn, challenging traditional understandings of order. Overdrawn thin white lines point a structured assembly of varied activities in specific locations. Crates with a product are on display here but not there. Buses are on a slow-go here but pass through there. People walk faster through one path, those browsings have narrower passages to meander. There is order, reason, and structure in the interstices or even in the absence of infrastructure. Every element is purposefully located. And because of this precise arrangement, Koolhaas argues, it works.

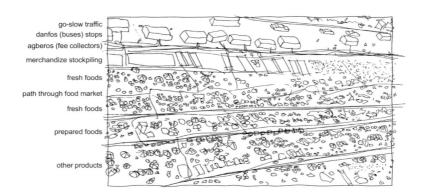

Figure 2.12 Tracing and labeling (by author) of a photograph by Koolhaas/OMA (1997) in Michael (2016) showing order in a Lagos informal market.

Urban informality: mainstream theories and visible alternatives 55

The reception of Koolhaas' ideas outside of architecture circles was ruthless. Scholars despised his perspective referring to it as ahistorical (indifferent to the colonial baggage), insensitive (for it disregarded the lack of choice those living in poverty experience), perverse (because romanticizing chaos justifies the retreat of government action), and also elitist (his use aerial photographs taken from a helicopter was deemed disgustingly top-down) (Ewenzor, 2002; Gandy, 2005; Packer 2006; Myers 2011, among others). This hostility was not easy for Koolhaas to cope with, even though he had long been well familiarized with torrential critiques being "the world's most controversial architect" (Ouroussoff, 2012). Despite the pushback, Koolhaas continued having varied and deep engagements with Lagos, producing over the last three decades more than seven books, that, unfortunately, never got published (Figure 2.13). Asked about this paralysis, he unconvincingly called it "an extended gestation" forced upon by what he saw were "moralizing arguments" (Koolhaas in: Haak, 2004).

There is no reason to deny there is truth in the criticisms. Plus, Koolhaas did himself no favor by hiding from print. However, revisiting his unpublished material reveals that to a certain extent, his opponents did not really hear what he was actually saying, they distrusted his methods, architecture's abductive visual research methods. Critics boxed out aesthetic registries from permeating mainstream theories on informality, shutting the door to radically new ways of thinking. But conservatism ought to be recognized when it happens. Prominent African postcolonial scholars like philosopher Achille Mbembe, vindicate Koolhaas approach (Mbembe and Nuttall, 2008:6) and

Figure 2.13 Seven unpublished books finished by Rem Koolhaas and Kunle Adeyemi and Harvard University (Michael, 2016). Reproduced with permission.

56   *Urban informality: mainstream theories and visible alternatives*

others even take his views as blueprints for a new disciplinary approach to Southern urbanism (Pieterse, 2013:26).

The next and last story in this chapter is diametrically opposed to that of Koolhaas. An architect from the South rather than the North, a dedicated researcher and designer who successfully introduced his research findings into municipal policies, thus shaping many cities in his home country, Colombia, and perhaps beyond. The misunderstanding about his research is less about misinterpretation than about incomplete absorption of the full scope of his ideas.

2.4.2 Samper's doctrine: standardization for desegregation and the wealth of the poor

Halfway through my college studies in 2001, while doing an academic exchange at Mexico's national university, I discovered, quite serendipitously, a book by German Samper that became my self-endorsed textbook. Samper is perhaps Colombia's most influential architect. Designer of iconic skyscrapers in the biggest capitals, the Bank of the Republic, the country's largest library, Cartagena's national convention center, the Gold Museum holding our invaluable preColumbian treasures, not to name the most beautiful and intimate concert hall. As if that was not enough, he was a devoted urbanist and housing specialist, trained with Le Corbusier in Paris and then wise enough to contradict his mentor. It is no coincidence that I learned to appreciate Samper's thinking far from home in Mexico, where I attested how in so many levels Latin America is one, how the commonalities in urban informality far surpass the differences, and how its research demands looking into what is usually looked down to. I understood the power of this downward look while standing among thousands of students at a Zapatista rally at UNAM: *Nosotros, quienes somos el color de la tierra, pensamos que la mejor forma de asomarse al mañana es mirando hacia abajo.* "We, who are the color of earth, think that the best way to peek into tomorrow is by looking down" (Subcomandante Marcos, 2001 [*translated by the author*]). Citing Unamuno, Samper insisted too on the downward inner look: "Instead of saying forward or upwards, say inside. Recognize yourself so you can shine" (Samper, 1974:12).

The lesson that drilling down within as the best way forward is everything but straightforward for someone like me, educated in scholarly disciplines that were not shaped by native scholars. I became an architect (and a philosopher) studying the intellectual legacy of the West, or more precisely, the North, rather than admiring thinkers from my land. The experience of being formed with ideas and authors from the North is indistinguishable from the effort of forcing their relevance to Southern realities. This effort places the burden of interpretation (and translation) on the reader. We, Southern students, tend to be forgiving with authors from the North. We are used to inadvertently blame ourselves and our defective background for any limitations in the exposition of a theory. Instead, reading theorists from the South is

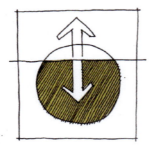

- Mirar hacia afuera es, generalmente, captar formas externas sin conocer su contenido.
- Mirar hacia adentro es conocer nuestra realidad de donde podemos encontrar soluciones propias.

○ Looking outward one usually grasps forms without content.
○ Looking inward, one gets to know our own reality and find our own solutions.

(Paraphrased by author)

Figure 2.14 Inward and outward research gaze (Samper, 1974). Translated by the author, reproduction with permission.

the opposite experience for students of the South. We understand faster, and we see the applicability of the theory better. But although Southern ideas are usually more pertinent, we tend to doubt their soundness. The easier it is for us to grasp them, the more demanding we are, even unforgiving. Reading Samper while translating selected passages into English helped me reverse this unforgiveness, reading appreciatively.

Samper explained his theory with exceptional clarity in writing, drawings, schematic maps, diagrams, and conceptual graphs. He also introduced his doctrine into city regulations that have long endured. Further still, Samper tested and refined his theories using brick and mortar, in more than 20,000 housing units. His rigorousness, meticulosity, generous publications, and professional commitment to informal urbanization spanning 50 years are hardly rivaled. Unlike most architects that research this topic, Samper did not change gears to delve into the study of informality. He incorporated ethnographic and statistical elements into his practice, but he did research as an architect, deploying architecture's own research methods and narrative registries, most notably drawing. He called this kind of work *laboratorismo urbano* (Samper, 1997:15), that is, "urban histology" or the study of urban tissues. Histology studies the microanatomy of cells and tissues as seen through a microscope, understanding the relation between formal structure and function through visual examinations, often revealed through coloring. Samper's urban histology studied housing, which composes 80% of the urban fabric (Samper,

1997:14), unconcerned about the epidermic aesthetic looks (O'Byrne and Salcedo, 2012:145) and delving instead into the relation between urban structure and function. Samper's emphasis on tissues, in urban patterns rather than in looks, is how he contributed, as an architect, to urban regulations.

Samper's theory of urban informality springs from the basic fact that in our countries, informality is the "immense majority" (Samper, 1997:204) (Figure 2.15). In fact, he argued that because of the magnitude of urban informality, there is a moral obligation to incorporate it into the planning apparatus (Samper, 1997:204), which he effectively did. For Samper, informality was not only a fascinating topic but a professional duty for architects of any developing country (Samper, 1997:204), and he took on this research as a permanent second career. It started in 1958, supporting his wife Yolanda Martinez who promoted La Fragua, the first self-help, progressive, and productive neighborhood in Latin America (Samper, 1997:22). From this moment on, he was convinced of the benefits of informal housing (it evolves progressively, it is productive, frees families from paying rent, averts professional fees), and aware of the challenges of informal urbanization (insufficient parks and communal areas, lack of concern for seismic building standards, upgrading over costs for the government) (Samper, 2003:207). Concerned with the need of balancing these benefits and costs, Samper became an advocate of urban standards.

In 1971, few years after his term at the city council (1965–1968), Samper participated in a pioneering study that laid the ground for a new regulation for "progressive urbanization." At the time, the concept of self-help housing or progressive construction was already in circulation in Latin America (see Chapter 4), but progressive urbanism, or the idea that road, sanitation, and electrical infrastructure for urban neighborhoods can be built in stages,

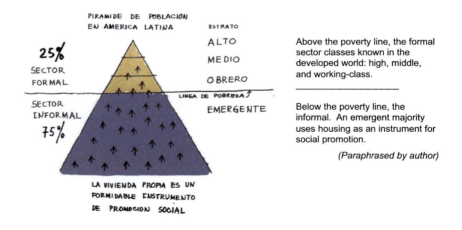

Figure 2.15 The social pyramid in Latin America (Samper, 2015[1965]). Translated by the author, reproduction with permission.

was revolutionary. The national and local governments commissioned this study to a leading economist, three engineers, and Samper, who developed a manual detailing the minimal technical specifications for progressive urbanization. The rationale was that reducing the costs of formal urbanization was the only way to compete against a mushrooming informal urbanization. The purpose was to redesign the regulations in place, which followed unworkable Western benchmarks, into more realistic and reasonable minimum standards (Consultécnicos, 1971). Furthermore, Samper realized that the previous standards (the Accord 65 of 1967 resulting from Le Corbusier's 1951 Pilot Plan) institutionalized a system of segregated densification (Samper, 1974:13; Samper, 1997:19), where the rich live in large plots and low densities in the North, and the poor lived in smaller plots and higher densities in the South (Figure 2.16). It was this classist view of density coded into the city's plan that Samper's regulatory efforts helped dissolve.

The *Minimum Rules (Normas Mínimas)* study, as it is widely known, "reconciled seemingly antagonistic features: on one side standardization parameters, and on the other self-help strategies" (Tarchópolus, 2012:239). Although Samper believed formal and informal housing were fundamentally different, for instance, informal houses grow but formal ones do not (Samper, 2011:225), the *Minimum Rules* standards had an equalizer effect.

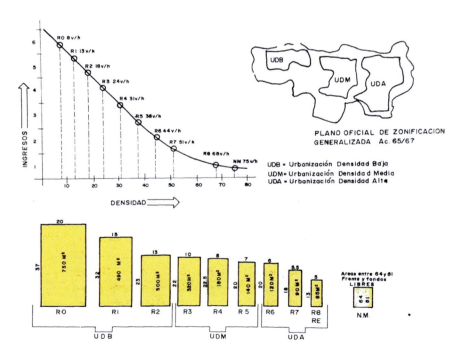

Figure 2.16 Bogotá's institutionalized spatial segregation by density in Accord 65 of 1967 (Samper, 1974:13).

"Since the 1970s *Minimum Rules* has both, attracted informal developments into legal parameters, and it has also served as a guide for formal developments" (Tarchópolus, 2012:239). Local urban scholars overwhelmingly agree that the 1971 *Minimum Rules* study left an enduring mark in the country's urbanization. But few dare to point out that they made the city, by design, look more informal. Today, in Bogotá the formal and the informal city fabric look confusingly alike, to the point they are indistinguishable (Figure 3.12).

Critics to Samper's minimal rules follow two main lines. The most common argues that the standards level down urban spatial qualities overall. Of special concern was the reduction of plot fronts from six (the informal standard) to three meters (Saldarriaga, 2005). A less common critique is that the rules have an overemphasis in new developments, disregarding the existing built areas (Molina et al., 1983 in Arteaga, 2012:228). With time, this second critique proved more relevant as the city grew less by "explosion": expansion of new informal settlements in the periphery) and more by "implosion": saturation via infill, subdivision, and densification of old informal peripheries. In graphic terms, line 2 in Figure 2.17 became steeper over time (Samper, 1974:14), meaning housing supply by implosion was higher than anticipated.

Samper's contribution to the *Minimal Rules* has been incompletely understood. Local policymakers enthusiastically embraced the savings in urbanization costs derived from the reduction in road areas and the increased densification via the low-rise high-density model (first introduced by Horacio Caminos at MIT and mastered by Samper). Also, both formal and informal developers celebrated that plot sizes were larger than in traditional

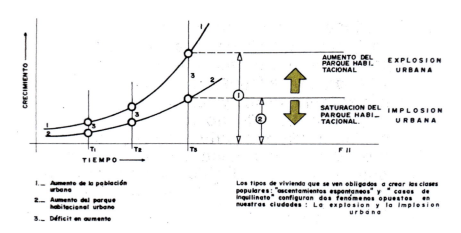

Figure 2.17 Housing supply by explosion (new settlements) and implosion (sublets and tenements) (Samper, 1974:14).

social housing projects (Figure 2.18). Samper believed architects should do research in order to quantify (Samper, 1974:15), this task of counting ought to be the basis for urban policy, determining desirable and realistic standards.

But not all of Samper's principles made it to the final 1973 Decree, fundamental aspects were watered down in later regulations. In Samper's urban histology, housing makes the majority of the urban tissue, but it is inseparable from the communal areas and services, which give form and function to the urban structure. His standards established generous provisions for communal areas and defined parameters for their location. However, over time, these shares have only shrunk from 15% to 8% (Arteaga, 2012:228). Today, even when the areas are reserved, "the social infrastructure never comes" (Arteaga, 2012:224), because it is "seen as a cost and not a social benefit" (Arteaga, 2012:229). The result is an unusually high-density city (Angel et al., 2016), of small yet generous plots that end up accommodating the communal services that are not offered by the city inside private homes. I will delve into this process in more detail in the next chapter.

Samper respected urban informality enough to bring closer the rest of the city to its standards. In a way, his was a task of recognizing the knowledge and wealth hidden in what seems poor. "What is constructed by the informal

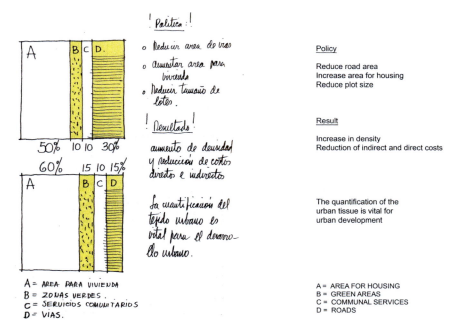

Figure 2.18 To quantify space is the link between research and policy: The transformative urban policy of the Minimal Rules (Samper, 1974:16). Translated by the author.

62 Urban informality: mainstream theories and visible alternatives

sector represents an immense wealth that is still not valued enough, to the point that we can talk about the wealth of the poor" (Samper, 2003:204). To understand the wealth of urban informality, to be able to see it, Samper insisted that house stories are the main avenue. "The term informal only makes sense if we penetrate into the family universes" (Samper, 2012:280). "Simple stories with short comments give the best insights into urban informality, rather than heavy, abstract, and boring statistics. Here some stories" (Samper, 1997:213). He offered some in his books, and he also revisited stories form John Turner in Peru, Teolinda Bolivar in Mexico, and others. "At the end, one is left with the impression that all those histories are a single one. Latin America is a unity..." (Samper, 2003:215). In the next chapter, I will tread this path walking the reader through some house stories and interviewing the houses through its residents and its images.

★

This chapter has offered a broad view of the theoretical landscape of urban informality moving from dominant approaches centered in conventional development economics, to alternative views concerned with looking appreciatively into previously overlooked areas: household economics, secondary multitasked activities, and seemingly disorganized occupation of liminal spaces. I end this review by arguing for a microscopic look into informal patterns that may render a quantifiable and more colored (rather than grayed) knowledge of my city, which is exactly what I attempt to cover in the following chapter.

References

Adelman, Jeremy. (2008). "Observando a Colombia: Albert O. Hirschman y la Economía del Desarrollo", *Desarrollo y Sociedad*, 62, Bogota, pp. 1–37.

Alsayyad, Nezar. (2004). "A 'New' Way of Life", In Roy, Ananya and AlSayyad, Nezar (eds) *Urban Informality: Transnational Perspectives from the Middle East, Latin America, and South Asia*. Lexington Books, Lanham, MD, pp. 7–30.

Angel, Shlomo, Jason Parent, Daniel L. Civco, and Alejandro M. Blei. (2011). Lincoln Institute of Land Policy, Cambridge [Previously published as: "The Dynamics of Global Urban Expansion", World Bank, 2005].

Arruñada, Benito. (2008). "How Doing Business Jeopardizes Institutional Reform," *European Business Organization Law Review*, 10:4, pp. 555–574.

Arteaga, Isabel. (2012). "El centro comunitario como parte integral de la producción de vivienda económica: una revisión del papel de los equipamientos en las normas mínimas de 1971", In Ediciones Universidad de los Andes, *Casa+casa+casa=ciudad?*, Universidad de los Andes, Bogota.

Bangasser, Paul E. (2000). *The ILO and the Informal Sector: An Institutional History*, International Labour Office ILO, Geneva.

Barry, Michael. (2015). *Property Theory, Methods, and the Continuum of Land Rights*, UN Habitat, Nairobi.

Bevington, William. (2007). *A Visualization Based Taxonomy for Informative Representation: Introduction and Overview. Part 1*, Parsons Institute of Information Mapping, The New School, New York.

Biles, James. (2009). "Informal Work in Latin America: Competing Perspectives and Recent Debates", *Geography Compass*, 3:1, pp. 214–236.

Bonnet, Francis, Vanek Joann, and Chen, Martha. (2019). *Women and Men in the Informal Economy – A Statistical Brief*, WIEGO, Manchester.

Boeke, Julius. (1942). *The Structure of Netherlands Indian Economy*, International Secretariat, Institute of Pacific Relations, New York.

Bolívar, Teolinda, Guerrero, Mildred, and Rodríguez, Marcelo. (2017). Casas de infinitas privaciones "Germen de ciudad para todos?" CLACSO/Abya-Yala, Quito

Bromley, Ray. (2000). "Street Vending and Public Policy: A Global Review", *International Journal of Sociology and Social Policy*, 20:1/2, pp. 1–28.

Buckley, Robert, and Kalarickal, Jerry. (2006). Thirty Years of World Bank Shelter Lending: What Have We Learned? *The World Bank*, April 2006.

Callon, Michel, and Kalliskan, Koray. (2009). "Economization, Part 1: Shifting Attention from the Economy Towards Processes of Economization", *Economy and Society*, 38:3, pp. 369–398.

Carré, Françoise, Negrete, Rodrigo, and Vanek, Joann. (2015). "Considerations for the Revision of the ICSE-93", ILO Working Group for the Revision of the International Classification of Status in Employment", May 6–8, 2015, Geneva.

Carrizosa, Maria. (2003). *La analítica del tú ante la pseudocomunicación en el debate Gadamer – Habermas*, Centro de Estudios Socioculturales CESO, Universidad de Los Andes, Bogota.

Castells, Manuel, and Portes, Alejandro. (1989). "World Underneath: The Origins, Dynamics and Effects of the Informal Economy", In Portes, A., et al. (eds) *The Informal Economy: Studies in Advanced and Less Developed Countries*, John Hopkins University Press, Baltimore, MD, pp. 11–37.

Chayanov, Alexander. ([1924]1985). *La organización de la unidad económica campesina*, Ediciones Nueva Visión, Buenos Aires.

Chen, Martha. (2006). "Rethinking the Informal Economy: Linkages with the Formal Economy and the Formal Regulatory Environment", In Guha-Khasnobis, B., Kanbur, R. and Ostrom, E. (eds) *Linking the Formal and Informal Economy*, Oxford University Press, London, pp. 75–92.

Chen, Martha. (2012). *The Informal Economy: Definitions, Theories and Policies*, WIEGO Working Paper no. 1, Cambridge.

Chen, Martha, Roever Sally, and Skinner Caroline. (2016). "Urban Livelihoods and the New Urban Agenda", *Editorial, Environment and Urbanization*, 34, pp. 1–12.

Chen, Martha, and Carré, Francoise. (eds) (2020). *The Informal Economy Revisited: Examining the Past, Envisioning the Future*, Routledge, London. https://doi.org/10.4324/9780429200724

Collier, Paul, and Gunning, Jan Willem. (1999). "Why Has Africa Grown Slowly?" *Journal of Economic Perspectives*, 13:3, pp. 3–22.

Consultécnicos. (1971). "Estudio de normas mínimas de urbanización, servicios públicos y servicios comunitarios. Primera parte: normas físicas y aspectos generales" (report to ICT, DAPD and DNP), Revista Escala 65, Bogota.

Davis, Mike. (2006). *The Planet of Slums*, Verso, London.

De Soto, Hernando. (1989). *The Other Path: The Invisible Revolution in the Third World*, Taurus, London.

64 *Urban informality: mainstream theories and visible alternatives*

De Soto, Hernando. (2000). *The Mystery of Capital: Why Capitalism Triumphs in the West and Fails Everywhere Else*, Basic, Print, New York.

Dovey, Kim, and King, Ross. (2011). "Forms of Informality: Morphology and Visibility of Informal Settlements". *Built Environment* (1978–), 37:1, pp. 11–29.

Edgcomb, Elaine, Losby, Jan, Else, Jon, Malm, Erica, Kingslow, Marcia, and Kao, Vivian. (2002). *Informal Economy Literature Review*. ISED and Aspen Institute, New York.

Elyachar, Julia. (2012). "Next Practices: Knowledge, Infrastructure, and Public Goods at the Bottom of the Pyramid", In *Public Culture 24:1*, Duke University Press, Durham, NC, pp. 119–125.

Ewenzor, Okwui. (2002). Under Siege, Four African Cities, Freetown, Johannesburg, Kinshasa, Lagos: Documenta 11, Platform 4, A Conference and Workshop Held in Lagos, Goethe-Institut Inter Nationes, March 16–20, 2002, Verso.

Feldstein, Martin. (2017). "Underestimating the Real Growth of GDP, Personal Income, and Productivity", *Journal of Economic Perspectives*, 31:2, pp. 145–164.

Ferguson, James. (2007). "Formalities of Poverty: Thinking about Social Assistance in Neoliberal South Africa", *African Studies Review*, 50:2, pp. 71–86.

Fergusson, Bruce, and Navarrete, Jesus. (2003). "A Financial Framework for Reducing Slums: Lessons from Experience in Latin America", *Environment and Urbanization*, 15:2, pp. 201–216.

Flórez, Nieto, and Elisa, Carmen. (2002). *The Function of the Urban Informal Sector in Employment: Evidence from Colombia 1984–2000*, Documento CEDE, Universidad de Los Andes, Bogota.

FAO – Food and Agriculture Organization. (2007). *Promises and Challenges of the Informal Food Sector in Developing Countries*, FAO, Rome.

Gallin, Dan. (2007). *The ILO Home Work Convention Ten Years Later*. Global Labour Institute, Manchester.

Gandy, Mathew. (2005). "Learning from Lagos", *New Left Review* 33, pp. 37–52.

Geertz, Clifford. (1978). "The Bazaar Economy: Information and Search in Peasant Marketing", *American Economic Review*, 68:2, pp. 28–32.

Gershuny, J. I. and Pahl, R. E. (1981). *Work Outside Employment: Some Preliminary Speculations*, Informal institutions, Saint Martins, New York.

Gershuny, Jonathan. (2009). "Harvey's Hypercodes and the 'Propogram': More than 24 Hours Per Day?" *Electronic International Journal of Time Use Research*, 6:2, pp. 193–199.

Gershuny et al. (2017). *CAPTURE24: Testing Self-report Time-use Diaries Against Objective Instruments in Real Time*, Center for Time Use Research, University of Oxford, Oxford.

Gershuny, Jonathan, Bitman, Michael, and Bauman, Adrian. (2019). "A Short History of Time Use Research; Implications for Public Health", BMC Public Health 2019, 19:607, Creative Commons.

Gilbert, Alan. (2002). "On the Mystery of Capital and the Myths of Hernando de Soto: What Difference Does Legal Title Make?" *International Development Planning Review*, 24:1, pp. 33–66, Liverpool.

Gilbert, Alan. (2004). "Love in the Time of Enhanced Capital Flows Reflections on the Links between Liberalization and Informality". In Roy, Ananya and AlSayyad, Nezar (eds) *Urban Informality: Transnational Perspectives from the Middle East, Latin America, and South Asia*. Lexington Books, Lanham, MD; Center for Middle Eastern Studies, University of California at Berkeley, Berkeley, CA, pp. 33–66.

UN Habitat (2006, May 1). About GLTN. Global Land Tool Network. Retrieved January 10, 2023, from https://gltn.net/about-gltn/.

Goldin, Claudia. (1995). "The U-Shaped Female Labor Force Function in Economic Development and Economic History", In Schultz, T. Paul (ed) *Investment in Women's Human Capital and Economic Development*. University of Chicago Press, pp. 61–90.

Goldin, Claudia. (2021). "How the Pandemic Could Make the Future Brighter for Women in the Workplace", *Wall Street Journal*. https://www.wsj.com/articles/pandemic-women-workplace-future-11638302927

Granovetter, Mark. (1985). "Economic Action and the Problem of Embeddedness", *American Journal of Sociology*, 68, pp. 481–510.

Guyer, Jane. (2004). *Marginal Gains: Monetary Transactions in Atlantic Africa*, University of Chicago Press, Chicago, IL.

Harris, J. and Todaro, M. (1970). "Migration, Unemployment and Development: A Two-Sector Analysis", *American Economic Review*, 60:1, pp. 126–142.

Hart, Keith / ILO. (1973). "Informal Income Opportunities and Urban Employment in Ghana", *Journal of Modern African Studies*, 11:1, pp. 61–89.

Hart, Keith. (2010). "Africa's Urban Revolution and the Informal Economy", *Vishnu Padayachee, The Political Economy of Africa*, pp. 372–387.

Hart, Keith. (2011). "The Informal Economy: A Story of Ethnography Untold", The Memory Bank RSS, Keith Hart's Blog, Entry: January 8, 2011, Accessed December 16, 2012.

Haak van der, Bregtie. (2014). "Architect Rem Koolhaas interviewed about Lagos", *Submarine Channel Vimeo*.

Henry, S. and Sills, S. (2006). "Informal Economic Activity: Early Thinking, Conceptual Shifts, Continuing Patterns and Persistent Issues", *Crime, Law and Social Change, Springler*, 45:4–5, pp. 263–284.

Hirschman, Albert. (1992[1970]). "Exit and Voice, an Expanding sphere of influence", In Hirschman, Albert (ed) *Rival Views of Market Society*, Harvard University Press, Cambridge, MA.

Gereffi, Gary, Humphrey, John, and Sturgeon, Timothy. (2005). "The Governance of Global Value Chains", *Review of International Political Economy*, 12:1, pp. 78–104.

Hussmanns, Ralf. (2003). *Defining and Measuring Informal Employment*, Bureau of Statistics, International Labour Office, Geneva.

Hussmanns, Ralf. (2004) *Measuring the Informal Economy: From Employment in the Informal Sector to Informal Employment*, Policy Integration Department, Bureau of Statistics, International labour Office, Geneva.

Hussmanns, Ralf. (2007). "Measurement of Employment, Unemployment, and Underemployment: Current International Standards and Issues in Their Application", International Labot Organization, Geneva. https://www.ilo.org/global/statistics-and-databases/WCMS_088394/lang--en/index.htm

IFC – International Finance Corporation. (2017). "Doing Business, Measuring Business Regulations", World Bank Group. http://www.doingbusiness.org/

ILO – International Labor Organization. (1993). "Resolution Concerning Statistics of Employment in the Informal Sector", *Fifteenth International Conference of Labour Statisticians*, Geneva (January 1993).

ILO – International Labor Organization. (2003). "Resolution Concerning Decent Work and the Informal Economy", General Conference of the International Labour Organization 90th Session, Geneva.

66 *Urban informality: mainstream theories and visible alternatives*

ILO – International Labor Organization. (2015). Resolution # 204: Transition from the Informal to the Formal Economy Recommendation, 104th ILC session, June 12, 2015, Geneva.

ILO – International Labor Organization. (2018). "Women and Men in the Informal Economy: A Statistical Picture", 3rd edition, Geneva.

Jackson, C. and Palmer-Jones, R. (1998). *Work Intensity, Gender and Well-being*, United Nations Research Institute for Social Development (UNRISD), Geneva, 96:iii.

Joshi, A. and Moore, M. (2004). "Institutionalised Co-production: Unorthodox Public Service Delivery in Challenging Environments", *Journal of Development Studies*, 40:4, pp. 31–49.

Jutting, Johannes and Laiglesia, Juan. (2009) "Is Informal Normal? Towards More Better Jobs in Developing Countries", *OECD Development Centre*, March 24, 2009.

Kanbur, Ravi. (2014). "Informality: Causes, Consequences and Policy Responses", Working Paper, Cornell University, Ithaca, NY.

Kanbur, Ravi. (2020). "Assessing Taxation and Informality: Disaggregated Frameworks Matter", In *The Informal Economy Revisited: Examining the Past, Envisioning the Future*, Routledge, https://doi.org/10.4324/9780429200724

Kenyon, Susan. (2010). "What Do We Mean by Multitasking? – Exploring the Need for Methodological Clarification in Time Use Research", *International Journal of Time Use Research*, 7:1, pp. 42–60.

Guha-Khasnobis, B., Kanbur, R. and Ostrom, E. (eds) (2006). *Linking the Formal and Informal Economy*, Oxford University Press, Oxford.

Koolhaas Rem Arc en rêve centre d'architecture and Harvard Project on the City. (2001). Mutations: Rem Koolhaas Harvard Project on the City ... [Et Al]. Barcelona Bordeaux: ACTAR : Arc en rêve centre d'architecture.

Koolhaas, Rem. (2002). "Fragments of a Lecture on Lagos", In O. Enwezor, Koolhaas, Rem, Kwinter, Sanford, Boeri, Stefano, Tazi, Nadia, Arc en rêve centre d'architecture, Obrist, Hans Ulrich, Chung, Chuihua Judy, Inaba, Jeffrey, Leong, Sze Tsung, Harvard University Graduate School of Design (eds) *Under Siege: Four African Cities — Freetown*, Johannesburg, Kinshasa, Lagos: Documenta 11, Platform 4.

Koolhaas, Rem, Pierre Belanger, Chuihua Judy Chung, Edgat Claijne, Joshua Comaroff, Michael Cosama, David Hamilton, Jeffery Inaba, Lan Ying IP, Jeannie Kim, Gullivar Shepard, Reshma Singh, Nathaniel Slayton, James Stone and Sameh Wahba. (2002). *The Lagos Project, Project on the City 4*, Harvard Design School, Unpublished manuscript.

Levy, et al. (2012). "(In) Formal and (Un) Productive: The Productivity Costs of Excessive Informality in Mexico", IDB Working Paper Series 34, Washington.

Lewis, Arthur. (1954). "Economic Development with Unlimited Supplies of Labor", *The Manchester School*, 22:2, Manchester, pp. 139–191.

Lubell, H. (1991). *The Informal Sector in the 1980s and 1990s, Organisation for Economic Co-operation and Development*. Development Centre, Paris.

Lipton M. (1984). "Family, Fungibility and Formality: Rural Advantages of Informal Non-farm Enterprise versus the Urban-formal State", In Amin, S. (ed) *Human Resources, Employment and Development Volume 5: Developing Countries*. International Economic Association Series, Palgrave Macmillan, London.

Madrick, Jeff. (2001). *The Charms of Property*, The New York Review of Books, New York.

Malthus, Thomas. (1798). *An Essay on the Principle of Population*, Project Gutenberg. J. Johnson, London.

Maloney, William. (1997). "Labor Market Structure in LDCs: Time Series Evidence on Competing Views", International Bank for Reconstruction and Development Working Paper March 29, 1997.

Maloney, W. F. (2004). "Informality Revisited", *World Development*, 32:7, pp. 1159–1178.

Mbembe, Achille and Nuttall, Sarah. (2008). *Johannesburg: The Elusive Metropolis*, Duke University Press, Durham, NC.

Meagher, Kate. (2013). "Unlocking the Informal Economy: A Literature Review on Linkages Between Formal and Informal Economies in Developing Countries", WIEGO Working Paper #27, April 2013.

Michael, Chris. (2016). "'Lagos Shows a How a City Can Recover From a Deep, Deep Pit': Rem Koolhaas Talks to Kunlé Adeyemi", Interview, *The Guardian*, Rockefeller Foundation, February 26, 2016.

Mitchell, Timothy. (2005). "The Work of Economics: How a Discipline Makes Its World", *European Journal of Sociology*, 46:2, pp. 297–320.

Mitchell, Timothy. (2008). "The Properties of Markets Informal Housing and Capitalism's Mystery", Institute for Advanced Studies in Social and Management Sciences University of Lancaster, Working Paper No. 2, Lancaster.

Molina, H., Salazar, J. and Salguero, M. (1983). *Alternativas para la construcción y el mejoramiento de vivienda en barrios de desarrollo progresivo en relación con las pautas de poblamiento y morfología de los asentamientos*, CPU – Universidad de los Andes, Bogota.

Moser, Caroline. (1978). "Informal Sector or Petty Commodity Production: Dualism or Dependence in Urban Development?" *World Development* 6:9–10, pp. 1041–1064.

Mumford, Eric. (2000). *The CIAM Discourse on Urbanism, 1928–1960*, MIT Press, Cambridge, MA.

Myers, Garth. (2011). *African Cities: Alternative Visions of Urban Theory and Practice*, Zed Books, New York.

Nash, Terre. (1995). Who's Counting? Marilyn Waring on Sex, Lies and Global Economics (film), National Film Board of Canada, online.

Navarrete, Pablo. (2017). *From Survival to Social Mobility: Supporting the Informal Economy in Santiago de Chile*, The London School of Economics and Political Science, PhD thesis, London.

Negrete, Rodrigo. (2002) "Case Studies on the Operation of the Concept of 'Informal Employment' as Distinct From 'Informal Sector Employment'", Paper Presented at the 6th Meeting of the Expert Group on Informal Sector Statistics (Delhi Group), September.

Nohn, Matthias. (2011). "Mixed-Use Zoning and Home-Based Production in India", WIEGO Technical Brief (Urban Policies) No 3, WIEGO, Boston.

O'Byrne, Maria Cecilia and Ángel, Marcela (eds). (2012). Casa + casa + casa = ¿ciudad? Germán Samper: una investigación en vivienda, Universidad de los Andes, Bogota.

O'Byrne, Maria Cecilia, and Salcedo, Juana. (2012). "Autoconstrucción dirigida, vivienda productiva y ejercicios sobre la densidad", In Casa+casa+casa=ciudad?, Universidad de los Andes, Bogota.

Ortiz, Enrique. (1996). "Towards a City of Solidarity and Citizenship", *Environment and Urbanization*, 8:1, pp. 13–20.

68   *Urban informality: mainstream theories and visible alternatives*

Ostrom, Elinor, Kanbur, Ravi and Guha-Khasnobis, Basuded (eds). (2006). "Beyond formality and informality", In *Introduction to: Linking the Formal and Informal Economy*, Oxford University Press, Oxford.

Ouroussoff, Nicolai. (2012). "Why is Rem Koolhaas the World's Most Controversial Architect?" *Smithsonian Magazine*, September 2012.

Packer, George. (2006). "The Megacity: Decoding the Chaos of Lagos", *The New Yorker*, November, New York.

Payne, G., Durand-Lasserve, A., and Rakodi, C. (2009). "The Limits of Land Titling and Home Ownership", *Environment and Urbanization*, 21:2, pp. 443–462.

Perry, G. et al. (2007). *Informality: Exit and Exclusion*, World Bank, Washington, DC.

Pieterse, Edgar and Simone, AbdouMaliq. (2013). *Rogue Urbanism: Emergent African Cities,* Jacana Media & African Center for Cities, Cape Town.

Polanyi, Karl. (2001[1944]). *The Great Transformation*, Beacon Press, Boston.

Portes, Alejandro, and Haller, William. (2005). "The Informal Economy", In Neil, Smelser. (ed) *The Handbook of Economic Sociology*. Sage, New York, pp. 403–425.

Prahalad, Coimbatore Krishnarao and Hart, Stuart L. (2001). "The Fortune at Bottom of the Pyramid", *Strategy + Business*, I:26, January 10, 2002.

Rakowski, Cathy, ed. (1994). *Contrapunto: The Informal Sector Debate in Latin America Albany*, State University of New York Press.

Ricardo, David. (1817). *The Principles of Political Economy and Taxation*, Dutton, New York.

Rodgers, D., Beall, J., and Kanbur, R. (2009). *The International Labour Organization and the Quest for Social Justice, 1919–2009*, International Labour Office, Geneva.

Rodgers, D., Beall, J. and Kanbur, R. (eds). (2012). *Latin American Urban Development into the 21st Century: Towards a Renewed Perspective on the City*, Palgrave Macmillan, Basingstoke.

Roitman, Janet. (2004). *Fiscal Disobedience: An Anthropology of Economic Regulation in Central Africa*, Princeton University Press, Princeton, NJ.

Routh, Supriya. (2011). "Building Informal Workers Agenda: Imagining 'Informal Employment' in Conceptual Resolution of 'Informality'", *Global Labour Journal*, 2:3, pp. 208–227.

Roever, Sally, and Rogan, Michael. (2017). "Urban Regulation and Income Stability for Self-employed Workers", 5th Conference of the Regulating for Decent Work Network, ILO, Geneva, July 3–5, 2017.

Roy, Ananya. (2004). *Urban Informality: Transnational Perspectives from the Middle East, Latin America, and South Asia*. Lexington, Berkeley, CA, Center for Middle Eastern Studies, University of California at Berkeley.

Roy, Ananya. (2005). "Urban Informality: Toward an Epistemology of Planning", *Journal of the American Planning Association*, 71:2, pp. 147–158.

Roy, Ananya. (2009). "The 21st Century Metropolis: New Geographies of Theory", *Regional Studies*, 43:6, pp. 819–830.

Roy, Ananya. (2009). "Why India Cannot Plan Its Cities: Informality, Insurgence and the Idiom of Urbanization", *Planning Theory*, 8:1, pp. 76–87.

Roy, Ananya. (2010). "Small Worlds: Democratization of Capital and Development", In *Poverty Capital, Microfinance and the Making of Development*, Routledge, New York, pp. 1–40.

Saldarriaga, Alberto. (2005). *Vivienda, Habitabilidad y Sostenibilidad*, Pontificia Universidad Javeriana, Bogota.

Samper, German. (1974). *Conferencia del Primer ciclo de actualización y ampliación de conocimientos de la Sociedad Colombiana de Arquitectos*, Revista Escala 79, Bogota.

Samper, German. (1997). *Recinto urbano: La humanización de la ciudad*, Ediciones Escala, Bogota.

Samper, German. (2003). *La evolución de la vivienda*, Ediciones Escala, Bogota.

Samper, Diego (ed.). (2011). *German Samper*, Panamericana, Bogota.

Samper, German. (2012). "Hacer ciudad en la ciudad, más allá de los macroproyectos", In Ángel, Marcela, and O'Byrne, María Cecilia (eds) *Casa+casa+casa=ciudad?*, Universidad de los Andes, Bogota.

Samper, German. (2015). German Samper Arquitecto, www.germansamper.com

Santos, Milton. (1977). "Spatial Dialectics: The Two Circuits of Urban Economy in Underdeveloped Countries", *Antipode*, 9:3, pp. 49–60.

Sassen, Saskia. (1994). "The Informal Economy: Between New Developments and Old Regulations", *The Yale Law Journal, New Haven*, 103:8, pp. 2289–2304.

Sassen, Saskia. (2000). "The Global City: Strategic Site/New Frontier", *American Studies*, 41, pp. 79–95.

Sassen, Sassen. (ed). (2002). *Global Networks, Linked Cities*, Psychology Press, New York.

Sassen, Saskia. (2004). "The Global City", In Nugent, David and Vincent, Joan (eds) *A Companion to the Anthropology of Politics*, Blackwell, Malden, pp. 168–178.

Sassen, Saskia. (2010). "The Global City", In Bridge, G., and Watson, S. (eds) *The Blackwell City Reader*, Wiley, Malden, MA, pp. 126–132.

Sethuruman, Salem V. (1976). "The Urban Informal Sector: Concepts, measurement and policy", *International Labour Review*, 114:1, pp. 69–81.

Simone, Abou Maliq. (2010). *City Life From Dakar to Jakarta*, Routledge, New York.

Sindzingre, Alice et al. (2006). "'The Relevance of the Concepts of Formality and Informality: A Theoretical Appraisal', In Guha-Khansnobis, Basudeb, Kanbur, Ravi and Orstrom, Elinor (eds) *Linking the Formal and Informal Economy: Concepts and Policies*, Oxford University Press, Oxford, UNU-WIDER Studies in Development Economics and EGDI.

Singer, Hans, et al. (1972). *Comprehensive Mission Report to Kenya. Employment, Incomes, and Equality: A Strategy for Increasing Productive Employment in Kenya*, International Labour Organization, Geneva.

Singer, H. W. (1970). "Dualism Revisited: A New Approach to the Problems of Dual Society in Developing Countries", *Journal of Development Studies*, 1970, pp. 60–75

Smith, Adam. (2000[1776]). *The Wealth of Nations*, Modern Library, New York.

Staats, Bradley R. and Gino, Francesca. (2012). "Specialization and Variety in Repetitive Tasks: Evidence from a Japanese Bank", *Management Science*, 58:6, pp. 1141–1159.

Standing, Guy. (2014). "The Precariat and Class Struggle", *RCCS Annual Review. Revista Crítica de Ciências Sociais*, p. 103.

Subcomandante, Marcos. (2001). "Discurso del Subcomandante Marcos en la UNAM pronunciado el 21 de marzo de 2001", Comité Clandestino Revolucionario Indígena-Comandancia General del Ejército Zapatista de Liberación Nacional, Ciudad de México.

Tarchópulos, Doris. (2012). "Entre el Plan Piloto y las normas mínimas: inicio y avance de una línea de investigación en vivienda", In Angel, Marcela and O'Byrne, Maria Cecilia (eds) *Casa+casa+casa=ciudad?* Universidad de los Andes, Bogota.

Tokman, Victor. (1978). "An Exploration into the Nature of Informal – Formal Sector Relationships", *World Development*, 6:9–10, pp. 1065–1075.

Turner, John. (1972). *Freedom to Build: Dweller Control of the Housing Process*, Macmillan, New York.

UN General Assembly. (2017). "Report From the High-level Panel to Assess and Enhance UN-Habitat Effectiveness", Session 71, Agenda item 20, New York, August 2017.

UN Habitat. (2018). "Metadata for SDG Indicator 11.1.1 Proportion of Urban Population Living in Slums, Informal Settlements or Inadequate Housing", SDG Indicators Metadata Repository, UNDESA-UNSTATS.

UNSD – United Nations Statistics Division. (2015). "About us".

UNSNA – United Nations System of National Accounts. (1993). System of National Accounts, Commission of the European Communities, International Monetary Fund, Organisation for Economic Co-operation and Development, United Nations, and World Bank, Brussels, New York, Paris, Washington, paragraph 1.42, 56. https://unstats.un.org/UNSDWebsite/about/

Varley, Ann. (2010). "Modest Expectations: Gender and Property Rights in Urban Mexico", *Law and Society Review*, 44:1, pp. 67–100.

Varley, Ann. (2012). "Postcolonialising Informality?" *Environment and Planning D: Society and Space*, 1:1, pp. 4–22. University City London, Print.

Vanek, Joann. (1974). "Time Spent in Housework", *Scientific American*, 232:5, pp. 116–121.

Vanek, Joann, et al. (2014). "Statistics on the Informal Economy: Definitions, Regional Estimates and Challenges", Working Informal Migrant Entrepreneurship and Inclusive Growth Migration Policy Series (68), WIEGO, Cambridge, MA.

Vanek, J., Bonnet, F., and Chen, M. (2019). *Women and Men in the Informal Economy: A Statistical Brief*, WIEGO, Manchester.

Waring, M. and Steinem, G. (1988). *If Women Counted: A New Feminist Economics*, Harper and Row, San Francisco, CA.

Waring, Marilyn. (2018). *Still Counting: Wellbeing, Women's Work and Policymaking*, 73, Bridget Williams Books, Wellington.

Wilthagen and Tros. (2004). "The Concept of Flexicurity: A New Approach to Regulating Employment and Labour Markets", *European Review of Labour and Research*, 10:2, pp. 166–186.

Yiftachel, O. (2009). "Theoretical Notes On 'Gray Cities': The Coming of Urban Apartheid?" *Planning Theory*, 8:1, pp. 88–100.

3 Space–use intensity in informal settlements in Bogotá

Home to eight million people, Colombia's capital Bogotá sits on a high and cold plateau of the Andes. The city fans out from the mountains in the east to the meandering wetlands along the Bogotá river on the west. My hometown Bogotá, a contradictory and dense city of "inscrutable doors" (Blair, 1924) is the setting of this chapter. The chapter is structured in three sections delving into what I have termed "space–use intensity." The first section prepares the ground to *define* the concept, the second one to *document* it, and the third one to *explain* it. I must warn the reader that while the thematic arc of this chapter seems quite narrow, that is, a single concept, the narrative registries are intentionally broad, as they seek to complement rather than supplement each other.

3.1 Defining space–use intensity

This first section locates my "space–use intensity" concept within a specific lineage of urban theory: Jane Jacob's defense of mixed–use against modernist urban planning. While mixed–use and space–use intensity are not synonyms, mixed–use is a good entry point to unpack the concept. This section also discusses some issues faced by available measures that strive to make operational Jacobs' conceptual analysis. I end this section outlining the key components and affiliations of my space–use intensity concept.

3.1.1 Jacobs' mixed–use

There is a broad agreement in the literature (Grant, 2002; Xie, 2012), among many others, that the issue of urban land–use intensity became prominent in the writings of Jane Jacobs. In her *Death and Life of Great American Cities*, "mixed–use" emerges as one of four conditions for healthy vibrant cities, the kind people want to live in. The other three factors are: density (of population and activities); small–scale, pedestrian–friendly streets (what today is called "walkability"); and preservation of old buildings into the city fabric (so harshly criticized by Glaeser, 2011). These four principles contain Jacob's seminal critique of modernist urban planning, which has come a long way

DOI: 10.4324/9781003297727-3

72 Space-use intensity in informal settlements in Bogotá

since the archetypical duel between her and her nemesis Robert Moses. After 30 years, it was her ideas that became mainstreamed into the urban planning discipline, inspiring not only communities and planners, but also influencing health professionals (see Putnam and Quinn, 2007, among others), retail specialists, and the international sustainable development community at large (UNGA, 2015).

For Jacobs, the first condition for city diversity is having a mix of primary uses. She defines this mixed-use condition as follows: "The district, and indeed as many of its internal parts as possible (1), must serve more than one primary function; preferably, more than two (2). These must ensure the presence of people who go outdoors on different schedules (3) and are in the place for different purposes, but who are able to use many facilities in common (4)" (Jacobs, 1961:152) (numbering added). There are at least four crucial ideas to unpack from this definition. First, there is the assertion that mixed-use is desirable at different scales not only at the neighborhood level but also within "as many of its internal parts." This means that not only a city must have mixed-use districts, but districts must have mixed-use streets. Moreover, taking this rationale two steps further (as my research does) mixed-use streets have mixed-use buildings, and mixed-use buildings may have mixed-used spaces. We can refer to this characteristic as *granularity*. Granularity is perhaps the most overlooked characteristic of mixed-use research, and it is crucial to my analysis.

The second argument she makes is that mixed-use gets better the more mixed it is, that is, if it includes more than two different uses. It is one thing to welcome retail into a residential neighborhood, and it is even better when other different uses come into play. Having residential and retail uses in the same building is the most conventional of mixed-use forms. We can call this a low-range mixed-use. Now, a wide-range mixed-use entails having a combination of uses that are less expected, like a library in a residential street. Range contributes to enhance diversity and cityness, Jacobs insists. This assortedness of uses speaks about the *range* of mixed-use.

The third crucial element in the definition of mixed-use is its role in spreading people in *time*, a central issue in Jacobs' theory. The idea is that a granular and more diverse range of uses distributes activities over longer periods of *time*, ensuring people use spaces at different moments throughout the day. Hence, increased mixed-use leads to increased time-use. It is notable how this very powerful idea was only partially explored by her and the literature thereafter. Indeed, the time-use benefits of mixed-use have been mostly circumscribed to Jacobs' prominent "eyes-on-the-street" approach to security. A residential area with some offices and shops is safer both during the day and at nights, as compared with a business-only district, which is not able to put people on the streets at nights. Secure sidewalks are precisely what modern planning and housing lacks, and in this sense her contribution to Oscar Newman's game-changing defensible space theory (Newman, 1971) is

Space-use intensity in informal settlements in Bogotá 73

instrumental, even if it ended being regrettable[1]. But security is not the only reason why the relationship between time-use and mixed-use is strategic. I would venture to say that productivity lies at the hinge between these two, which is why Jacobs got into *The Economy of Cities* (1969) so soon after *The Death and Life of Great American Cities* (1962), and continued reflecting on this topic for decades to come, as shown in other groundbreaking—yet overlooked—books: *Cities and the Wealth of Nations* (1984)[2] (which furthers her critique to Smith) and *The Nature of Economies* (2000) (which draws a parallel between economics and ecosystems).

The last element in her characterization of mixed-use refers to the *interaction* between uses that takes place when one space has different purposes and is able to share facilities. Diverse uses relate with each other in a way that generates urban and economic vitality. The mix of uses produces complementarity and economic cooperation (Jacobs, 2061:153), in other words, synergy. What is most interesting about this idea is the productive or enhancing capacity of mixed-use: "workers and residents together are able to produce more than the sum of our two parts" (Jacobs, 1961:153). This Aristotelian "more-than-the-sum-of-its-parts" principle is strikingly similar to the concept of agglomeration and indeed equally instrumental to her economic theory. Via the interaction between uses, resources, and ideas, the total sum of activities is more than that of each of the independent elements. It is this capability of "creating something out of nothing" (Jacobs, 2000:165) that lies at the core of healthy diverse cities like the ones Jacobs advocates for. This extra output produced at the local level is the very reason why, according to Jacobs, economic growth should be focusing not on mass production (as Smith argued) but on differentiated production (Jacobs, 1969:239). "Division of labor, in itself, creates nothing" (Jacobs, 1969:82) she said, whereas a city, by definition, is "a settlement that generates its economic growth from its own local economy" (Jacobs, 1969:262). Surprisingly, little did she know at the time that cities generate more than 80% of the world's Gross Domestic Product (GDP). In a way, the statistical evidence that proves her theory correct emerged well after this book, and even today it is difficult to amass as there is no internationally agreed method to measure GDP at the city level.

Anticipating critiques to her plea for diversity, Jacobs explains that the understanding of mixed-use as causing urban decay and congestion is nothing

---

1 Newman's theory of defensible spaces became the theoretical support for the "broken window theory" which has been misused in cities around the world to justify extreme policing techniques (Kelling and Wilson, 2012).

2 Jacobs was convinced that if she would ever be remembered as an important thinker of her time it would be for *Cities and the Wealth of Nations*, rather than for *The Death and Life of Great American Cities*. She assured her most relevant contribution was the explanation of how of economic expansion (rather than development), happens. (Jacobs, 2001). In this sense, perhaps Jacobs legacy as a barefoot feminist economist is yet to be fully unraveled.

74　*Space-use intensity in informal settlements in Bogotá*

but a "misconception, and a most simple-minded one" (Jacobs, 1961:229). She calls the belief that "mixed-uses look ugly" a myth. A dangerous myth deeply cemented in zoning regulations without a clear understanding of how mixed-use actually works. "Intricate minglings of different uses in cities are not a form of chaos. On the contrary, they represent a complex and highly developed form of order" (Jacobs, 1961:222). The problem is to assume dysfunctional disorder from visual complexity. This spurious association has important repercussions. Quoting Jacobs, Scott elaborated this same argument in *Seeing Like a State* (1998), stating that high modernism assumes functional and efficiency from visual order (Scott, 1998:4); and, taking it one step further, Roy quoted Scott's reference to Jacobs in her critique to slum upgrading policies (Roy, 2005:150). To break up with this misleading association, Jacobs calls for a different way of looking: "To see complex systems of functional order as order, and not chaos, requires understanding... once they are understood as systems of order, they *look* different" (Jacobs, 1961:376). My inquiry into mixed-use practices in informal settlements in Bogotá intends to do just that. Offer an understanding of this complexity so it may look, through our eyes and to our minds, differently.

3.1.2 Mixed-use mix-ups

Jacobs vindication of mixed-use has steadily gained ground in urban planning since it was first articulated. This mainstreaming process was accelerated thanks to its embrace by New Urbanism (Calthorpe, 1993; Duany and Plater, 2000), others, transit-oriented development (Cervero, 2006), others), smart-growth narratives, and also due to its public health implications (Frank et al., 2005). Recognized mixed-use benefits like increased walkability, sharing of facilities, decrease in motorized trips, and even crime reduction, have gained it a central space in sustainable development discourses and tactics. Referred to as "the holy grail of urban planning" (Dovey and Pafka, 2017:262), "Mixed-use has become a mantra in contemporary planning, its benefits taken for granted. [Yet,] Few question its premises or endeavor to clarify its meaning" (Grant, 2002:71). It took another decade for the potential disadvantages of dense mixed-use urban areas to regain visibility in urban circles. A good summary of drawbacks of density of mixed uses is what is known as the "paradox of intensification": "in locations where intensification occurs, greater concentrations of traffic [as well as noise and overcrowding] tend to occur, and this worsens local environmental conditions" (Melia et al., 2011). While an important warning, the paradox of intensification is far from definite, evidence is inconclusive and often contradictory. These problems stem from theoretical fragmentation (Dovey and Pafka, 2017:250), and differences in the way mixed-use are defined (Grant, 2005) and measured (Gehrke and Clifton, 2016).

Often times, both praise and critiques of mixed-use get tangled up with that for density, and understandably so since many of the arguments, both for and against, overlap. Both high mixed-use and high densities bring about shorter commutes and stimulate alternative modes of transport, yet both tend to concentrate pollution and traffic. Density, not mixed-use, is associated with higher per capita energy consumption patterns if it is achieved via high rises (Godoy et al., 2018). On the other hand, mixed-use rather than density is associated with rising property values (Cervero and Duncan, 2004) among others. In this ongoing scholarly debate, attention is more often placed on new construction rather than on existing buildings, and more on developed countries than on developing ones. The emphasis of my research counters this tendency: low rise rather than high rise, existing buildings rather than new, developing economies rather than developed, and more importantly, the emphasis is less on density and mores on mixed-use.

Below I will discuss four problems that the analysis of mixed-use faces. First, the lack of a stable standard of the number or type of uses that should be considered for analysis. Second, the fact that variations in the unit of analysis can so radically affect the results of the extent of mixed-use found in a specific area. Third, the legibility limits of engaging in complex mapping exercises. And last, the important yet insufficient differentiation between horizontal and vertical mixed-use.

3.1.2.1 Number of components

Mixtures are substances where two or more components intermingle without losing their properties. In cities, the primary uses we broadly talk about are residential, industrial, commercial, and recreational. Urban mixtures of uses, as any other mixtures, are much more common than pure elements, which makes talking about measuring mixed-use much like measuring the everydayness. Fuzzy and elusive, to say the least. Perhaps the most basic problem facing mixed-use analysis is that the components of the urban mix (i.e. residential, industrial, manufacturing, community, commercial, educational, transport, institutional, recreational, etc.) are not fully agreed on, there is no broadly recognized international standard. These are constructed categories with much overlap and ways to group them, so each city defines and subdivides them differently. For instance, New York establishes 18 use groups, while Bogotá has 26. Even the same city may modify this classification at different times, for different areas or for different motives, as will be shown in the case of Bogotá in Chapter 4. A literature review on this issue showed the use of at least 100 different categories (Lee and Moudon, 2006 in (Dovey and Pafka, 2017:250)). But such punctiliousness is hardly intelligible because, as Miller famously demonstrated, human cognitive retention and judgment is compromised beyond seven categories (Miller, 1956). This is one of the appeals—and also shortcomings—of indexes, that they are able to crunch down multiple variables into one-dimensional concepts.

3.1.2.2 Unit of analysis and boundary problems

A recent systematic effort to assess different measures of land-use mixture is that of Song and Rodríguez. Motivated by the gap between a burgeoning consensus on the benefits of mixed-use in urban planning, transport, health studies, and urban economics and the paucity of research on it (Song and Rodríguez, 2005, 2013), they compare different land-use mix measures taken from a variety of disciplines to understand their strengths and limitations. The detailed mathematical analysis is beyond the point here, but it is worthwhile calling attention to the persistence of the boundary problem across the majority of indexes.

The size and layout of the units of analysis can substantially affect the results of land-use measures. To explain this, Song et al. distinguish between integral and divisional measures of land-use mix. Integral measures (like percentage and proportions, the Balance index, and the Entropy index) are not sensitive to distributional patterns within the area of analysis. "By definition they mask micro-scale variation. Land-use patterns of great diversity and great homogeneity are considered as a whole and averaged out" (Song et al., 2013:3). As a consequence, larger areas appear more mixed than small ones, simply because of their scale. On the other hand, divisional measures are more difficult to calculate and communicate but they do take into account distributions within an area by further subdividing it. However, once the subdivisions are established (using administrative divisions or a simple regular grid, as in the graphic examples above), even these measures suffer from the Modifiable Areal Unit Problem (MAUP) (Figure 3.1). The MAUP is a common yet scarcely dealt with the problem in statistical analysis where the shape and the size of the boundaries of the spatial unit of analysis can radically affect the results. An easy way to think of it is as gerrymandering. Clearly, this statistical problem can lead to unfair, deceiving results. Now, imagine a situation where the boundaries are not formal but informal. This is precisely what is at stake in the cases I will document in Section 3.2.

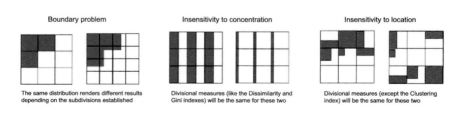

Figure 3.1 Common problems of land-use mix measures. Adapted from Song et al. (2013).

3.1.2.3 Mapping gymnastics

Like many others, Dovey and Pafka are concerned with the lack of conceptual clarity of available mixed-use measures and the corresponding difficulties in measuring it consistently. But their approach is quite different. They opt for maps rather than indexes because, in their view, maps enable an empirical understanding of cities that no other instrument provides. Maps "like x-rays of a city... enable us to expose different kinds and levels of mix in a non-linear manner" (Dovey and Pafka, 2017:263). In a direct reference to Jacobs' seminal account, they add: "rather than reducing a mix to an index, mapping reveals a *mix of mixes*" (Dovey and Pafka, 2017:249). Only via mapping, they assure, can the analysis of mixed-use (or functional mix as they call it) "focus on the *interconnection* [or interaction, to use Jacobs' words] between functions rather than the functions in themselves" (Dovey and Pafka, 2017:249).

Now, without getting too involved in the procedural gymnastics of their exercise, let me briefly illustrate Dovey and Pafka's maps comparing the different mix of mixes in Bogotá with that of New York. First, the researchers color-coded all categories of uses in each city's cadaster according to Hoek's live/work/visit triangle (Figure 3.2. right). With these colors, they produced maps where each hectare of the city is assigned a color depending on the mix of uses available at a walking distance from it (Figure 3.2. left). The different colors in these new maps show the type of uses in the mix. Then, the lighter the colors are, the more mixed the uses will be (Figure 3.3). Finally, each hectare was plotted in a live/work/visit triangle, summarizing the mix of mixes in each city (Figure 3.4). The summary diagrams show that "Bogota has a patchwork of every kind of mix where mono-functional areas disappear ... the neighborhoods of central Bogota are distributed across almost the entire triangle, showing a far greater range of mixes" (Dovey and Pafka, 2017:262),

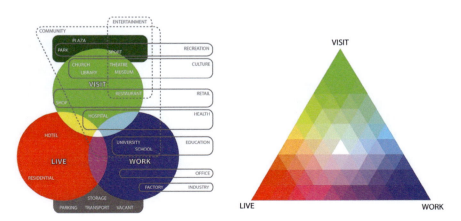

Figure 3.2 Coding uses along a primary Live/Work/Visit triangle (Dovey and Pafka, 2017).

78 *Space-use intensity in informal settlements in Bogotá*

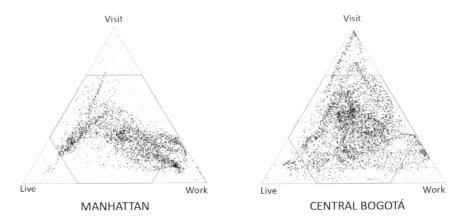

Figure 3.3 Functional Mix in Manhattan (left) and Bogotá (right) (Dovey and Pafka, 2017).

Figure 3.4 Diagram of the mix of mixes in each hectare (Dovey and Pafka, 2017).

than in Manhattan. This means that Bogotá has either zoning regulations that are more open to mixed-use, or less capacity to enforce them.

Dovey is concerned with the legibility and ease of readability of maps, but the extent to which his gradient maps and their corresponding triangular summary diagrams are successful is not that clear. The researchers themselves struggle interpreting the final diagrams and decidedly brush away evident inconsistencies (Dovey and Parka, 2017:262). They promise to produce maps that work as analytical cross sections of the city as a means to rendering clear urban complexity. This aim is undoubtedly compelling and promising, especially in the hands of an experienced urban researcher as Dovey, but the gymnastics of the process, make the final visualization at odds to deliver clear messages from the processed data. This analysis does not reveal, for instance, how is it that the interaction between uses is *more* than the mere depiction of uses. What or how much does it add? In contrast to this approach I put forward a stripped down, low-tech cross-sectional diagram that gives prevalence to simplicity: easy to draw, to read, and to interpret.

3.1.2.4 Horizontal and vertical mixed-use

Another basic but often ignored distinction when it comes to analyzing mixed-use is the difference between horizontal and vertical mixed-use. Generally, horizontal mixed-use zoning refers to different single use buildings that are adjacent to each other or within the same block, and vertical mixed-use zoning refers to different uses stacked inside the same building. Regulations take into account horizontal mixed-use more frequently, but vertical mixed-use is far more common in practice. In part, this has to do with the fact that horizontal mixed-use takes advantage of most of the benefits of mixing uses (sharing of resources and promoting walkability), while "avoiding the financing and *coding complexities* of vertically layered uses" (Blackson, 2013), as shown in Figure 3.5. Increased availability of cadastral and floor-area data is slowly pushing forward this frontier (Dovey and Pafka, 2017:250), as are digital visualization capabilities. It is, indeed with a mix of frustration and excitement for the new technological possibilities, that surveyors recognize that: "no country in the world has a true 3D cadaster" (FIG, 2018).

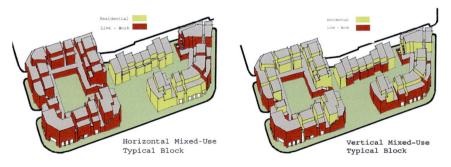

Figure 3.5 Horizontal mixed-use and vertical mixed-use (Blackson and PlaceMakers, 2013).

80 *Space-use intensity in informal settlements in Bogotá*

As this frontier moves forward, it is important to recognize that there can be horizontal mixed-use within the same building, whenever different rooms of the same building have different uses. One might also find different uses in the same room at different moments in time, or even simultaneously. It is also possible to further subdivide a building or a room and recognize different uses within. My research explores this. That spaces multitask seems to imply that mixed-use data is not discrete but continuous. This is a far-reaching difference. If mixed-use data is continuous, then in theory it could be measured, rather than counted. One could talk of the extent of mixed-use, not just its presence or absence. Ultimately, it is a matter of establishing the level of resolution at which the data can be captured and for what purpose.

3.1.3 Origin and components of space-use intensity

3.1.3.1 Origin

As referenced in Chapter 2, my concept of space-use intensity is inspired by the way time-use research deals with the issue of multitasking. Tracing this origin is fundamental for at least three reasons. The first one is that both time-use and space-use studies share the same ulterior purpose. In time-use research, analysis of time budgets by different population groups, particularly by gender, provides evidence that expands traditional accounts of productivity and renders visible the contribution of non-monetary economic activities to the economy (Gershuny, 2009; Vanek, 2014). In the same vein, space-use research also renders visible previously overlooked activities that are fundamental in understanding the performance of certain urban areas.

The second reason is that in time-use research on multitasking, there is enough clarity on the impact of data collection and data recording instruments on the overall results. For instance, time-use research is cognizant of the fact that survey takers tend to perceive as natural certain activities (Kenyon, 2010:57) and do not report on them, which is why experts have devised new technologies to reduce respondent burden and to improve data quality (Gershuny et al., 2017). For example, when time-use day-after interviews are supplemented with images, tallies of discrete activities performed during the day are more than twice the non-image prompted reports (from 19.2 activities to 41.1 activities, as reported by Gershuny et al., 2015). Similarly, data from my qualitative research will show the tally of uses in a space is more than twice (actually more than seven times), those reported by the official cadastral surveys.

The third reason is conceptual. Both time-use and space-use research on multitasking reveal that intensification in fact occurs, which means time and space-use are not zero-sum games. If secondary and additional activities are accounted for, new activities do not replace existing ones but are added. In fact, time-use research shows people can, in fact, use more than 24 hours a day (Kenyon, 2008; Gershuny, 2009). The same logic is at stake in space-use,

Space-use intensity in informal settlements in Bogotá   81

if additional uses are accounted for and recorded, spaces are found to be used more intensely, so the same floor area ends up being used at more than 100%. Later in the chapter, I will provide some examples of how these non-zero-sum realities take place.

3.1.3.2 Components

There are two components in space-use intensity: the amount of different *types of uses* and the amount of different types of *users*. The type of uses refers to what Jacobs' called range of mixed-use, or the breath and variety of types of uses. A building can be said to have a low mixed-use range when it has residential and commercial uses. And, it may have a high mixed-use range when more uses are added to the mix (i.e. light industries are added to the residential plus commercial mix) or when less expected uses share a space (i.e. a public library is added to a residential building). Of outmost importance here is establishing a short list of use types under which activities observed will be categorized. I apply five types of uses: residential, industrial, commercial, services, and recycling. The first four emerge from the main "economic destinies" used by Bogotá's cadaster (IGAC, 2003; Amaya, 2019), which in turn come from a Colombian adaptation of the International Standard Industrial Classification of all Economic Activities, ISIC (UNDESA, 2002) and (DANE, 2005:84). I add a fifth use type that I label "recycling" following recurrent field findings as well as literature on informal employment categories (Chen, 2012).

The second component of space-use intensity refers to different groups of users that share a space. This has a direct relationship with Jacob's "granularity" concept. Granularity of mixed-use is the presence of more than one use in as many urban scales as possible. We can understand this as different households that share a house, different businesses within the same property, or a mix of those. To account for this, I embrace the cadaster category "use-unit." Use-unit is an analytical devise that helps differentiate different types of uses and of users within a building that does not have a horizontal property regime. For example, a single-family house has one use-unit and a single-family house that rents a shop has two use-units, but if the family owns and runs the shop itself, then it is a single use-unit. Now, a multi-family building has as many use-units as independent households. This will become clearer when I illustrate it with specific examples. For the moment, let me add that the more diverse the *types of uses* a building has, the *more use-units* it is likely to have. However, a building may have many *use-units* but very few *types of uses* no mixed-use at all, as in the case of a building purposed for rental housing.

Jacobs' understanding of mixed-use also considers "time spread" a notion that speaks to how a mix of uses extends activities over different moments of the day. If uses are different, they may be complementary, the same space can have less idle time, and be occupied for larger swaths of time. For example,

82 *Space-use intensity in informal settlements in Bogotá*

a garage space can be rented only at nights, guaranteeing that the same area of the house can be used as a beauty salon space during the day[3]. While both components of space-use intensity are at stake here, it is the different types of uses that lead to a greater time spread. Finally, the last of Jacobs' components, "interaction," refers to the ability of different uses to have relationships with each other. For example, a roommate can help keep an eye on a baby while the mother runs an errand. More interaction is likely to happen when there is a greater diversity of *type of uses* and a higher amount if *use-units*. Note that in understanding interaction, both the *types of uses* and the number of *use-units* are necessary, which goes to say that these two components are the basis to understand other characteristics.

In sum, space-use intensity can be defined by both spatial components range and granularity (types of use and of users respectively), and time components (schedule and interaction). My research is focused on all of them but documents with greater detail the spatial components.

3.2 Documenting space-use intensity

As described in the introduction, the aim of this chapter is to define, document, and explain what I have termed "space-use intensity." The empirical findings at the center of this endeavor derive from semi-structured interviews to residents in consolidated informal settlements Bogotá, Colombia. The main data collection tool I developed to answer this question was what I call "house interviews," as opposed to "residents' interviews." It may sound incongruous to perform an interview on a house, rather than on a person, as objects or places cannot speak for themselves directly to exchange their views with the interviewer. But as much as the house interviews did entail having semi-structured conversations with residents, the main objective was less a depiction of people's feelings and the personal stories and more to record how their spaces are being used and why. Objects in space, furniture, tools, materials, clutter, or any trace of the activities that usually take place there, were as important—if not more—as the words of the people I spoke with. In the same vein, spaces that I was not allowed to get in were treated as interesting cues, much like silences or topics people decidedly avoid in a regular interview.

3.2.1 Getting inside: Access and sampling

3.2.1.1 Access

Access to the house interviews was established via personal connections rather than through organizations. Below I explain the rationale for this being so

---

3 Credit is due for this particular example to German Samper (see Chapter 2), one of the greatest Colombian architects of all times, whose contributions to design paralleled his pathbreaking research efforts to social housing.

and make a few comments about how positionality awareness helped secure, maintain or deepen research access.

Getting invited into a person's home, being allowed to tour the different rooms it has, and having the possibility to ask questions about non-wage income, is not an easy place to arrive at as a researcher. I managed to do this after a few failed attempts of gaining access via community boards, local universities, and through an NGO. It became evident that ensuring access to a large group of houses was not as valuable to my research as having a trustworthy conversation at each of them. Looking back, I see these dead-end efforts accessing some houses as a steep learning curve in fine-tuning my rapport-building strategy, making it more transparent to ensure communication would flow more naturally. After all, rapport is not something a researcher builds one-sidedly, but something that emerges smoothly from a two-way relationship. Going into the field without holding hands with any organization turned out to be an advantage. It bought me freedom not to carry any political baggage (which I would have needed to declare openly if helped by the community board), nor academic liability (which I would have needed to counter disciplinary biases in place), or moral ideologies (as I would have needed to engage in the specific rituals the NGO works within the ground).

With this lone freedom, I followed up on personal contacts. I reached out to people directly connected to friends and family, putting my research interest as the opening line for my approach. This forced me to directly embrace my outsider positionality and play it to my advantage as best as I could. There are two dimensions of this positionality awareness that are relevant: social (gender, race, class, etc.) and knowledge values. Let me begin with those referring to knowledge and values.

One of the rewrites for the oral informed consent protocol helped me arrive at a simplified version of my research interest, devoid of any language that would reinforce the drastic imbalance in educational backgrounds between me and my interviewees. Framed in the simplest natural language, the enunciation goes as follows: "I want to find out how people use the spaces in their house when they work or when they have a business at home because I think there should be better public policies to support them." This enunciation proved useful in balancing my position, as well as in easing and maintaining access. By critiquing policy for falling short, I immediately placed myself on their side, arguing for the government to do more in their favor. This enunciation also helped me play down the importance of academic knowledge, a prompt I often brought up later in the conversation. After all, I was in their home to learn from them whatever books nor any university teacher could teach. Finally, I should mention that I shared my impression they needed to be helped not because of their lack of economic resources, but on the contrary because their homes are noteworthy assets generating income that supports a wide-range of needs, most importantly, social protection needs.

84 *Space-use intensity in informal settlements in Bogotá*

Now, with regard to social positionality, I would say that class was the loudest power imbalance I dealt with in establishing access to the sites. In a third of the cases, I connected to the residents through a family member of mine who was the employer or regularly paid services from the interviewee. I should add that while I belong to the lower-to-middle class in New York, in Colombia I am part of the socioeconomic elite. Of course, this sets an uneven ground for conversation which I wanted to offset somehow. Not having myself a house or a business of my own, I showed interest in their housing and business accomplishments, which helped open up the conversation. When the conversation allowed it, I shared that being an immigrant in New York entails traveling down the socioeconomic ladder. This way, I was not hiding my privileged background but revealing the lack of privilege in my daily life. Getting to my interviews by public transport was also instrumental in leveling the ground. I took these two or three extra hours of travel, as a time that helped tune out from my outsider perspective. In the two neighborhoods that interested me the most, I shared meals with interviewees, and in one of the houses, I was invited to spend a night, which I did.

Both race and gender positions were more silent in my approach. While I do not openly thematize gender, being a woman and a mother helped empathize with many interviewees, 84% of which were women. As mentioned before, the feminization of informal home-based work (Chen, 2014) and of multi-tasking (Floro, 1995) is abundantly clear in the literature. On the other hand, race and ethnicity were less instrumental if not silent in my approach. All but two of my interviewees were racially mixed. I interviewed one woman from the Amazon region of Guainía, who explained her grandparents belong to an indigenous tribe, though she distanced herself from sharing that same ethnic identity. In the case of the one black interviewee, her family was mixed. Bogotá is predominantly "mestiza," a blend between Spanish and indigenous descents. This means that in Bogotá it is easier to travel across the socioeconomic spectrum finding mestizos with undistinguishable physical differences, something that is less likely to happen in countries like Argentina, Bolivia, or Mexico (where people talk about "whitexicans" as a clearly distinct elite). Interestingly, the Colombian census does not distinguish between white and mestizo. The latest census established that in Bogotá 97% of the population is either white or mestiza (DANE, 2018). Personally, I proudly identify myself as mixed, mestiza, especially as I have darker skin than my siblings. It is true that this combined ethnic category confounds race issues, and invisibilizes differences instead of celebrating its heritage. Particularly since 2005, Bogotá has seen a resurgence of reivindicatory indigenous urban histories from the peripheries (González, 2004; García, 2011), among others. These movements counter the systematic erasure during colonial times, their purposeful omission during independence times, and the modern-era identity silencing and disregard. However interesting these new histories are, in my approach, race did not represent a strategic entry point. I can only state that my race did not set me apart from the interviewees.

3.2.1.2 Sampling

The sampling approach was a mix of theoretical sampling and snowballing. Snowball references from one interview to another one proved instrumental, guaranteeing access to almost half the interviews. A few extreme cases were included for the sake of validity checks on what are deemed more typical cases. The fact that this is an exploratory fact-finding research rather than an extensive collection of statistically representative evidence, made it viable to accept the tradeoff between scope and evenness of the sample size, in favor of depth and quality of rapport. Hence, the sample of houses visited was not an even sweep within a predefined area, but a scattered selection across Bogotá's "old periphery" (Ward, 2015). Besides accessibility and personal security considerations, the houses were chosen based on a basic criterion: they were consolidated informal settlements in Bogotá's old periphery.

I embrace a useful distinction between incipient and consolidated informal settlements that Ward's Latin American Housing Network establishes in his comparative research of 11 Latin American cities in nine countries (see Figure 3.6). Settlements of incipient development are those more recently formed, with minimal urban infrastructure, with buildings often having non-permanent materials, and usually located further away on the newest peripheries of the city. In the case of Bogotá, they are often outside the administrative perimeter of the city. By contrast, consolidated informal settlements were formed 30 or more years ago, usually have regularized tenancy, basic urban infrastructure, and services, and buildings have three or more floors. There are two subtypes of consolidated informal settlements: central and old peripheries. Those centrally located, like classical Brazilian favelas or Argentinian villas, usually have smaller plots and irregular street layouts. On the contrary, "old peripheries" are in what was once the outskirts of the city but now belong to the intermediate ring. They display reticular street layouts,

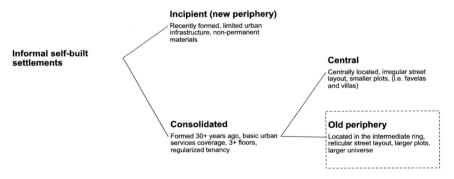

Figure 3.6 Subtypes of informal settlements in Latin America and choice of this research's focus. Adapted from Ward (2015).

86 *Space-use intensity in informal settlements in Bogotá*

larger plots, and represent a larger universe of informal settlements, and in fact of the whole residential fabric, and of the low-income rental options in cities. They represent "the principal means of land and housing acquisition for low-income ownership outside of the formal market in Latin America and elsewhere" (Payne, 2013; Ward, 2015:3).

An alternative distinction is made by expert scholars in Bogotá, particularly architects, between sloped versus flat settlements (Ceballos, 2019). They argue this distinction is useful in determining the chances a neighborhood has to properly integrate with the rest of the city. Sloped sites face more challenges because of their non-reticular street grids, propensity to landslides, as well as added structural requirements. Neighborhoods in slopes are more likely to be disconnected from public transport. It should be noted that Bogotá is surrounded by mountains along the east and southwest. Its functional center runs parallel to the eastern mountains. This means that sloped neighborhoods are more likely to be either central or new peripheries, rather than old peripheries, which to a large extent are flat. Hence, for the purposes of my research, the old periphery classification remains most useful.

Below a list of the 19 house interviews performed between March 10 and July 30, 2019, four of which were visited twice (Table 3.1). As shown in the table and in the map below, all but one of the houses are in Bogotá's periphery, and 79% belong to the old periphery categorization. In terms of the physical conditions, 74% of them are stratum 2 (remember Bogotá divides residential buildings into six categories, one being the most precarious and six the most well-off[4]). As mentioned earlier, 84% of my interviewees were women. And, in terms of the access mode, 37% of the interviews were via an employee of my family, and 47% of them were reached by snowballing. This sample size is aligned with what some scholars reviewing accepted guidelines for different types of qualitative studies reference as acceptable for single case grounded theory studies (i.e., 15–30) (Marshal et al., 2013).

The data collection was finalized in all of these 19 houses, yet the final sample used for the analysis excluded five houses in order to compose a coherent sample of houses located in consolidated informal settlements in Bogotá. Among the remaining 14 houses is a house located in the neighboring municipality of Soacha. Separated from the administrative boundary of Bogotá only by a street, there are notable differences in the quality of the infrastructure. Interestingly, houses on the Bogotá side of the street have sidewalks, paved streets, and better access to public education than the houses on the Soacha side of the street. The houses in the final sample are on average at least 32 years old, considering the date of when the neighborhood urban layout was acknowledged in a city's legal document.

---

4 Colombia's novel yet highly debated stratification system is discussed in Chapter 4.

Space-use intensity in informal settlements in Bogotá 87

Table 3.1 List of house interviews and key sample characteristics

	Code name	Neighborhood	Visit date	Strata	Periphery type	Gender	Access mode
1	Susy	Aures II	+3/11/2019	2	old	female	direct work
2	Ana	Aures II	+3/11/2019	2	old	female	snowball
3	Nataly	Aures II	+3/11/2019	2	old	female	direct work
4	Marlen	Bellavista	3/12/2019	2	old	female	direct work
5	Teresa	Villa Nueva	3/14/2019	2	old	female	direct other
6	Maria	Sierra Morena	6/5/2019	2	old	female	snowball
7	Alba	Caracolí	6/5/2019	1	new	female	snowball
8	Joana	El Oasis	6/5/2019	1	new	female	snowball
9	Virginia	El Oasis	6/5/2019	1	new	female	snowball
10	Alex	El Oasis	6/5/2019	1	new	male	direct work
11	Emily	Vida Nueva	6/5/2019	2	old	female	direct work
12	Ines	Alfonso Lopez	7/19/2019	3	old-old	female	direct other
13	Lucy	Patio Bonito I	+7/28/2019	2	old	female	direct other
14	Leo	Patio Bonito III	7/28/2019	2	old	male	snowball
15	Jorge	Patio Bonito I	7/28/2019	2	old	male	snowball
16	Rosa	Patio Bonito II	7/29/2019	2	old	female	direct work
17	Julie	Patio Bonito II	7/29/2019	2	old	female	snowball
18	Isabel	Bachué	7/31/2019	2	old	female	direct work
19	Jose	La Gloria	7/30/2019	2	old	male	direct other

+ These houses were visited more than once.

3.2.2 What to look for and how: Data collection tools and data analysis procedures

Three key data collection tools were used: observation (which became increasingly focused as the research advanced), informal semi-structured interviews, and photographs (of the outside of the building and of each space inside, whenever allowed to and without interrupting the flow of the conversation). The data collection and analysis process were iterative and multistage, following the nine steps described below.

88 *Space-use intensity in informal settlements in Bogotá*

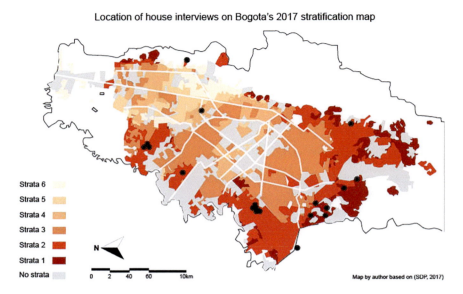

Figure 3.7 Localization of house interviews on Bogotá's (2017) stratification map by the author based on SDP (2017).

1 *Notebook jottings.* I wanted to travel light into field, using as few props as possible during the interviews. I got a set of plain rigid notebooks that I did not require any support and used pens that fit into the notebook spiral. Some of my questions entailed dates and money amounts, so I blamed my poor memory for the need to take out a notebook. While taking out pen and paper, I did the oral informed consent. Notes were taken in Spanish. The jottings were intermingled with schematic spatial layouts (Figure 3.8). Multiple plan views, one per floor, proved better than cross sections at this stage.
2 *Photographs.* When the conversation was evolving and questions about other rooms of the house were raised, I asked permission to be toured around the house, and while on it, I asked permission to take photographs. I was allowed to do so in two-thirds of the houses. Photograph shoots were taken quickly and almost carelessly, in an effort to play down their seriousness, and prioritize the flow of the conversation. Pictures of the outside were taken at the end, and if not allowed, I used Google Street Maps to have a visual record of each interview.
3 *Day-after fieldnotes*: On the same day or the day after at the most, I typed out and translated my Spanish handwritten notes directly into English. These notes were perfected with additional information and subsequent visits if any, and from few audio recordings of interviews. These notes

Space-use intensity in informal settlements in Bogotá 89

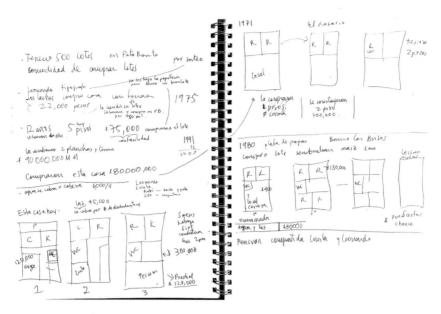

Figure 3.8 Sample of notebook jottings with schematic layouts of house #13 (Author, 2019).

also included tables with economic information (both in pesos and dollars, assuming a conversion rate of $3,000 Colombian pesos for US dollar), direct quotes, and other related information.

4 *Cross-sectional diagrams*: Using the information from the schematic layouts and hints from the conversation, I mapped all the data I gathered on uses and users in schematic cross sections (Figure 3.9). These simple diagrams are vertical views of the building where the floors of the building are represented as stacked boxes. The street is always depicted to the left-hand side. The different uses are drawn as circles placed left to right on each floor resembling their relative location to the windows. I used standard color codes for the various types of uses: yellow for residential, red for commercial, purple for industrial (what in New York zoning is referred to as manufacturing), blue for services, and green for both recycling and urban agriculture. The letters on the colored circles represent different users within the property (what Bogotá's cadaster calls "use-units"). For example, if a house uses one of its rooms as a shop, it will have the same letter (because it is the same household) but different colors (because it has different types of use: residential and commercial). These diagrams were progressively updated after completing steps 5–7 described below.

90 *Space-use intensity in informal settlements in Bogotá*

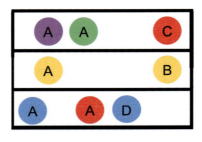

Figure 3.9 Cross-sectional diagram of observed uses in house #6 (Author, 2019).

5 *Cadastre data look up.* Bogotá's cadaster online geographic information system (IDECA) was used to check information on each plot visited. This information was visualized in the same cross-sectional fashion. Other relevant information extracted from the cadaster was: number of floors, number of use-units, and a reference to the neighborhood's urban legal status. For informal settlements that is the date of their legalization decree, and for formal ones the registration date of the urban plans at the city planning office. In either case, the date of this legal document is a hint to establish the approximate age of the settlement.

6 *Detailed reading of photographs.* A third iteration of each house field record added a detailed reading of the photographs taken. This proved to be more productive than anticipated. I was able to trace additional activities not disclosed in the conversation, that I was able to corroborate via WhatsApp messages with the interviewees. For example, the photograph of the patio in Alba's house (#7) showed men's clothes drying (Figure 3.10), but no man lived in the house. Following up on this I found out that she regularly washes laundry for neighbors for a fee. The color-coded cross-sectional diagrams were updated when new information of this type emerged.

7 *Second column reflections on fieldnotes.* The entire fieldnotes of each house record were formatted into one column. In this second column, I included detailed reflections, connected ideas or feelings, emerging categories, or side notes. This exercise facilitated the transition from data collection into analysis.

8 *Visual record of each house interview.* For each house interview I completed a visual record (Figure 3.11) that includes an exterior photograph and two cross-sectional use diagrams: one with the information that rests on the cadaster and the other with the uses I observed. The key to read the diagram with the observed uses tells the story of the specific uses found within each house. The record also has two boxes with textual

Space-use intensity in informal settlements in Bogotá 91

Figure 3.10 Photograph of the patio in house #7 (Author, 2019).

information. One is an identification box that contains: the interview number, the code name of the interviewee, the neighborhood where the house is located (addresses are intentionally left out), the number and year of the neighborhood's urbanization legal document, the estimated used area of the building (in squared meters), and date of the interview. The other box contains a list of emergent use-related categories: use-units (shown in capitalized letters), types of uses (shown in colors), the count of different uses observed (that is the number of circles in the legend that are different), and the maximum number of types of uses per use-unit (the maximum number of colors that a circle with the same letter has).

9 *Emerging categories summary table*. The information on the analytic box in the visual records from each house interview was logged into a summary table, allowing some interesting findings that will be discussed at the end of this chapter. For instance, one can observe that despite them being characterized as such, the buildings visited are far from single-family residential homes. On average, they hold more than seven different

92 *Space-use intensity in informal settlements in Bogotá*

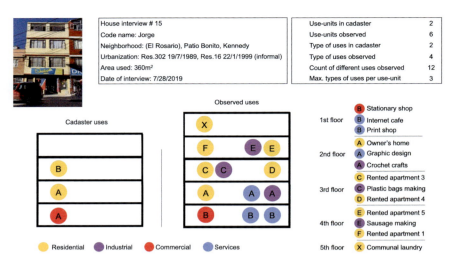

Figure 3.11 Visual record house #15 (Author, 2019).

Table 3.2 Emerging categories summary table

	Code name	Use-units in cadaster	Use-units observed	Type of uses in cadaster	Type of uses observed	Count of discrete uses	Max. discrete uses per use-unit
1	Susy	2	5	2	5	11	3
2	Ana	1	3	1	2	5	3
3	Nataly	1	2	1	2	3	2
4	Marlen	1	5	1	4	8	3
5	Teresa	1	1	1	4	7	4
6	Maria	2	4	2	4	8	5
7	Alba	1	1	1	3	4	3
13	Lucy	1	2	1	5	9	5
14	Leo	2	12	2	2	13	2
15	Jorge	2	6	2	4	12	3
16	Rosa	2	2	1	3	4	3
17	Julie	2	3	2	4	6	3
18	Isabel	1	2	1	4	5	4
19	Jose	1	11	1	3	13	3
	Average	1.43	4.21	1.36	3.50	7.71	3.29

uses within them (second to last column), making them multipurpose buildings. Also, when considering single-household units within these buildings, on average it may have more than two additional uses besides the residential (last column).

3.2.3 Five house-stories: from narratives to diagrams

In this section, I will walk the reader into a set of the houses I visited in Bogotá's old periphery, two in Patio Bonito neighborhood on the southwest borough of Kennedy, and the other two in Aures II on the north-west borough of Suba. All of them are located an hour and a half from Bogotá's central business district by Transmilenio bus system. The selection of these four houses is quite purposeful. Both these residential neighborhoods share an informal housing development and sit in counties that have the highest densities in the city[5] (Gonzalez, 2013). Today, they both have very similar street-life and self-built constructions look indistinguishable from one another (Figure 3.12). However, Patio Bonito's urban layout originated informally while Aures is the result of a state-planned formal urbanism project. This alone is a very important fact not only from an urban policy perspective, but from a theoretical point of view. Informal housing in Aures speaks already of the logical impossibility or at least the practical difficulty of achieving full formality for a neighborhood that began as a formal urban project of "sites and services" (to follow the World Bank's lingo) or "progressive development" (to follow Bogotá's). In the same vein, Patio Bonito went to great strides to claim urban services provision (most famously a strike in 1995) but has today fully formalized urban services blurring the formal/informal distinction altogether.

3.2.3.1 Lucy's house. Patio Bonito, Kennedy

Lucy is a spartan woman in her late sixties, with deep wrinkles, bony cheekbones, and olive skin. Even bundled up in thick sweaters, one can tell she is

Figure 3.12 A corner of the commercial street in Patio Bonito (left) and Aures II (right) (© Google Street View, 2018).

---

5 Patio Bonito's Urban Planning Zone (UPZ) has the highest population density in Bogotá which is already one of the densest cities in the world, with 577 people per hectare. El Rincón UPZ, where Aures II is located has the second highest: 462 (Gonzalez, 2013). It is worth noting that density was not an intentional criterion for selecting the case studies, as explained earlier.

94 *Space-use intensity in informal settlements in Bogotá*

very thin. She spends most of her time in the first floor kitchen, the coldest room in the house. Sharp in manners, she commands her guests to receive her many attentions without uttering many words. Lucy was very generous with her time, fed me lunch, and shared with me the story of her house, which can only be understood in connection to two other houses of hers, all of them in Patio Bonito.

Lucy and her husband Leo arrived in Patio Bonito from Los Laches, a historic informal settlement in Bogotá (records of it exist before 1685 (Ibañez, 1891:108)). They shared a house with Leo's sister but wanted to find a place of their own. Leo was a typesetter while Lucy worked at a glass engraving factory. In 1971, Leo was hired to print some paperwork for an urbanization project. Five hundred plots were being sold far from the center near the Bogotá river, their specific location would be assigned by raffle. Leo got interested and offered to do the printing for free in exchange for being allowed to pick a well-located plot. So, he sold his part of the Los Laches house to his sister and with this money bought a plot for USD\$25 in what would become, many years after, a commercial street in Patio Bonito.

Most plots in Patio Bonito were sold by Mariano Porras, a well-known "pirate urbanizer," second only to Rafael Forero Fetecua. Pirate urbanizers were common informal urban developers in Bogotá between the 1960s and 1990s. They usually bought more affordable rural plots or took possession of at-risk areas or public lands, sold standard plots of 6 by 12 meters[6] in blocks with minimum street widths and with no public services. Back in 1971 when Lucy bought the plot, Patio Bonito was not a suitable area for urbanization because it was a low-lying area in the floodplain of the Bogotá river. Nonetheless it was deemed to become a good investment because Corabastos, the main produce wholesale market in the city, would be established nearby. Pirate urbanizers were well connected, knew about it, and banked on this knowledge.

Pirates sold the plots with makeshift titles as part of self-help housing projects. Very likely, Leo's typographic work helped give the project an aura of legitimacy, one of many strategies to blur its informality. Pirate urbanizers made hefty margins (between 80% and 90% of the cost of the land according to experts (Torres, 2017:66)), and they also amassed substantial political capital. Through informal urbanization projects in the Patio Bonito and Unir neighborhoods, Porras became a prominent figure, got a city council seat and also ran for Congress. Pirate developers have been responsible for tens of thousands of housing "solutions" in Bogotá (Gutiérrez, 1988). Quite imperfect solutions they were, often locking people into other types of informalities (Torres, 2018), but housing solutions nonetheless. For instance,

---

6 At the beginning, using the same standard sizes as those mandated by law, was a strategy to blend in their illegality. In fact, "pirate urbanizers have continuously adapted to regulations, weakening urban policies" (Torres, 2012:467), translated by the author.

these plots are usually better than those attained by land invasions. Having followed minimal urban regulations, they have better prospects of achieving full legalization than invasions and tend to develop faster (Torres, 2017:66). For instance, Patio Bonito urbanization has been the subject of recurring legalization decrees in 1982, 1985, 1989, and 1999 (IDECA, 2019), a practice that I detail in other studies. While Porras, as well as other pirate urbanizers, ended up in jail for deceiving buyers into informal occupations, the practice is far from forgotten. Today's "tierreros" sell even smaller plots, further away from serviced areas (Montenegro, 2019) and have no intention of building any community engagement or political base.

Lucy, her husband, and their two children, lived in this first house for 32 years. In the beginning, all they could afford to build was a shack with dirt floors and no kitchen. With time they managed to raise two floors and a usable rooftop. The whole first floor was soon rented out. It had a shop facing the street and two rooms in the back. The second floor and the rooftop were for Lucy's family only. In 2003, Leo sold this house for US$30,000 and bought the one they currently live in for US$27,000. Like the first house, this one also had two floors plus a rooftop, but it was located in a non-commercial street. Since self-built houses are constantly in construction, calculating the costs and hence the rate of return on investment is close to impossible. Regardless, their asset more than tripled in 30 years (adjusting the initial cost of the plot to the Colombian inflation rate from 1971 to 2003). The secret to this business was the constant influx of extra money from another property, also in Patio Bonito, that Leo and Lucila bought in 1983 when Leo got his inheritance.

This other plot has always been secondary to Lucy's family, they have never lived there. In the beginning, they cropped the land. "We had maize, potatoes, carrots, onions, herbs, it was good," says Lucy. Construction began soon after and went on for many years, at a slow permanent pace. Today, the house has three floors and a rooftop. The first floor has two rooms in the back and a "tienda" (small shop selling snacks, sodas, and beer) facing the street. The monthly rent for this first floor is US$134. The second and third floors have four rooms each. There is a shared bathroom per floor. There are no kitchens. Lucy dislikes that, not because tenants end up improvising makeshift cooking areas, but because "I would prefer that people feel better in their place, but Leo doesn't think it important." The rooftop is accessible to all tenants. As in most houses I visited, this is the place for laundry, pets, storage, and reclaimed construction materials, and when the neighbors get along well, it can serve as a communal social area. Because this house is not on a commercial street, residential are more profitable than commercial rents despite being less steady, Lucy explained. Room tenants often get hung up, like Mr. Santos, who sells lottery in the streets and depends on the money that his children send him to pay the rent each month. Each of the eight rooms is rented at US$43, which adds US$450 per month for the whole house, after utilities. This is almost twice what she receives from her pension, US$250 per month. This house is, without a doubt, a fundamental supplement to Lucy and Leo's pension with which they could barely get along.

The third house, the one bought in 2003, is where Lucy and her family live now (Figure 3.13). Facing the street, the first floor has a rented garage space (at US$40 per month). In the back, there is the kitchen, a social area, a bathroom, and a narrow patio in the rear end. It is in this cold back end of the first floor that Lucy spends most of her days. The second floor has three rooms and a bathroom. Lucy and Leo have a big room facing the street. In the back, there is a room for their 30-year-old son Leo, and the other one is for their daughter Rubi, aged 42. Leo is a creative type: long haired, dreamy, and absentminded. He has his woodworking shop right there in his room (Figure 3.14). Rubi is very reserved and quiet. She regularly takes care of neighbors' babies, loves sewing, and seldom leaves her room.

Figure 3.13 Lucy's houses in Patio Bonito: Current state of former house (left), secondary house (center), and Lucy's home (right) (Author, 2019).

Figure 3.14 Lucy's glass engraving table (left), access to rented rooftop (center), and Leo's room and wood workshop (Author, 2019).

Figure 3.15 Lucy's home (center) and next-door neighbors (left and right) (Author, 2019).

The top floor has a terrace in the front, and a room, kitchen, and bathroom in the back, which cannot be seen from the street (Figure 3.15). The whole third floor is rented at US$100 per month plus utilities (unlike the arrangement in their second house, here water is charged at US$2 per head and electricity is US$15 if the tenant does not have too many home appliances). Access to this floor is not independent. Lucy said this is not an issue, it helps keeping a close eye on the people living there. For example, the previous tenant, a man from Cali who sold "cholados" (shaved ice with fruit flavorings and condensed milk) in a pushcart, was problematic. He frequently took his cart upstairs, something he was not allowed to do. Then, he rented a washing machine and began doing his "family" laundry, for a fee of course. To make things worse, he started bringing strangers into the house, until at one point six people were sleeping in his room. This was the end of it. He was playing difficult, but when plumbing problems began, there was a clear excuse to make him leave.

Lavish water consumption was not only an issue due to the monthly cost, which could ultimately be transferred to the tenant, but because it runs against Lucy's own nature. "I've always saved, it is part of my way of being. I don't buy unnecessary clothes; I don't throw away food. I reuse water." When in the patio, she walked me through the herb garden and her water-saving strategies: "I collect water from the washing machine and use it to clean the floors. I collect water from the sink and use it in the toilets." There was also a neatly organized space for reusable plastics: "we wash every plastic bag and reuse it or give it to the recyclers well separated." Recycling is done with care and pride in Lucy's house. They save only what is necessary for reuse, most they clean and give, or sometimes sell, to Ben, the waste picker in charge of

98 Space-use intensity in informal settlements in Bogotá

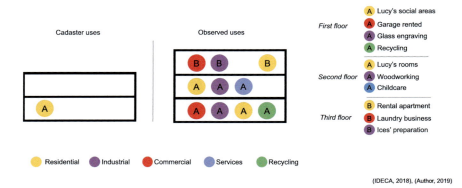

Figure 3.16 Cross-sectional diagrams of cadastral and observed uses Lucy's house (#13) (IDECA, 2018; Author, 2019).

their block.[7] She repeated that she is always adding up little things and saving. For instance, she receives half of Leo's pension, a part of the rents on their second house, and all the rents from their own house. She also tells me that when her son got his first payment, he gave her US$1,000 so she would see the ocean for the first time. Instead, she decided to save the money for his woodworking studies. Part of it, she lends at 4% interest, cashing an extra US$15 each month. "The thing is that we are economists," Lucy clarifies.

The contrast between the information that rests on the cadaster with the observed uses is striking in a variety of ways (Figure 3.16). First in terms of the number of use-units, this house has two households (A and B) instead of one. Also, in terms of the diversity of uses, five types instead of just residential. And finally, in the amount of uses within the same use-unit. Lucy's use-unit has six different uses and the tenants use-unit has at least three different uses. Also notable is how difficult it is to tell, from looking at the façade of the house, that there are so many economic uses within this simple-looking single-family house. There are no physical cues that might lead one to believe that there is such an intense economic activity taking place inside this inconspicuous house.

3.2.3.2 Susy's house #1. Aures, Suba

Susy has big bottle-bottom glasses that make every other trait of her less prominent. It is difficult to tell her age, but she is likely well into her sixties. Copper skin and short, over-dyed black hair, Susy never married. Her only

---

7 In 2019, Bogotá was paying 18,000 associated informal waste-pickers (Parra, 2019) for their service collecting and sorting solid waste, a noteworthy advance towards the recognition of the contribution of informal work to city-wide wellbeing.

son runs a tire shop, but she prefers not to visit him. Instead, she enjoys spending time with her ex-daughter-in-law's family, who live in Aures. Susy was a domestic worker all her life, now she only takes cherry-picked day jobs that pay well. Oddly interested in pedigree, she talks with great pride and detail about the various high-class families she worked for: their ancestries, power marriages, political appointments, and travels. Susy lives by herself in a rented apartment on the second floor of a roasted chicken corner joint, in Aures' main commercial street.

I say hers is an apartment because this is the way people refer to it, but this living arrangement is hardly what one thinks of when speaking of an apartment. In informal settlements in Bogotá, an apartment is a rented living space within someone else's house. Susy's apartment is disjointed: she uses four spaces separated from each other, the bathroom and the laundry area are shared with other tenants and her bedroom and the kitchen are private. There is no living or dining room, she does this in the bedroom. Having the residential spaces separated means she has a key for each space: one for the street door, one for a gate to the second floor, one for her kitchen, another one for her room, and the last one for the rooftop, where she does the laundry and where she leaves her dog when going out.

Her bedroom is spacious, it accommodates the refrigerator and the pantry that do not fit in the kitchen down the hall (Figure 3.17). Her room also has two queen beds because she enjoys having friends and family stay over as often as possible. In fact, when I decided to stay the night in Aures, Susy would not accept that I stayed elsewhere, despite the plans I had. Susy's granddaughter often stays the night with her. Together they prepare no-bake cheesecakes. Cheesecakes are good business because they are quick and cheap to make, as there is no electricity use. They only spend US$10 on ingredients to produce 30 pieces, which they sell at US$1 each. Together, they make US$20 on each

Figure 3.17 Susy's apartment in Aures: Outside view (left), room (center), and kitchen (right) (Author, 2019).

batch. This is good pocket money for both of them, plus, they enjoy their time together.

Susy shares the bathroom with the other tenants on the second floor: an insurance office, and a soap shop. This has never been a problem. The other tenants barely use the bathroom, and she showers every morning before the commercial spaces open for business. This mixed-use arrangement intertwines space-use across schedules, so there is less idle time. Susy knows the other tenants well enough to maintain common agreements about the use of space. Plus, "they are women, which helps," she adds. In fact, Susy confesses having admiration for their entrepreneurialism and is quite engaged in the businesses of these two women. For instance, Susy had become a door to door saleswoman for the soap business. "These are not regular soaps like those commercial brands. They are highly concentrated, so you have to explain to people how to use them. I am quite good at this," she explains, admitting yet another one of her side businesses. This practice also reveals that the interaction between different uses not only happens at the neighborhood level as Jacobs described but also within the same building, adding granularity and hence intensity to the use of space.

The busiest and most profitable space of Susy's building is the rotisserie restaurant on the first floor. This business uses the whole first floor. This commercial space has independent water and electricity meters from the second floor, making it formal in terms of usage in the face of the building regulations. According to the landlord lady, the monthly rent of the restaurant is USD$400, five times that of Susy's and the insurance office, who pay US$80 each. The restaurant has an open area for customers to dine in, a bathroom, and a storage area with direct access through the restaurant and also by the street. The restaurant tenants also use half of the rooftop. One section they use to store coal, wood, cooking oil, and refreshments. The other section is for storing chicken bones and trimmings that will be recycled: they get sold

Figure 3.18 Non-residential uses in Susy's house: Rotisserie (left), insurance office (center), and soapmaking laboratory (right) (Author, 2019).

Space-use intensity in informal settlements in Bogotá 101

to produce bone flour. This supply chain follows a full circle: bone meal is the main ingredient in chickens' diets like the ones roasted downstairs.

The soap business pays USD$140 for the store on the second floor and the laboratory space in the rooftop. This business on the second floor, run by two women, has six different products: laundry soap, dish soap, glass cleaner, multisurface spray, bathroom disinfectant, and an anti-grease. They store large plastic cans with sodium hypochlorite and smaller jerrycans of formaldehyde in what can be said to be an open-air laboratory on the third floor (Figure 3.18). The third-floor rooftop has unfinished flooring and no walls, or at least walls and roofing of non-permanent construction materials. This is ideal for having good ventilation, and further, having no permanent enclosure, all uses in the rooftop go unnoticed from the street view. This is important so these activities pass under the radar of property assessment officers. The soapmaking business also uses another section of the rooftop as a recycling area for plastic bottles. Here, they clean, sort, and test each bottle and label it before they fill it and put it on display on the second-floor shop.

Susy is also involved with activities taking place at the insurance office. This office sells health and pension insurance to: "taxi drivers, housewives, construction workers, security guards, and independent vendors and workers" reads a sign by the entrance to the restaurant on the first floor. Insurance offices like these are quite common in consolidated informal settlements, which comes as no surprise since the working arrangements of residents are mostly independent or informal. This office sells USD$16,700 per month at this location alone, as exposed in a board planner hanged on the wall. Susy is not involved with the insurance deals, but she comes into this office every other Wednesday night when the room transforms into a religious space. In fact, this location is known in the neighborhood as the "prayer house," and apparently, it is an active community gathering venue. Insurance agency during the day and church at night, this room hosts a broad range of seemingly incompatible uses. A wall of this office has a wall scribbling saying: "God

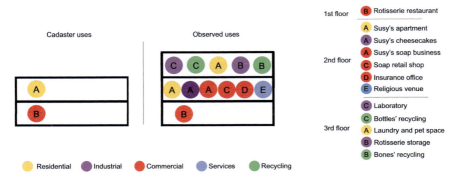

Figure 3.19 Cross-sectional diagrams of cadastral and observed uses in Susy's house (#1) (Author, 2019; IDECA, 2018).

102 *Space-use intensity in informal settlements in Bogotá*

protects and *multiplies* every day," both a good-fortune omen and a reminder of what is happening in this very space.

Similarly, the contrast between the information that rests on the cadaster with the observed uses documented is striking, but in this Aures case, there is an even further intensification of space-use than in the house in Patio Bonito. In terms of the number of use-units (shown as different capital letters), this property has four instead of the two logged in the cadaster (Figure 3.19). This is twice the number of use-units that in Patio Bonito while having the same area in the same number of floors. Now, in terms of the diversity of uses, here we have five types instead of two (residential and commercial). Furthermore, when considering the range of uses, or the variance in the different types of uses, this house shows a broader spectrum. This is not a simple mixed-use between residential and commercial. It is fair to argue that having a laboratory and a church alongside the residential use is remarkable. Finally, regarding the amount and granularity of uses within the same use-unit, we observe here more tenants engaging in a broader variety of activities and also interacting more with one another.

3.2.3.3 *Ana's home-based enterprise, Aures II, Suba*

Ana picked up her passion for cooking 20 years ago while covering for her sister at her previous work. She got hooked ever since. Four years ago, Ana started a catering business called Pic Nic in partnership with her daughter and her son-in-law. Their main client is a television filming company that works mainly in Bogotá but has eventual shootings across the country. Pic Nic caters to them at any filming location. A regular service includes five meals: breakfast, morning snack, lunch, afternoon snack, and dinner for 200 people, that is 1,000 meals per day. Pic Nic charges US$23 per person, making US$4,600 per day of service. There are at least 10 filming days per month. This is US$46,000 of gross income on this client alone. Besides the food itself, their fee also covers transport, a mobile kitchen, tents, waiters, dining furniture, and dinnerware. Pic Nic works around the clock to meet long filming sessions with unusual schedules. They are readily flexible to accommodate more people to the table, extra services when the filming takes longer, or travel to different locations if needed. Ana's son-in-law manages deliveries and directs on-site service. Ana's daughter is the bookkeeper, though not a very good one. Ana is the hands-on brain of the kitchen operation: buying, designing the menus, portioning, cooking and overseeing other cookers, setting up, and packing. When I called her the "Chef" she immediately blushed and added shyly: "Yes, I guess that's what I am."

On my visits to Ana's house, she was always so busy that we could not sit down for an interview. Instead, I shadowed her at different times of the day and the night. Despite being so modest she enjoyed talking with me about her much-cherished work, proudly showing me around the house and her neighborhood's suppliers. She was also more than open to record audio and video.

Ana works like an ant and sleeps very little whenever there are services to get out. It is no coincidence that her business is at her house. When it is busy, she sleeps a couple of hours whenever there is a spare moment, often before noon. Besides her room, there is an extra room used by any of the nine regular workers or temps who do not have enough time or money to go home and be back at work by 1:00 am, when things must get started for a regular service (Figure 3.20). The schedule is the king in Ana's work-life.

On the first floor of Ana's house, there are six spaces. Facing the street there is an area where trays and crates get ready to be loaded into the truck, which I invariably found parked outside the very narrow street. In lieu of the garage, there is a storage space for tents, coal, furniture, and workers' bikes. The first floor also has two different kitchens, a portioning table by the side of two home refrigerators, and a storeroom for chafing dishes. On the second floor, there are three rooms: Ana's room, the workers' room, and a room that is rented out to one of the workers. Ana's room has a spare mattress often used by her son. One bathroom is for Ana alone and everyone else shares the second bathroom. On the second floor, there is also the office. It has a filing cabinet, a computer that was not in use, the ironing table for the tablecloths, and many create with snacks. The third floor, not visible from the street, is a partially covered rooftop. It holds a dishwashing space, a communal laundry area, a charcoal grill, and gas stove for deep frying.

Ana loves the neighborhood not only because it is where she and her family have lived for many years, but also because it is so convenient. She makes all of the purchases locally whenever it is needed. In fact, there is not even a pantry at Ana's house. The commercial street down the block has a variety of shops to choose from with everything she needs in good quality and quantity (Figure 3.21). I accompanied Ana to the produce shop and the meat and dairy shop. At the produce shop, she was greeted with warmth and respect as she is the most valued customer, spending US$3,400 per month on fruits and vegetables alone. Surprisingly, she is not the biggest customer

Figure 3.20 Ana's catering business: Packing area (left), main kitchen (center), and Ana's room (right) (Author, 2019).

Figure 3.21 Ana's home–business: night street view (left), street (center), and produce shop and butchery across the street (right) (Author, 2019).

at the meat and dairy shop, even though she spends there about US$6,000 every month.

Ana rents this house for US$430 per month from a retired schoolteacher. As is usual practice according to other interviewees, this is slightly higher (less than 10%) than what it would cost if the house was for residential purposes alone. Ana uses the house for living, as a working space, and also sublets a room, and quite evidently, there are a few economic benefits from this mixed-use. Ana's business does at least 10 services per month, so the gross monthly income is US$46,000 at a minimum. Even discounting 10 salaries, this means that the house's rent represents 2.6% of the gross monthly income, which is quite inexpensive by any standard.

At some point on our tour of the house, I noticed the son-in-law making efforts to keep a couple of kittens out of my sight. Of course, the elephant in the room was mice. This was after I had asked Ana whether the business had any permits they must get and renew, to which she candidly said: "I can't remember how often is it that one must *sacrifice* (sic) before the INVIMA.[8]" This was no pun or play-on-words of Ana but an honest phonetic misunderstanding of hers where the word "certify" was replaced by "sacrifice" (in Spanish the two words sound slightly more similar: "certificar" and "sacrificar"). The answer was elusive. They do have a business registry and a health registry as vendors, but of the full range of permits and licenses that they should comply with these two permits represent merely 8% of the total (CONPES, 2019). Their business is far from being fully formal-

---

8 INVIMA (Instituto Nacional de Vigilancia de Medicamentos y Alimentos) is the national institute that issues compliance permits for medicines and foodstuffs producers and vendors.

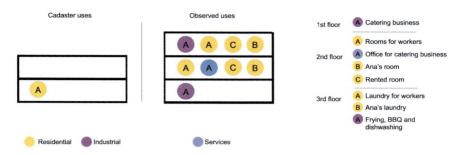

Figure 3.22 Cross-sectional diagrams of cadastral and observed uses in Ana's house (#2) (Author, 2019; IDECA, 2018).

ized. Furthermore, this is taking into account only the business permits, not the building permits.

The cross-sectional diagram of Ana's house reveals that, once again, the difference between the information that rests on the cadaster and the observed uses is quite large (Figure 3.22). Whereas this house is seen by the cadaster as a single-family residence, in reality, two households (use-units B and C) share the space with a business (use-unit A) that produces food, has related services, and also incorporates a residential use (A). While in this house the range of different uses is not as large as in Susy's home, here we see a high level of interaction between the residential and industrial uses. This business would hardly function well if it did not offer on-site sleeping arrangements for a few of its workers. Also notable in this case is the close relationship between the business and the commercial offerings in the neighborhood. As mentioned, this food preparing business does not even have a dedicated room to store food but instead, it buys purchases fresh ingredients every day from local vendors down the block.

3.2.3.4 Rosa's home in Patio Bonito, Kennedy

Rosa is 50 years old and has a youthful, independent spirit. She married a divorcee and never wanted kids of her own. Her husband has a disabled son with his first wife, but the boy lives with his mother most of the time. As a teenager, Rosa came to Bogotá from Huila because the farm she grew up in was taken over during a moment of spiked armed conflict with the then guerrilla group FARC (Spanish acronym for Revolutionary Armed Forces of Colombia). Once in Bogotá, she settled in Patio Bonito. At first, she had to rent but "all the grumbling around utility bills and water consumption was exasperating" and she adds: "so I saved and saved."

By 2007 she had amassed US$4,000, which was more than enough for the down payment of a house (in fact, it was close to 40% of the total cost of what the minimum social housing is in Colombia by legal definition[9]). Despite the fact that she qualified to receive a public subsidy, she could not use it to buy the house she wanted in Patio Bonito, because housing subsidies are given to developers rather than beneficiaries when they buy newly constructed projects (a model that is wrongfully called the "subsidies to the demand") (Torres, 2020:173; Carrizosa, 2020:356). Rosa did not hesitate when refusing the subsidy. There is no question that the house the Patio Bonito real estate agent found for her was a better choice in the short term and especially long term. Unlike the public housing offerings, the Patio Bonito house is bigger, better located, and it can be expanded. This story, of a deserving, yet, refused housing subsidy is quite common. In fact, at least four of my interviewees found themselves taking this same decision.

Sitting on a standard six by 12-meter plot, Rosa's house originally had a single floor with fiber cement roofing. It cost her US$7,300 in 2007. With time and continued efforts from her and her husband, they managed to change the roof for a concrete slab. "This was great, because we could put a prefabricated house in the rooftop and started renting" she explains. Ever since, Rosa has always rented one of the two floors. Right now, her own house is on the second floor and she rents part of the first floor to a family of three (Figure 3.23.) Rosa's home: inverted ziggurat streetscape (left), entrance (center), and access to the second floor (right) (Author, 2019). Rosa charges a monthly rent of US$117 plus utilities, which are separated. Water is US$37

Figure 3.23 Rosa's home: inverted ziggurat streetscape (left), entrance (center), and access to second floor (right) (Author, 2019).

---

9 Colombian Law 1753 of 2015 defines a priority social housing (VIP by its Spanish acronym) as one that costs less than 70 minimum monthly wages (US$13,160 in 2015). The law also establishes the top cost for a social housing to receive governmental subsidies is 135 minimum monthly wages (US$25,380 in 2015). The top tier social housing threshold was adjusted upwards in 2019 to 150 minimum monthly wages (about US$36,150).

per person per month and the electricity has an independent meter. "I know it's cheap—she says—but I don't want them to get hung up." The first floor also has a garage for her husband's rented taxi. He became a taxi driver after having worked for 14 years at a tile shop. He was let off his job as soon as he completed the 1,300 working weeks required to get a pension. However, he is still too young to start receiving a pension, so he was left without wage nor pension. Rosa hopes that when the pension starts to come in, they can change the roof sheets for another concrete slab, in order get an extra apartment for rent: "This is everyone's idea here" says Rosa.

Rosa cleans houses and businesses on a day-to-day basis. She has five regular clients, one per day of the week. She enjoys the work with the businesses, because "I pick up the trades." Over the last 18 years, she has worked at a beauty salon. As a side business, she sells the beauty products they carry. Rosa also works for a furniture décor shop. She has been there for five years. She likes it a great deal and has learned fast. Not only is she allowed to deal with clients frequently, but she also puts into practice many of the decoration tactics in her own house, like the custom-made cabinet that separates the kitchen from the social area, the canvas pendant lamp, or vinyl stencils that "liven up the stair wall" (Figure 3.24)

Three years ago, the same real estate agent who sold her this house offered to buy it back from Rosa for US$40,000. It felt good to know that it was worth five times more, but "it felt better still to decline the offer," she says, adding "I like it here." I also learned that the property tax is exactly 10% of this commercial value, US$400. "It used to be less (US$333), but one day they found the house had two kitchens. That is when they raised the tax." She does not quite remember which one came first, the second meter for electricity or the 20% property tax raise. In any case, the two are most likely connected, since she cannot recall any cadaster house visit.

Figure 3.24 Rosa's social area (left), custom-made cabinet by kitchen (center), and vinyl butterflies' wall decor (right) (Author, 2019).

108 *Space-use intensity in informal settlements in Bogotá*

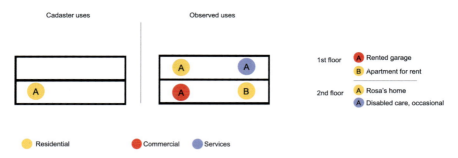

Figure 3.25 Cross-sectional diagrams of cadastral and observed uses in Rosa's house (#16) (Author, 2019).

Houses like Rosa's almost invariably construct each floor's concrete slab slightly bigger than the floor below, generating a small cantilever of about a foot all along the street front. Consecutive cantilevers produce inverted ziggurat volumes. These inverted ziggurats are the exact opposite of conventional setbacks and generate the opposite effect. They limit the exposure to the air and light, and bring closer the houses that are on the opposite side of these already narrow streets. Streets like these end up having a characteristic homogenous urban frontage. This is a common practice in consolidated informal settlements in Bogotá, a pervasive micro invasion of public space. A seemingly minor detail, the strategy makes the available area of each floor 2.5% larger than the one below, adding a usable area equivalent to a full-size bed per floor. An extra area of 1.8 square meters is by no means insignificant especially if compared with the size of a minimum subsidized social housing unit (35 square meters). Thanks to the inverted ziggurat invasion, an informal house has 5% more usable area per floor (see the right-hand side photograph above). All the houses I visited with more than one floor have such cantilevers.

In Rosa's house, the difference between the information that rests on the cadaster and the observed uses is not as large as in the previous three cases (Figure 3.25). Not long ago the cadaster registered that this house holds two households, shown above as use-units A and B. It did so recently even though this house has held two households for almost 10 years. Now, in terms of the different types of uses (range) coexisting in the house, these are completely undetected by the cadaster. In any case, Rosa's house has one of the most simple configurations of observed uses of all the houses I visited.

3.2.3.5 *Alba's home in Caracolí, Ciudad Bolívar*

Alba's house is located in Bogotá's new periphery, making it very different from the other houses in my sample. It is one of the two negative cases included to deepen the analysis by comparison. Clinging from a precarious unpaved road in the southwest mountains of Bogotá, this house is far from Bogotá's center. Only one street separates Caracolí neighborhood from the adjoining Soacha municipality. Being so close to the intermunicipal administrative boundary seems to accentuate the feeling that this is a forgotten territory for both local governments, at least in terms of accessibility and policing. Compared to the stories before, Alba's house story gives a glimpse into what those other houses in consolidated informal settlements must have gone through some 20 or more years ago. In a way, Alba's house interview description allows for some sort of time-travel.

Ciudad Bolívar has a rich convoluted urban history that is still in the process of being written and re-written with different voices (Gomez, 2014). It is a living laboratory for unresolved urban issues and promises in migration, land encroachment, social mobilization, environmental justice, micro-trafficking, participatory action research, paramilitarism, and so on. Bypassing these complexities is of course unfair. But this is not the story I will focus at the moment. For now, I ask the reader to continue through the house interview narration bearing in mind that this is indeed a loaded territory, in the frontline of many evolving conflicts.

Access to Alba's house is by a steep unpaved street that is not accessible to cars and is difficult to walk through, especially when it rains (Figure 3.26). The corner cross street, though, is paved and quite busy with commercial activity, notably more second-hand shops (of clothes, appliances, and even discarded produce) than you would find in other locations. Alba lives in this house with her mother and her sister, who has two boys, ages four and seven. There are no men around. She never met her dad and her two older brothers are "enlisted" (from the tone of her voice it is not sure if both went into the army or to some other armed group). The three women rent this house for US$122 per month. The house has one floor and a leaking tin roof. As observed in the façade photograph, a makeshift electricity connection and a water tank in the roof suggest that utilities are not completely formal.

Figure 3.26 Alba's house in Caracoli: façade (left), street (center), and training school for security guards on nearby corner (Author, 2019).

There is, however, an official address street sign. It is also worth noting that the house has two front doors, meaning the owners have plans to subdivide the house and rent two units independently in the future.

Alba's family is from Guainía in the Amazon. Her mother arrived in Caracolí 10 years ago, whereas Alba arrived very recently. She used some savings from her grandmother to pay for a security guard training that offered job placement (see the sign of this "office" on the photograph above right). Alba paid in advance but, she did not receive any training, job offer, nor any explanation. By now, she is convinced this office is a scam but is afraid to ask for her money back. At the moment, she is taking care of her two cousins. Before she arrived in Caracolí the kids were being looked after by the neighbor, who also happens to be the owner of the house. Alba's sister used to pay $82 per month so the neighbor would take care of the children "from 6:30 am to 6:30 pm, not including food nor toilet paper." The neighbor was supposed to take them to school at noon and then pick them up at four in the afternoon, "but who knows if she did or if they went by themselves, most likely they never left the house." So, at least while Alba does not get a job, because she is taking care of the cousins, she is contributing to the household's income those $82 per month that her sister does not have to pay.

Alba did not mention the two businesses in her house when I asked her directly. These came up later, as follow-up questions. When I saw the elliptical trainer machine in the back, she mentioned in passing that more than her or her sister, other neighbors use it for a fee (Figure 3.27). I learned about the clothes' wash and fold business months after my visit, when reviewing the photographs. I followed up with her when noting men's clothing drying in the line, which is curious since no man lives in the house. There was a lot Alba did not share with me, and this silence loomed heavy for both of us during our conversation. Perhaps this is the reason why after I left, she decided to share a WhatsApp message that was recently sent to her (Figure 3.28).

Figure 3.27 Alba's room (left), corridor and gym (center), and kitchen (right) (Author, 2019).

Space-use intensity in informal settlements in Bogotá 111

The message, distributed two weeks before my first visit to Caracolí, orders a mandatory curfew and announces a new round of "social cleansing" in the neighborhood: "we will be cleaning all Venezuelans and crackheads... after 11 pm there should be no spoiled Venezuelan motherfucker outside, nor any vicious kids we see outside. After 11 "PUM," we put them down.... Let the killing begin, it's the only way." I was told messages like this are common here. Most are allegedly connected to the Black Eagles, a right-wing organization that emerged after the demobilization of the far-right paramilitaries between 2004 and 2006. In fact, residents of Potosí, the neighborhood to the south of Caracolí, call Caracolí "*Paracolí*" to reference the dominance of paramilitary groups there. In contrast, Potosí is known for being home of a left-wing school and community organization (Instituto Cerros del Sur), inspired in Freire's *Pedagogy of the Oppressed* (Freire, 1970).

As can be seen in the diagrams in Figure 3.29, in Alba's house there is a difference between the information that rests on the cadaster and the observed uses. Alba's home is certainly used for much more than just living, it holds

Figure 3.28 Social cleansing threat in Caracoli circulating on WhatsApp. (Urrea, 2019) translated by the author.

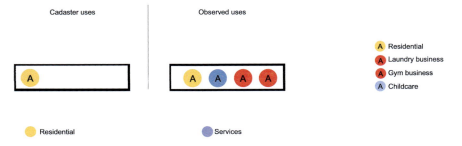

Figure 3.29 Cross-sectional diagrams of cadastral and observed uses in Alba's house (#7) (Author, 2019; (IDECA, 2018).

informal laundry and gym businesses, as well as childcare service. These commercial uses are hidden from public view in the far end of the plot. They are only offered to acquaintances. These uses take advantage of the residential space to support the household's livelihood and are indeed instrumental to it. This case is also interesting in that Alba's mother does not pay the rent for the house by herself. Her two daughters, if they are to live with her and because they already turned 18, must contribute to the monthly expenses. This practice is not uncommon, co-payment arrangements for people in the same household or use-unit happened in more than half of the houses I visited.

3.3 Explaining space–use intensity: discreteness and non-porousness

The objective of the house narratives of Lucy, Susy, Ana, Rosa, and Alba was not that of thick description, typical of an ethnographic study. These stories were important here not only for the sake of revealing the color, richness, and complexity of social meaning. My interest in description is more pragmatic, it is a necessary step to gather the fine-grained information contained in the set of cross-sectional diagrams. In a similar fashion, these diagrams are not only produced with the ultimate goal of visualizing data. They are, in turn, instrumental in producing tallies of different space-use categories in these houses. The diagrams proved central in this process as "instruments for reasoning about quantitative information" (Tufte, 2001).

The graphics eased the translation of the field notes into categories with basic quantitative information, a process that entailed various research feedback loops between description, visualization, and tallying. Below I include a visual summary of the cross-sectional diagrams of observed uses (Figure 3.30), followed by a table with the descriptive statistics of the key space-use intensity variables and their categories (Table 3.3), which I explain in greater detail below.

As foreshadowed earlier in this chapter when analyzing Jacobs' ideas, space-use intensity has two fundamental categories: granularity and range. I will explain in greater detail each of them and then show how they interact in order to fully account for the intensity of use.

3.3.1 Intensity as the count of discrete uses

3.3.1.1 Granularity: use-units within

Granularity is mapped in my cross-sectional diagrams with capital letters that stand for different "use-units" within the building. The term "use-unit" comes directly from Bogotá's cadaster. Despite the fact that this cadaster

Space-use intensity in informal settlements in Bogotá 113

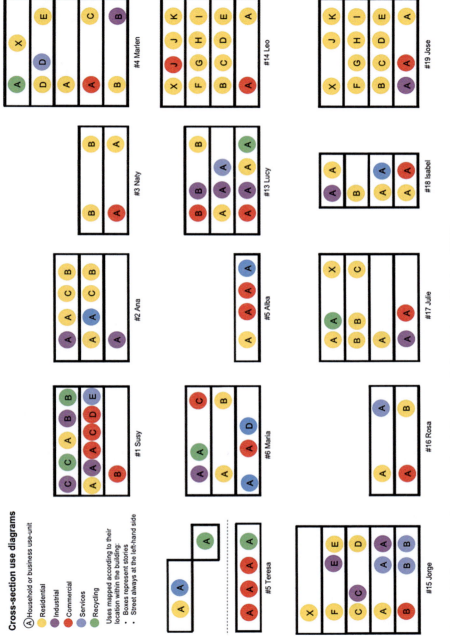

Figure 3.30 Summary of cross-sectional diagrams of observed uses (Author, 2019).

114 *Space-use intensity in informal settlements in Bogotá*

Table 3.3 Descriptive statistics of space-use intensity variables

	Min.	Max.	Avg.	Std. Dev.
Granularity				
Use-units in cadaster	1	2	1.43	0.51
Use-units observed	1	12	4.21	3.45
Use-units per floor	0.5	3	1.25	0.75
Range or diversity				
Type of uses in cadaster	1	2	1.36	0.50
Type of uses observed	2	5	3.57	0.94
Types uses observed per floor	1.5	4	2.55	0.90
Intensity or depth				
Residential uses observed	1	11	3.57	3.34
Industrial uses observed	0	3	1.14	1.17
Commercial uses observed	0	4	1.50	1.02
Service uses observed	0	3	0.93	1.00
Recycling uses observed	0	2	0.57	0.76
Count of discrete uses	3	13	7.71	3.45
Density of uses observed ×100	2.08	6.11	4.05	1.32
Maximum discrete uses per use-unit	2	5	3.29	1.07
Related variables				
Urbanization origin: formal (1) or informal (0)	0	1	0.36	0.50
Age of legal urbanization	1,963	2,007	1,988	11
Number of floors observed	1	5	3.14	1.17
Total area in use as observed (m^2)	72	360	207	98.59
Cadaster value of the block (USD/m^2)	9.7	587	306	182.79

is recognized in the region as a highly advanced one (Erba and Piumetto, 2016:13), and despite the fact that use-units are an important analytic variable for this organization's analytic products (Amaya, 2016); there is no explicit definition for the term in the organization's glossary. However, implicit in their database and in conversations with technical staff (Amaya, 2019), it is clear that "use-unit" is a loosely estimated subdivision within the plot, the smallest spatial unit of measurement in the cadaster's database. Granularity is the extent to which a system is broken down into small parts, it is the "extent to which a larger entity is subdivided. For example, a yard broken into inches has finer granularity than a yard broken into feet" (WikiGis, 2009). In geographic information systems, as well as across disciplines like computing, physics, business, photography; granularity is described as being coarse or fine. In this case, use–units add fine–grain to Bogotá's cadaster, adding detail and hence deepening data analysis.

Even though all the houses visited are single–family residential units in Bogotá's cadaster, official data recognizes that some plots have more than one use within them. The cadaster records this as use–units, ascribing an estimated area to a part of the plot's area. This is usually done after a field visit by a cadaster officer, who without necessarily entering into the property, follows some visual cues, like the existence of: "more than one address sign with different nomenclatures, more than one utility meter, large doors, high ceilings, or trusses" (Amaya, 2019). Before 2004, Bogotá's cadaster used to do "recognition brigades" sending hundreds of people to the ground to gather this type of information in "cadastral formation forms" (see Annex #2). But swiping an eight million city by foot with an army of cadastral surveyors is a cumbersome never-ending task, so the cadaster started updating its records relying on secondary information like utilities' databases, real estate ads, and building permits records. "Nothing is better than field recognition," acknowledges a cadaster technician, who, while proud of the potency of the use–units measure, accepts this information is inherently incomplete (Amaya, 2019).

As shown in the second row in the table, the average official count of use–units in the sample is more than one: 1.43. This number is smaller than the average of observed use–units, which was 4.21. The difference in these two numbers suggests there are almost three times (2.95) more use–units per plot more than what the cadaster acknowledges there is. Collecting more fine–grain data might not always be necessary or desirable. Nonetheless, this number shows that the extent of what remains invisible is considerably large.

3.3.1.2 Range or diversity of uses

The second category is the *range* of uses. As explained at the beginning of the chapter, range refers to the scope of mixed–use a residential building incorporates, so it is a traditional understanding of the diversity of uses. Diverse uses are identified in my diagrams with five different colors (again, yellow for residential, red for commercial, purple for industrial, blue for services, and green for recycling and urban agriculture). Accordingly, the summary table records range as the simple count of different colors in the visual record of each house. If a color appears more than once, it is only counted once. In my sample, the maximum range of use is 5, and the minimum is 1. A range of one tells a house is used strictly for residential purposes, so any number above one is considered mixed–use. As shown in the table, the average official range in my sample is more than one: 1.36. However, as in the case of granularity, this number is also smaller than the average of what was observed, 3.5. Even if just applicable within my sample, this number makes

116 *Space-use intensity in informal settlements in Bogotá*

an important statement. Residential areas are only so at about 30%. As early as 1967, Bogotá openly welcomes mixed-used areas in its plans, particularly within houses with an informal origin or that are self-built. Nevertheless, the difference in these two range averages suggests the extent of diversity is much higher than anticipated. There are two and a half (2.6) more types of uses per plot more than what the cadaster concedes there is.

High range of use speaks very clearly of the extent of economic utilization of the residential spaces. In every single one of the 14 houses in my sample I observed some economic use of space. In fact, the total count of non-residential types of uses is 35 and of those, only two were non-economical: a prayer house (house #1) and informal policing (house #6). All other uses were economical either in monetary terms (like having a shop or business) or non-monetary (like childcare or recycling). What I find is consistent—though notably higher—than what recent studies surveying hundreds of residents in consolidated informal settlements in Bogotá report. For instance, Camargo reports 65% of economic use (rented spaces, shops, or home-based work) of residential space (Camargo, 2017), while Torres finds 85% (Torres, 2019). High shares of economic use of residential are far from unique. To reference a distant example, in the large Bodija sites and services project in Ibadan, Nigeria, this percentage was found to be 89.9% (Okewole, 1998:160). In my modest sample of 14 houses, there are 33 economic uses, making the extent of economic use of residential space higher than 100% (236%). The intensity category is introduced to help make sense of this apparent impossibility.

3.3.1.3 *Intensity or depth*

Both granularity (use-units within a plot) and range (diversity in type of uses observed) are fundamental components of space-use intensity. The first step in understanding what intensity is, going back to my diagrams, is adding the total count of circles that have different letters (use-units) and different colors (diverse uses) in each house. This is the total count of different or discrete uses. Each house has a number of use-units (ranging from 1 to 11), and each use-unit has a number of different uses it engages in (ranging from one to five). The total count of all different uses in my sample is 108. Of those, 50 are residential uses. This means that in this set of residences, the actual residential use represents less than half (46%) of the total uses. This alone is an outstanding fact. It leads to believe that in consolidated informal settlements, a house is not a house. A house is a lot more than a place of residence. All houses of course have at least a residential use in one of its use-units, but they have much more happening than that, as the first bar graph below reveals. One residential use per house represents as little as 7.7% and as much as 25% of the total uses in the house (Figure 3.31). The following bar graph shows the composition of the total count of discrete uses in the sample. The colors reflect the different types of uses. The number of partitions within each bar shows the number of use-units (Figure 3.32).

Space-use intensity in informal settlements in Bogotá 117

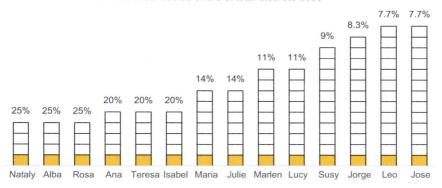

Figure 3.31 First residential use-unit as share of total discrete uses (Author, 2019).

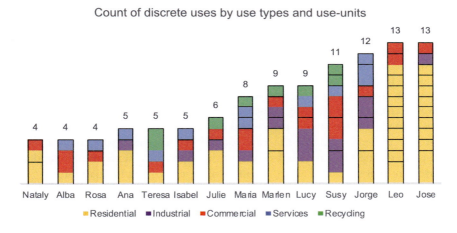

Figure 3.32 Count of discrete uses by use types and use-units (Author, 2019).

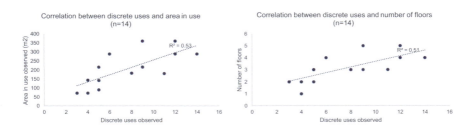

Figure 3.33 Relationship between discrete uses and area-based measures (Author, 2019).

118 *Space-use intensity in informal settlements in Bogotá*

Naturally, the bigger the houses, the easier it will be for the count of different uses to be higher. This is why it is important to consider an area-sensitive measure. Many types of densities could be calculated on the houses in my sample, like use-unit density, or density of use, which is the one I opted for. It must be stressed that I am not referring to density of use (in singular) that takes into account either granularity or range, but rather density of uses (in plural) that takes account of both, by means of the variable "discrete uses." The second number needed to calculate density is some kind of area–related denominator. Unfortunately, while my study located each discrete use in a specific floor of the building, I did not calculate the area that each discrete use occupies of the total area in use. The two area-based variables I have are the number of floors and the estimated area in use. Following a 1972 city decree on minimal plot sizes, most plots in this type of neighborhoods (and in my sample) have 72 square meters: six meters in front by 12 meters in depth. Using information gathered through field notes, I compared the relationship between discrete uses with both the estimated area of the building in use and the number of floors.

As observed in the graphs in Figure 3.33, though the correlations are not strong, the area in use seems to be slightly more important than the number of floors. The fact that having more area is more relevant is unsurprising. However, what is in fact quite interesting, is that the number of floors is almost as important. This hints that having an extra floor can often be of more use-value than having a bigger plot. Adding space vertically with additional floors facilitates partitioning use-units and giving them independent access. This is an insight repeatedly mentioned in the interviews, people seem to have a precise understanding of the value added of an extra floor. For example, Isabel mentioned it was only because of the extra floor with an independent apartment that she could afford paying college tuition for her daughter.

But the density of uses is not all there is to intensity of use. Besides the simultaneous consideration to both range and granularity, in the notion of intensity there is an additional emphasis on the interaction between these two components. Interactions between and within uses happen due to frequency of contact in both space and time. Let me illuminate this statement with some examples. Susy might not have a side-job selling soaps if she was not sharing the bathroom of her "apartment" with the soap shop. In this case, a residential use-unit interacts with a commercial use-unit and as a result, it expands its range of uses adding a commercial activity it might not otherwise have. Susy complements the slim pension she gets with an extra occasional income. Another example is Alba's laundry business, which is likely to be more active because she also has a gym machine that neighbors use for a fee. In my diagrams, one can track such synergies by adding the number of circles that have the same letter but different colors. The variable "maximum discrete uses per use-unit" uniquely addresses the depth of space-use, showing the range of multitasking a use-unit can engage in. The numbers in my sample show that 79% of the houses visited have use-units that engage in three or more types of uses. Further research into this matter could detail: the specific area dedicated to each type of use (three-dimensional cadasters take this path), the dwelling time of each use (as in space utilization analysis (BCO, 2018) or the tiny house movement), or primary and secondary types of use of space (following the time-use studies approach).

At this point, it is important to recognize that there are a number of limitations to the study on the intensity of use. A salient one is that the count of discrete uses and use-units is very sensitive to the type and quality of rapport and intimacy that the observer is capable of ensuring. Being this a study into the private realm there is a lot that remains unseen. Estimating the extent of the unseen, that is, the question What should be counted? is as important as considering the questions Who benefits from counting? and Why count? Many agree that often times remaining unseen or blurring legibility is a low-profile, everyday form of resistance of the oppressed, it is one of the "weapons of the weak" (Scott, 1985: xvii). While this point merits further analysis, for now, let me state that not only are there activities people are unwilling to disclose, but there are also activities people are not aware, do not remember, or do not value as relevant. To address this, as mentioned earlier, there are a handful of cues about both range and granularity that can be discerned without the need to enter a house or to ask too many uncomfortable questions to the residents. In this sense, it is important that researchers or survey takers are at least aware that these categories exist and that they are meaningful. Despite this limitation, it is encouraging to see that the houses where I built better rapport (Susy #1 and Ana #2) are not necessarily the ones with the highest space-use intensity measures (Maria #6, Teresa #5, and Lucy's #13, where I did build high rapport).

Even though my sample is quite small and hence to a large extent, findings can be inconclusive, there are a few additional insights worth highlighting. Interestingly, the count of observed use-units, observed use types, and discrete uses higher in older neighborhoods, irrespective of them having a formal or an informal origin. Both neighborhoods that have an informal origin and a formal one, tend to increase their use intensity over time. While a high number of types of uses in a single use-unit are found across extremely different levels of consolidation, use-units tend to be higher the older the neighborhood is. However, among older neighborhoods, once a building has a fixed number of use-units, it can, via interaction, diversify its type of uses, hence deepening its space-use intensity. Also interesting is to note the fact that properties tend to gain value as they consolidate (of which the year of legal urbanization is a proxy for), a tendency that operates in reverse of formal neighborhoods. This is, however, a very weak relationship.

3.3.2 Cadastral knowledge

Despite the large discrepancies between my findings and the information on the cadaster, the use-units classification has been instrumental in arriving at

120 *Space-use intensity in informal settlements in Bogotá*

a more granular knowledge of the structure and growth of uses in Bogotá. Unfortunately, gaining knowledge depth has "not necessarily meant using it, nor achieving a better understanding of the city" (Florián, 2019). Taking full advantage of use-unit area measurements, Bogotá's cadaster published a series of 19 documents analyzing the dynamics of the "intensity of land-uses" in each of the city's boroughs (localidades) over a decade (Orjuela and Cogua, 2013:5). The level of detail and technical subtlety of this analysis is quite surprising. Unfortunately, this analytic knowledge is strictly reported without providing any synthesis and without aggregating the findings for the city as a whole. As a result, this knowledge is not translated into understanding. What appears to be happening is that there is a high level of empirical refinement in need of a theoretical framework. Without more robust theories to explain these realities, informing policy with this knowledge will be impossible. Unfortunately, the use-unit classification is still to be absorbed successfully into theory.

This process has started to happen in Bogotá at a slow pace and in an unarticulated fashion with another related classification of Bogotá's cadaster: Non-Horizontal Property (NPH for its Spanish acronym). Non-horizontal property refers to properties having more than one use-unit inside it that are not legally separated, so they do not have different owners, as condominiums do. Strategic urban planning and urban development documents in Bogotá are increasingly using this "non-horizontal property" classification as a proxy to refer to informal housing (DTS-POT, 2019:47) and (DDPDD, 2020:152). For instance: "An important part of the growth in the supply of housing in Bogotá is carried out without a license, in properties for residential use of non-horizontal property (NPH), this can be interpreted as informal growth that does not translate into new properties, yet it entails additional residential areas being constructed" (DDPDD, 2020:153). This is particularly true for lower income residents. I delve into this topic more at length elsewhere, but the main reason to mention it here is to call attention to the fact that granular knowledge of strategic cadastral categories as these ones, need to be critically adapted and also need to expand the vocabulary in use to make sense of the nature of urban informality in our cities.

3.3.3 *Intensity as the opposite of porosity*

Allow me to change narrative gears in order to delve more deeply into the conceptual meaning of intensity of use. Consider for a moment that intensity is the contrary of porosity. Porosity (from the Greek *poros*, passage) is a property of materials that let fluids pass through. Porous objects have a large aggregate of inner voids or a larger interstice's volume. Imagine houses are like buckets filled with rocks of different sizes and different types. There are air gaps, interstices between these rocks. The space occupied by the interstices is determined by the size and the amount of rocks in the bucket. This void space can be filled to a larger or lesser extent, making the bucket more or less porous. The more these interstices are filled, the more intensely space is used. Spaces that are intensely used are thicker and more difficult to pass through, that is, they are less porous.

As pores saturate, houses take in, and absorb the many services that dwellers do not find publicly. Any service that is not met by the city, is satisfied this way. Absorbing urban responsibilities, these houses clog their inner pores and become more productive and more intense. Intensification takes advantage of spatial porosity, occupying residual voids, and stifling every pocket of air. Space-use intensification frees oneself from depending on public services but asphyxiates the private realm. Unlike other types of violent choking, the porosity fill-up of these houses is yet unspoken for. Speaking for intensification or about it is marred with controversy, in part because while forbidding, it is also beneficial and quite promising. Intensification takes out air but adds value, increasing carrying capacity, and supporting life. As spaces saturate, not only are they more vibrant, but they also start playing social protection roles, and filling the gaps left by absent or insufficient public urban services.

The concept of porosity helps explain the existence and capacity of the spaces within, helps assess the extent of residual voids (that are not empty, so are better called pores) and their role as pockets storing productivity, minute stock. Porosity can accurately describe what cannot be seen at plain sight. Houses in neighborhoods of progressive development extract the most out of them. People commonly mention a good house is one which one can "take out from," to the extent that *sacarle a la casa* is a broadly understood idiom for taking economic advantage of the pores of the house, making room within, squeezing it while maintaining it. Everyone wants a house that one can take out from, subdividing up or within. A better house is one that one can take out from more.

References

Amaya, Aureliano. (2016). *Análisis de variables incidentes para el tema de valorización índice de renta para la localidad de Kennedy*, Observatorio Técnico Catastral Distrital, Alcaldía Mayor de Bogota, Bogota.

Amaya, Aureliano. (2019). Personal interview, July 15, 2019, Bogota.

BCO – British Council for Offices. (2018). *Office Occupancy: Density and Utilisation*, BCO Research & Policy, AECOM – Ramidus, London.

Blackson, Howard and PlaceMakers, LLM. (2013). "Don't Get Mixed Up on Mixed-Use", *PlaceMakers*, April 4, 2013, http://www.placemakers.com/2013/04/04/mixed-up-on-mixed-use/

Camargo, Angélica. (2017). "Prácticas residenciales y movilidad social en barrios populares", PhD dissertation, Universidad Externado de Colombia, Colombia.

Calthorpe, Peter. (1993). *The Next American Metropolis*, Princeton Architectural Press, New York.

Carrizosa, Maria. (2020). "Six Countries and Twenty Years: A Transversal Reading of Latin American urban policy", In Cohen M., Carrizosa M., and Gutman M.

122 *Space-use intensity in informal settlements in Bogotá*

(eds) *Urban Policy in Latin America: Towards the Sustainable Development Goals?* Routledge, Oxford, pp. 352–354.

Ceballos, Olga. (2019). Personal interview, May 28, 2019, Bogota.

Cervero, Robert. (1996). "Mixed Land-uses and Commuting: Evidence from the American Housing Survey", *Transportation Research A*, 30:5, pp. 361–377.

Cervero, Robert, and Duncan, Michael (2004). "Neighborhood Composition and Residential Land Prices: Does Exclusion Raise or Lower Values?" *Urban Studies*, 41, pp. 299–315.

Chen, Martha. (2012). *The Informal Economy: Definitions, Theories and Policies*, WIEGO Working Paper #1, Cambridge.

Chen, Martha. (2014). "Informal Economy Monitoring Study Sector Report: Home-Based Workers", Women in Informal Employment: Globalizing and Organizing – WIEGO, Cambridge, MA.

CONPES – Consejo Nacional de Política Económica y Social. (2019). Política de Formalización Empresarial, CONPES # 3956, Departamento Nacional de Planeación, Web.

Davis, Mike. (2006). *The Planet of Slums*, Verso, London.

DANE – Departamento Nacional de Estadística. (2005). "Manual Técnico del Censo General 2005," República de Colombia, Web.

DANE – Departamento Nacional de Estadística. (2018). "Censo Nacional de Población y Vivienda 2018", República de Colombia, Web.

DDPP – Documento Diagnóstico del Proyecto de Plan de Desarrollo Distrital 2020-2024. (2020). *Bogota City Government*, February 28, 2020.

Desrochers, Pierre and Hospers, Gert-Jan. (2007). "Cities and the Economic Development of Nations: An Essay on Jane Jacobs' Contribution to Economic Theory", *Canadian Journal of Regional Science*, 30:1, p. 115+.

Dovey, Kim and Pafka, Elek. (2017). "What Is Functional Mix? An Assemblage Approach", *Planning Theory and Practice*, 18:2, pp. 249–267.

DTS-POT – Documento Técnico de Soporte del Plan de Ordenamiento Territorial. (2019). "Análisis de ordenamiento y gestión del suelo de la demanda de vivienda esperada", Secretaria de Planeación Distrital, document 3, annex 1.

Duany, Andres, Plater-Zyberk, Elizabeth and Speck, Jeff. (2000). *Suburban Nation: The Rise of Sprawl and the Decline of the American Dream*, North Point Press, New York.

Erba, Diego AAlfonso and Piumetto, Mario Andres. (2016). "Making Land Legible: Cadasters for Urban Planning and Development in Latin America", Policy Focus Report, Lincoln Institute of Land Policy, Cambridge, MA.

Florián, Alejandro. (2019). Personal interview, January 28, 2019.

FIG – Fédération Internationale de Géomètres. (2018). "3D Cadasters", FIG Joint Commission, Delft University of Technology, Web.

Floro, Maria Sagrario. (1995). "Women's Well-being, Poverty, and Work Intensity", *Journal of Feminist Economics*, 1:3, pp. 1–25.

Frank, Lawrence, Schmid, Thomas, Sallis, James, Chapman, James, and Saelens, Brian. (2005). "Linking Objectively Measured Physical Activity With Objectively Measured Urban Form". *American Journal of Preventive Medicine*, 28, pp. 117–125.

Freire, Paulo. (1972). Pedagogía del oprimido, Siglo XXI, Mexico.

García, Andrea del Pilar. (2011). *Por el derecho a construir la felicidad en Patio Bonito: Una experiencia de planeación y gestión colectiva que se construye día a día*, Corporación Grupo Enlace Social – Corpoges, Bogota.

García, Wilson. (2013). *Dinámica de las construcciones por usos en la Localidad Kennedy 2002-2012*, Unidad Administrativa de Catastro Distrital – UACD, Bogota.

Gehrke, Steven and Clifton, Kelly. (2016). "Toward a Spatial-temporal Measure of Land-use Mix", *Journal of Transport and Land Use*, 9:1, pp. 171–186.

Gershuny, Jonathan. (2009). "Harvey's Hypercodes and the 'Propogram': More than 24 Hours Per Day?" *Electronic International Journal of Time Use Research*, 6:2, pp. 193–199.

Jonathan Gershuny, Kelly, Paul, Thomas, Emma, Doherty, Aiden, Harms, Teresa, Burke, and Órlaith, Foster, Charlie. (2015). "Developing a Method to Test the Validity of 24-Hour Time Use Diaries Using Wearable Cameras: A Feasibility Pilot", *PLoS ONE Journal*, San Francisco, December 3, 2015.

Gershuny, J., Fisher, K., Gilber, E., Calderwood, L., Huskinson, T., and Cleary, A. (2018). "Using New Technologies for Time Diary Data Collection: Instrument Design and Data Quality Findings from a Mixed-Mode Pilot Survey", *Social Indicators Research*, 136:1, pp. 379–390.

Glaeser, Edward. (2011). *The Triumph of the City: How Our Greatest Invention Makes Us Richer, Smarter, Greener, Healthier, and Happier*, Penguin Press, New York.

Godoy, D., Steadman, P., Hamilton, I., Donn, M., Evans, S., Moreno, G., and Shayesteh, H. (2018). "Energy Use and Height in Office Buildings", *Building Research & Information*, 46:8, pp. 845–863.

Gómez, Nemías. (2014). *Partir de lo que somos: Ciudad Bolívar, Tierra, Agua y Luchas*, Alcaldía Mayor de Bogota, Secretaría de Gobierno, Memoria Histórica Local para la Construcción del Territorio, Bogota.

González, María Isabel. (2004). *Escuela-comunidad historia de la organización comunitaria en Potosí Jerusalén*, Ediciones Desde Abajo, Bogota.

González, Lina Maria. (2013). "Complementación y compensación de zonas verdes en áreas con tratamiento de mejoramiento integral", report from contract 130 of 2012, Secretaria Distrital de Planeación, Bogota.

Grant, Jill. (2002). "Mixed Use in Theory and Practice: Canadian Experience with Implementing a Planning Principle", *Journal of the American Planning Association*, 68:1, pp. 71–84.

Gutiérrez, Francisco. (1998). *La ciudad representada: Política y conflicto en Bogota*, Tercer Mundo Editores – IEPRI, Bogota.

Ibáñez, Pedro María. (1891). *Las crónicas de Bogota y de sus inmediaciones*, Imprenta de la Luz, Bogota.

IDECA – Infraestructura de Datos Espaciales de Bogota. (2019). "Unidades de uso", Catastro Bogota, www.ideca.gov.co, GIS database

Instituto Geográfico Agustín Codazzi – IGAC. (2003). "Manual General de Formación Catastral", IGAC, Excel table provided by Bogota's Cadaster.

ILO – International Labour Organization. (2018). *Women and Men in the Informal Economy: A Statistical Picture*, 3rd edition, ILO, Geneva.

Jacobs, Jane. (1992[1962]). *The Death and Life of Great American Cities*, Vintage Books, New York.

Jacobs, Jane. (1970[1969]). *The Economy of Cities*, Vintage Books, New York.

Jacobs, Jane. (1984). *Cities and the Wealth of Nations: Principles of Economic Life*, Vintage Books, New York.

Jacobs, Jane. (2000). *The Nature of Economies*, Vintage Books Canada, Toronto, ON.

Jacobs, Jane. (2001). "City Views", interview by Bill Steigerwald, Reason Magazine, June 2001, Washington, DC.

Kenyon, Susan. (2008). "Internet Use and Time Use: The Importance of Multitasking", *Time & Society*, 17, pp. 2–3, SSOAR, Open Access Repository, pp. 283–318.

Kenyon, Susan. (2010). "What Do We Mean by Multitasking? – Exploring the Need for Methodological Clarification in Time Use Research", *International Journal of Time Use Research*, 7:1, pp. 42–60.

Law 1753. (2015). National Development Plan 2014-2018, Congress of the Republic of Colombia, June 9, 2019.

Leighton, J. A. (1910). "On Continuity and Discreteness", *The Journal of Philosophy, Psychology and Scientific Methods*, 7:9, April 28, pp. 231–238.

Marín, María Natalia. (2014). "Ciudad Kennedy: una leyenda urbana en Bogota", In Caballero, et al. (eds) *Alberto Lleras Camargo y John F. Kennedy: amistad y política internacional: recuento de episodios de la Guerra Fría, la Alianza para el Progreso y el problema de Cuba*, Ediciones Uniandes, Bogota.

Marshall, Bryan, Cardon, Peter, Poddar, Amit, and Fontenot, Rene. (2013). "Does Sample Size Matter in Qualitative Research? A Review of Qualitative Interviews in IS Research", *Journal of Computer Information Systems*, 54:1, pp. 11–22.

Mavoa, Suzanne, Eagleson, Serryn, Badland, Hannah, Gunn, Lucy, Boulange, Claire, Stewart, Jpshua, Giles-Corti, Billie. (2018). "Identifying Appropriate Land-use Mix Measures for Use in a National Walkability Index", *Journal of Transport and Land Use*, 11:1, pp. 681–700.

Melia, S., Parkhurst, G., and Barton, H. (2011). "The Paradox of Intensification", *Transport Policy*, 18:1, Elsevier, pp. 46–52.

Miller, G. A. (1956). "The Magical Number Seven, Plus or Minus Two: Some Limits on Our Capacity for Processing Information", *Psychological Review*, 63:2, pp. 81–97.

Montenegro, Maria Trinidad. (2019). Personal interview, March 14, 2019.

Newman, Oscar. (1972). *Defensible Space: Crime Prevention Through Urban Design*, Macmillan, New York.

Okewole, L. A. (1998). "Environmental Restructuring in Planned Residential Setting: The Case of Bodija Estate", *Ife Planning Journal*, 1:1, pp. 97–106.

Orjuela, C. and Cogua, M. I. (2013). *Marco teórico y metodológico dinámica de la construcción por usos según localidades, años 2002–2012*, Unidad Administrativa de Catastro Distrital – UACD, Bogota.

Parra, Federico. (2019). Personal interview, August 5, 2019.

Putnam, Sara, and Quinn, Andrew. (2007). "Jane Jacobs and Urban Health", *Journal of Urban Health: Bulletin of the New York Academy of Medicine*, 84:1, pp. 1–2. doi:10.1007/s11524-006-9143-5

Roy, Ananya. (2005). "Urban Informality. Toward an Epistemology of Planning", *Journal of the American Planning Association*, 71:2, pp. 147–158.

Sampedro, Pablo. (2019). "What is the Difference Between Density and Intensity?" *Quora*, Web, Mar 4.

Samper, German. (2015). Personal conversation, New York, March 31.

Scott, James. (1985). *Weapons of the Weak: Everyday Forms of Peasant Resistance*, Yale University Press, New Haven, CT.

Secretaría Distrital de Planeación – SDP. (2017). *La estratificación en Bogotá: impacto social y alternativas para asignar subsidios*. Alcaldía Mayor de Bogotá.

Secretaria de Planeación Distrital de Bogota – SDP. (2018). *Boletín de Vivienda 2018: Seguimiento Mercado de Vivienda Bogota y Sabana*, Alcaldía Mayor de Bogota, Bogota.

Song, Yan, and Rodríguez, Daniel A. (2005). "The Measurement of the Level of Mixed Land Uses: A Synthetic Approach." Carolina Transportation Program White Paper Series, Chapel Hill, NC.

Song, Yan., Merlin, Louis, and Rodriguez, Daniel A. (2013). "Comparing Measures of Land Use Mix", *Computers, Environment, and Urban Systems*, 42, pp. 1–13.

Torres, Carlos A. (2012). "Legalización de barrios: acción de mejora o mecanismo de viabilización fiscal de la ciudad dual", *Bulletin de l'Institut français d'*études andines – *BIFEA*, 41:3, pp. 441–471.

Torres, Carlos A. (2017). "Ciudad informal colombiana", *Revista Bitácora Urbano Territorial*, 11:1, pp. 53–93.

Torres, Jorge. (2019). Personal interview, February 1, 2019.

Torres, Jorge Enrique. (2020). "Colombia. The singularity of housing policy in urban development". In Cohen, M., Carrizosa, M., and Gutman, M. (eds) *Urban Policy in Latin America: Towards the Sustainable Development Goals?* Routledge, Oxford, pp. 145–202.

UNDESA – United Nations Department of Economic and Social Affairs. (2008). *International Standard Industrial Classification of All Economic Activities*, Revision 4, United Nations, New York.

UNGA – United Nations General Assembly. (2015). *Transforming Our World: The 2030 Agenda for Sustainable Development*. General Assembly 70 session, September 25, New York.

Vanek, Joann, Chen, Martha A., Carré, Françoise, Heintz, James, and Hussmanns, Ralf. (2014). *Statistics on the Informal Economy: Definitions, Regional Estimates and Challenges*, Working Informal Migrant Entrepreneurship and Inclusive Growth Migration Policy Series (68), WIEGO, Cambridge, MA.

Ward, Peter. (2015). "Housing Rehab for Consolidated Informal Settlements: A New Policy Agenda for 2016 UN-Habitat III", *Habitat International*, 50, pp. 337–384.

Wilson, G. and Kelling, J. (1982). "Broken Windows", *The Atlantic Monthly*, 249:3, pp. 29–38.

WikiGIS. (2009). "Granularity", GIS Dictionary.

Xie, Jing. (2012). "Diversity and Mixed Use: Lessons from Medieval China", In Hirt, Sonia and Zahm, Diane (eds) *The Urban Wisdom of Jane Jacobs*, Chapter 11, Routledge, New York, pp. 150–167

4 The politics of urban formalization in Bogotá

Despite the efforts and good intentions of so many communities, activists, and local officials, the state of urban formalization policy in Bogotá is disappointing. The set of procedures it comprises seems to be designed to maintain the status quo rather than to actually upgrade it. Formalization presents itself as a highly technical normative system devoid of any political bearings. However, in reality, the urban formalization process is a labyrinth of byzantine rubrics that, more than difficult, is impossible to get across. Legal antics make a perfect crime, leaving no trace of wrongdoing, when in fact bottleneck after bottleneck, the result is obstruction. Whether by deliberate design, by default, or by inadvertent attrition, such deceit is nothing other than violence. Far from politically neutral, it is a veiled kind of violence that neither high nor middle class Bogotanians ever encounter, so ultimately, formalization policy is an artifact that reproduces and conceals Bogotá's systemic classism.

This chapter shares some details of the history of urban planning in Bogotá and gets into the technicalities of the local urban formalization policy, which, rather than a consistent body of regulations is a scattered set of procedures that are difficult to sequence so that informal settlements are recognized, improved, and integrated. The analysis draws on insights from more than 40 interviews with local experts, document analysis of regulations and their doctrine, as well as of local urban planning history accounts.

4.1 Formalization has its origins in the South

I use urban formalization as an umbrella term to include the various processes by which the local government deals with informal settlements, informal buildings, and informal businesses. While the informal phenomena and formalization intents are as old as the city itself, my analysis concentrates on the period between 1972 and 2016, the same one used in the literature review in Chapter 2. Two reasons make 1972 an excellent starting point for this task. First, 1972 was the year the Inter American Housing Center, CINVA (Centro Interamericano de Vivienda), finalized two decades of outstanding innovations in housing studies, urban development, and community

DOI: 10.4324/9781003297727-4

planning. The second reason is that in 1972, with the publication of a study on minimum standards, there was a fundamental shift in Bogotá's urban planning from a plan-based approach to a code-based approach. The 2016 end date was the moment when the Colombian Constitutional Court declared that inaction in slum upgrading policy represents an unconstitutional state of affairs, urging a fundamental policy change[1] that so far, remains elusive.

4.1.1 Self-help predates Turner

John Turner is globally recognized as the father of the self-help approach to urban development. However, digging into the local history in Bogotá, it becomes clear that these ideas had previous, unacknowledged, pioneers. Colombian history is marred with numerous breakthroughs getting silenced due to ideological reservations. The fate of CINVA is emblematic of this oblivion. Founded in 1952 with support from the Organization of American States (OAS), CINVA's legacy is yet to be fully acknowledged (Rivera, 2001). During its three decades of operation at the National University of Colombia, the center epitomized the vanguard of development studies in the region, championing an alternative paradigm of advocacy planning "from below" (Salazar, 2017:183), a decade before Davidoff mainstreamed these ideas into the Anglo discipline (Davidoff, 1965). Some noteworthy CINVA contributions are: the Participatory Action Research framework (led by the renowned sociologist Orlando Fals Borda); the CINVA-RAM, a low-fi low-cost portable manual press to produce earth compressed bricks (patented by the Chilean engineer Raul Ramírez); the operationalization of the national policy of community action—Acción Comunal-geared to slum upgrading (supported by the trailblazer urban historian and New Dealer Caroline Ware); and also, the conceptual and methodological advancement of "progressive development" of low-income neighborhoods and "directed self-help" construction of low-income housing. With the center's demise in 1972, two stripped-down versions of these concepts were popularized: "sites and services" and "self-help" (Salazar, 2017:117), under the banner of the anti-communist agenda of the Alliance for Progress (Offner, 2019:89). It is important to acknowledge, then, that 1972 marks the moment not when a self-help approach was conceived, but rather when a stripped-down version of it was continuously deployed.

---

1 The Court called out "a gap in the policy regarding the legalization and regularization of informal settlements". It argued that "The legalization and regularization of these settlements is a condition of possibility for the full effective enjoyment of the right to housing ... [it] contributes to the exercise of other related rights". The high Court also insisted that upgrading informal settlements "may be one of the most appropriate solutions to the unmet needs left by previous housing schemes which not only yielded insufficient results; but did not correspond to the magnitude of the problem" (CC373, 2016).

128　*The politics of urban formalization in Bogotá*

John F. C. Turner is, almost undisputedly, credited with conceptualizing and disseminating self-help housing in international urban development literature and practice. But by the time he started writing about this, the concept was already old[2]. In Bogotá, the first model neighborhood of progressive development (Acevedo Tejada) was finished in 1951 and incorporated industrial spaces within the houses (Acebedo, 2003). Soon after, CINVA published the paper "The Concept of Progressive Development" (Eyheralde, 1953), which had regional dissemination. In Bogotá, La Fragua neighborhood (a fitting name for it really forged this approach) initiated by Martinez and Samper 1958 with CINVA's support, was the first neighborhood of aided mutual help, progressive and *productive* development in the region. Turner did little to credit these ideas largely because he was not aware of them: "I read very little academic literature before 1965… I was totally absorbed by the practicalities and with very limited access to—or even awareness of—relevant literature" (Turner, 2000) in (Harris, 2003:491). Tracing back the full genealogy of the concept is beyond the point here, but it is important to note how easily ideas get labeled as being born in the North, when in fact they were not possible without ideas and practices in the South or at least without North-South interactions.

4.1.2　Shelved worldly plans and the unspoken centrality of informality

1972 was also the turning point when spatial planning in Bogotá shifted from a plan-based to a code-based approach. Before this, there was no shortage of grand urban plans for Bogotá. On one hand were the spatial master plans produced by CIAM architects Le Corbusier and Sert in which land-use was essential in defining the model of the city. The spatial master plan of Wiener and Sert in 1949 was a locally adapted version of Le Corbusier's 1947 plan for Bogotá. Distancing itself from the modernist strictures, Sert's plan was more open to mixed-use, mixed-income, pedestrian streets, civic centers, and low-rise housing (Salazar, 2017:48). On the other hand, was the rational economic development approach steered by Lauchlin Currie[3] (1969), where

---

2　Jacob Crane published about aided self-help housing in 1950 following his work in Puerto Rico (Crane,1950). The term got into international cooperation when Crane advocated for it before the US Senate on behalf of the HUD. Nigel Oram, British ethnographer with work in New Guinea as well in West and East Africa before the 1970s gives evidence of other forebearers of self-help (Oram, 1965). In Latin America and particularly in Bogotá, the practice and theorization of Samper is instrumental (see Chapter 2).

3　Canadian-born Keynesian economist. President Roosevelt's personal aide for China during World War II, and prominent Bretton Woods architect. After he was accused of communism in the McCarthy years in the US and his US visa was revoked, he settled in Colombia where he ran the National Planning Department (DNP). Not to be mistaken with Leonard Currie, Harvard architect and Walter Gropius disciple, who was appointed as the founding director of CINVA.

state-produced housing would "filter" from middle to low-income classes and planned "cities-within-cities" would decentralize employment, producing a more equitable future city (Currie et al., 1969). Despite these notable planning precedents and without underscoring their influence, Bogotá ended up prioritizing plans that were explicitly concerned with competing against a mushrooming informal housing supply. These ambitious plans with foreign last names brandishing an ideal city, ceded ground to more realistic plans whose objective was to harmonize with on-the-ground realities.

The tension between worldly and grounded plans is evident in Bogotá's incapacity to build a subway system. Subways invariably cost any city many times their annual budget. In this sense, they are always Quixotic plans, but always worth it. Bogotá's barren dreams of a subway began in the XIX century, and foreign plans for it have been routinely archived, the first French-inspired effort (1942), the British–American (1970), Japanese (1996), to name the most remembered. The capital has had a consistent incapacity to aspire (Appadurai, 2004), it has remained incapable of projecting itself freely and ambitiously into the future the way other cities have.[4] Responsibly recognizing informality and providing effective alternatives to it was central to the purpose of Bogotá's plans-turned-codes of the 1970s. In fact, the idea of competing against informality has remained central to urban policy in the country (DPU, 2006), as will be discussed later.

4.1.3 Pirate urbanizers: champions of gray

Urban planning in Bogotá has been deeply shaped (especially between the early 1970s[5] and the late 1990s) by the actions of a singular type of actor: informal urban developers broadly referred to as "pirate urbanizers." Pirates are quite renowned in Bogotá and most reached Council and Congress seats before getting jailed. Take for instance Saturnino Sepúlveda, a prolific priest, full-fleshed anarchist, and community advocate who was affiliated with the guerrilla; or the big Alfredo Guerrero Estrada—6.5 feet and 220 pounds—, a street vendor who learned the language of communitarianism in China while working there as a construction worker in the late 1960s; or Mariano Porras, who like the others built his political capital around grassroots mobilization while offering thousands of self-help housing alternatives; or Rafael Forero Fetecua, the most prominent of all. Their quirky stories reveal the logic of local class-based idiosyncrasies, and also the high stakes of the blurred lines between the formal and the informal.

---

4 Cities facing similar constraints, like Medellín and Quito, already have subways, even though many argue that they are less deserving of national efforts, because of their contribution to the national GDP.

5 By 1972 more than 45% of the city lived in pirate settlements (Vernez, 1975) in: (DPU, 2006:257).

130   *The politics of urban formalization in Bogotá*

Rafael Forero Fetecua was one of 11 children of a truck driver and a vegetable merchant. He was an avid soccer and chess player, who only got to finish third grade before he had to start working at the age of 10. Despite many difficulties, or perhaps because of them, Forero focused his many businesses on "the forgotten country" (Rodríguez, 2012:73), particularly on urban land and services for low-income communities. He was such a successful entrepreneur that by the 1980s owned one of the biggest public contractor engineering consortia in the country (Rodríguez, 2012:45) and was the majoritarian shareholder of the Workers Bank[6]. When the national tax authority imposed on him in 1988 one of the biggest penalties in the history of the country, the mainstream media estimated he was the tenth richest person in Colombia (Rodríguez, 2012:68). However, he surprised everyone when all of his capital was put under third parties. Forero Fetecua was not poor, but curiously enough, he was not rich either. Despite his money, his widespread recognition, and his political capital, he definitely mingled but could never integrate into the elite.

Forero began his involvement in urbanization projects because of his disenchantment with traditional politics that—he argued—"promised everything but got nothing for communities." Instead, he embodied a different type of politics: "politics is not talking, it is acting" Forero said (Gutiérrez, 1998:2). And he definitely did act. One of Forero's most significant projects was Ciudadela Sucre, an urban development of more than 5,800 plots on the hills of Soacha outside the administrative boundary of Bogotá. "What we looked for here—Forero claimed—was to give the poor a solution without taking over the State's obligations. The State has a responsibility toward the population, which it is failing with regard to social housing" (Rodríguez, 2012:62). Plots in Forero's urbanizations were either sold cheap or "exchanged plots for bicycles, for a TV, or for making love as they say" shared Evelio, a longtime collaborator of Forero (Gutiérrez, 1998:1). In addition, he had a permanent involvement building and supporting local community organizations. At first, he gave help through the official channels, the Juntas de Acción Comunal. Later, when noticing some were pocketing resources, he had a direct approach.

For years, Forero delivered many kinds of support to communities personally, on a case-by-case basis. He first began helping communities when learning of a pre-k where kids sat on bricks and slept on the floor, and since then never stopped being involved. In fact, "support" became the generic term

---

6 The Worker's Bank (Banco de los Trabajadores) was created with support from international donors to promote the development of unions in the country. With time, the drug lord Gilberto Rodríguez Orejuela, second only to Pablo Escobar, became the majoritarian shareholder. When Orejuela was convicted and extradited, the bank was nationalized and Forero Fetecua bought a large share of it. Though Forero was unrelated to the drug trafficker, the association between the two lingered in the public imagination (Rodríguez, 2012:60).

for a broad range of provisions that were distributed in these settlements. He lent his trucks, offered groceries, gave out cash, facilitated free doctor's consults and hair styling sessions, sold cheap construction materials, paid for religious ceremonies, organized job pools, and gave pensions to families in need (13,000 at some point!) (Gutiérrez, 1998:7). Not only did people sympathize with him, he was loved by many and regarded not only as a populist benefactor but almost as a hero. Beyond "support," Forero "emerged as the single *intermediary* between the urban poor periphery and the paved Bogotá" (Gutiérrez, 1998:4). He was the poor's broker. His support for the consolidation process of informal settlements bought him voting loyalty, and he offered these numbers to high-ranking politicians. Forero's "machinery worked, what is more important, endured because both "those below" and "those above" owed him favors" (Gutiérrez, 1998:10). Elites needed him, and the city government tolerated him, to a large extent because the housing crisis would have been worse without pirate urbanizations, which in fact were much easier to upgrade than the alternative invasions.

Forero's political movement was called the Popular Integration Movement (Movimiento de Integración Popular), a name that according to him emphasized that "the popular sectors must *integrate* around a leader (…because they) are dispersed" (Gutiérrez, 1998:3). The day the Movement was born 30,000 people arrived at a meeting called at an empty plot. However, "out of fear, the press reported only 15,000 attendees" (Gutiérrez, 1998:3). His massive support structure was regarded as powerful and dangerous. In 1984 on his first popular vote election the Movement received 36,800 votes, 1.8 times more than Galán,[7] who was most likely to become the next Colombian

Figure 4.1 Wedding of the daughter of Forero Fetecua (far left) attended by President Michelsen (far right) (Rodriguez, 2013).

---

7 Iconic liberal politician who was twice a salient presidential candidate. Self-declared enemy of Pablo Escobar (who tried to get into Galan's New Liberalism Movement). Galan, clearly the frontrunner that year, was shot to death at a presidential rally in Soacha in 1989.

132 *The politics of urban formalization in Bogotá*

president. In fact, it was the greatest number of votes a nascent political movement had ever won (Gutiérrez, 1998:3). Forero Fetecua's name and political recognition also had a considerable reach into the high echelons of Colombian society. For instance, in 1985 former President Lopez Michelsen attended Forero's daughter wedding (Figure 4.1). But being a millionaire, bank owner, congressman, and mingling with the privileged, never bought Forero Fetecua recognition as part of the elite. For instance, in 1991, only he was charged for a crime that both he and a fellow congressman, son of a former president (who would later become Housing Minister), had committed. Both loved and hated, Forero remained an outcast, a pirate until his death.

4.2 From plan-based to code-base planning

4.2.1 Competing with informality

The *Minimum Rules* study (Samper et al., 1971) was a pathbreaking urban planning approach, as discussed earlier in Chapter 2. It laid the ground for Accords 20 and 21 of 1972, and Accord 7 of 1979, the scaffolding of the urban formalization policy that is still enforced today. The aim of the *Minimum Rules* was to halt informal settlement formation by lowering the requirements and hence the costs of formal urbanization, so it could more easily compete with the informal supply. In particular, "water and sanitation infrastructure specifications were deemed overrated, directly copied from North American regulations, and unsuitable for our realities" (Ceballos, 2005). These standards revised downwards the technical specifications allowing for higher densities (of up to 100 houses per hectare), smaller plots ($72m^2$), and fixing a percentage of the developable area to be reserved for open spaces (18%) (Ceballos, 2005). More importantly, it embraced the fact that some areas could have *incomplete* urbanization and would improve their urban services *progressively* in time, with input from urbanizers, communities, and the local government. By opening the door for incomplete settlements of progressive development, the city had defaced its relationship with conventional urban plans. Simultaneously, it placed upgrading at the center of urban policy, channeling the efforts of both formal and informal providers (Stevenson, 1979:63).

Figure 4.2 visually summarizes the multiple formalization procedures that settlements need to go through in order to be brought into code. Types of settlements are organized from left—most informal—to right—more formal. Depending on their characteristics and levels of development, they are subject to different policy measures. Notably, even fully formal sites informalize as they consolidate and thus are also subject to formalization procedures. As shown, formalization is far from a streamlined path. Most often, processes are so long, confusing, and contested, that settlements can bounce back and forth between required procedures, falling into legal loopholes.

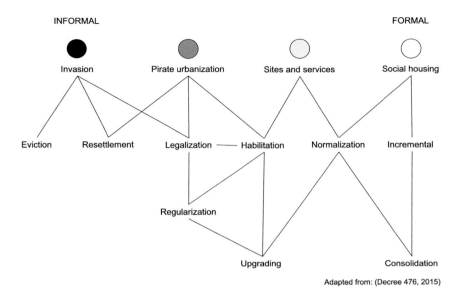

Figure 4.2 Map of formalization paths for different types of settlements. Adapted from: Decree 476 (2015) (by the author).

4.2.2 Urban treatments (1979): a second-level zoning

With Accord 7 of 1979, code-based planning went even further. On one hand, it enabled further densification (up to 180 houses per hectare) and instead of compensating with more open space areas, it allowed these to further shrink under co-ownership arrangements (Ceballos, 2005). But more strategically, the accord incorporated the notion of "urban treatments," which operated as a second zoning on top of the traditional land-use (Salazar, 2017:168). Urban treatments determine the type of regulation that is needed in each area of the city, contingent on its urbanistic qualities (morphological homogeneity, typological representativeness) and its real estate value (assessed based on the age of the buildings and their localization). The rationale was to give those areas with fewer urban qualities and less value, more flexible urban regulations. Areas under the "upgrading" urban treatment, like informal settlements and sites and services projects, were granted less stringent restrictions than historic preservation areas under the "conservation" treatment.

Figure 4.3 maps the full range of urban treatments and the modalities foreseen under each treatment, still at work in Bogotá's planning instruments. As in the visual above, here treatments are also organized from left (those for more informal areas) to right (those for more formal areas). This shows there is an inherent idea of progress and value, as will be detailed.

134 *The politics of urban formalization in Bogotá*

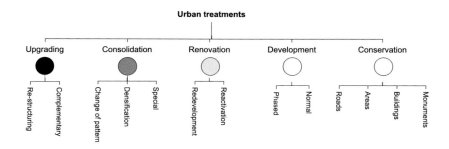

Figure 4.3 Mapping upgrading as one of five types of urban treatments. Adapted from: Accord 7 (1979) and Accord 6 (1990) (by the author).

The 1979 Accord established two preconditions for the system of urban treatments to operate well, which sadly got diluted in Accord 6 of 1990 and the next re-incarnations of the plan up to the current one (Salazar, 2017:166). The first condition was to define technical criteria to assess both the urban qualities (architectonic and the urban layout) and the property values. Property assessments in Bogotá work surprisingly well since 2003, when the Cadaster engaged in its first comprehensive update. Ever since property assessments are reappraised annually under punctilious criteria established by a national agency. As mentioned in Chapter 3, Bogotá's Cadaster is recognized regionally for its good practices. But on the other hand, the assessment of urban qualities is more problematic. These are developed by expert urbanists as part of doorstop diagnostic documents produced for each city plan, using undeclared criteria and unclear assumptions. Despite both of these components being equally instrumental in the definition of urban treatments, property value assessments are routinely contested by scholars, politicians, the media, and in lay people's conversations, while the assessment of urban qualities remains an inconspicuous black box.

The second condition for the urban treatments to function properly was that these were to be regarded as temporal categories in constant flux. Rather than locking urban areas into fixed treatments, the city was supposed to monitor its neighborhoods and constantly encourage transitions between different treatments. For example, Figure 4.4. from Accord 7 of 1979 shows the changes in conservation areas between 1900 and 2000. Note how the dark-shaded areas of historical heritage expand as time passes. In fact, recategorizing areas from one type of treatment to another would be one way the code-base plan would ensure its impact.

The politics of urban formalization in Bogotá 135

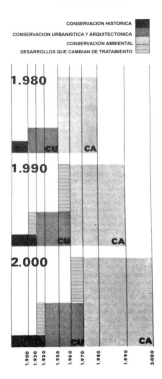

Figure 4.4 Dynamics of the conservation treatment from 1900 to 2000 (Escala 110, 1981).

The same logic applies to upgrading, even more so given that areas of progressive development were originally defined in temporal terms: they should transition from an incomplete state into urban completeness. However long (HfH-CENAC, 2014)[8] and costly (CEDE, 2007)[9] upgrading processes might be, these neighborhoods do improve their physical infrastructure quite drastically over time. Efforts by individuals, communities, NGOs, and government invariably raise the physical well-being of these areas as well as the

8 A 2014 survey of 5,000 residents of an informal settlement in Soacha (a municipality to the southwest of Bogotá) revealed that on average, it takes a family 25 years to complete 55 square meters of housing. Lower, yet high timeframes -11 years- have been reported Mexico City (Freire, 2007:6).
9 Estimates of upgrading over costs in Bogotá are high: upgrading is 6 times more expensive than an equivalent formal provision. Calculations for Rio de Janeiro report an average of 2.8 (Smolka, 2003).

136 *The politics of urban formalization in Bogotá*

quantity and quality of the services they receive. Despite this, local planners complain, with a tint of frustration that "No neighborhood ever gets out from upgrading to consolidation" (Yunda, 2019).

4.2.3 Upgrading is a leaky bucket

The city's upgrading program has long had the reputation of being slow and ineffective, a constant leakage of public efforts. It has also been observed that the city upgrading programs are often outperformed by non-governmental efforts (SCA, 2011), of which it fails to take full advantage of. Attention to the conceptual history of upgrading policy confirms that the impression that upgrading is an intractable policy problem is reinforced by the planning techniques themselves, via sluggish transitions between urban treatments. "Upgrading" areas do not move to "consolidation" nor "renovation" areas, and even less into "conservation" treatments. The city planning department is well aware of this problem.

We must transition areas from upgrading to consolidation treatment areas. Some areas are not upgrading any longer. There are transitions between these two [treatments], but these have not been recognized. We have to redefine what we mean by upgrading. Many of these areas already have basic urban services. If we do not redefine this, it would mean that this public policy is always bound for failure (Avendaño, 2019).

While upgrading areas in real life improve, in the urban codes they remain quite stagnant. The temporal definition of the urban treatments is overlooked, and by doing so, their capacity to plan and shape the city weakens. It does not help that there are no legal or technical instruments that allow the city to re-zone these areas outside of the 10-year lapses of the POT (Planes de Ordenamiento Territorial) master plans. In addition, community advocates in Bogotá are reluctant to let areas go off the upgrading urban treatment as this categorization grants access to a subsidy line which, however meager, may still represent a lifeline for potential improvements for these communities.

At the root of this contradiction is the inability to effectively assess the urban qualities and property values that emerge out of the progressive type of urbanism. The technical difficulties of assessing architectural and urban qualities are further marred with moral controversy. For example, discussing the Museum of Self-built City (Museo de la Ciudad Autoconstruida) currently in construction along the route of the new cable car in the slums of Ciudad Bolívar, some experts push for the recognition of popular housing as part of the urban heritage (Carvajalino, 2019; López, 2019), while others called it an absurd "celebration of a flawed model" (Ceballos, 2019) and even "urban porn" (Yunda, 2019). Attention to the transitions foreseen in the 1979 Accord would ensure acknowledgment of actual upgrades. This way, by the sheer passing of decades, upgrading policy could be less of a leaky bucket if the city effectively assessed the current urban qualities and actual value of its informal settlements.

4.3 De-politicization and technification of formalization policy

4.3.1 The rise and fall of the housing movement in Colombia

Slum upgrading policy in Bogotá is besieged with legal terminology and operates within the strict planning technicalities. But such legal technification is not how this policy was always characterized. For years, upgrading was less a process of carefully reconciling the de facto realities with normative regulations, and more a political community-building process. The process of de-politicization and parallel technification of the upgrading policy has everything to do with the rise and fall of the housing movement in Colombia, a link that is yet to be fully articulated in the literature of urban planning in Bogotá. Without delving too deep into this story, making this connection is important, because it helps make sense of why the intended purpose of the urban formalization policy has been de-politicized.

The rise and fall of the housing movement in Colombia are well exemplified in the fate of the Centro Nacional Provivienda (Pro-housing National Center), Cenaprov; the longest standing housing organization in Latin America (Naranjo, 2017:28). In the first and only history of this organization, Naranjo explains that during its first decade, Cenaprov built itself up as a communist social movement by organizing inner-city tenants and planning land invasions in the peripheries of Colombia's main cities. In the next decade (1971–1982), it created a design commission, led by activist academic Gilma Mosquera, the first black woman architect in the country. Cenaprov designed urban plans of model self-help neighborhoods around the country and provided technical support to communities in their struggle for urban services. Technical assistance complemented popular solidarity efforts allowing Cenaprov to compete with pirate urbanizers, who often presented themselves as false cooperatives (Mosquera, 1984:133).

The following decade (1983–1993) saw the apex of the national housing movement. Cenaprov was by far the biggest and more powerful, but many other organizations emerged with religious, philanthropic, or foreign-aid lines. This rich canopy of popular housing movements (Organizaciones Populares de Vivienda, OPV[10]) was the breeding ground for an ambitious urban reform project presented before Congress in 1984, which represented the highest point of the unitary housing movement. Alongside this process, the communist party (Unión Patriótica, UP) had grown a wide base, especially in informal settlements, unsettling the traditional parties. As Naranjo explains, in the next decade (1994–2004) the OPV model disintegrated. Thousands of secretive systematic assassinations decimated the UP between

---

10 OPVs were regulated in the Decree 2391 of 1989, which describes them as belonging to the "solidary economy", a third type of economy that is not formal nor informal, and that foresees communities buying and owing collectively urban land ("compra comunera" or community land trusts).

138   *The politics of urban formalization in Bogotá*

1987 and 1988. The UP genocide heralded the decline of the housing movement and the dissolution of much of its social tissue. By then, Cenaprov had already weakened from the inside, falling victim to its own success. Improper management of millionaire contracts that Cenaprov won in the aftermath of the eruption of Armero volcano (a 1985 tragedy of 20,000 deaths costing Colombia a fifth of its GDP) was definitive and tarnished the movement's original spirit.

Quite paradoxically, the final blow to the housing movement was the Political Constitution of 1991. This constitution represented a profound and euphoric historical transformation in many fronts. Not only was it a bipartisan effort to reimagine the nation as a decentralized, multicultural, and secular welfare state. In addition, the 1991 Constitution embraced social rights like the right to housing (Art. 51), and further, it embraced a revolutionary principle: the social and ecological function of property (Art 58). Moreover, the Constitution represented one of the very few successful reconciliation and peacebuilding endeavors with demobilized a leftist guerrilla (M-19). All in all, the new constitution was also a juncture toward an irreversible economic globalization and a profound neo-liberalization of the state.

During the boom of the unified popular housing movement, OPVs were first-line operators of housing subsidies: they organized the community, offered legal advice, led participatory design efforts, and followed through with upgrading works in informal settlements. It was an urban policy environment where the State had already rolled back, opening space not to the market, but to grassroots organizations. But when the new constitution prescribed the State the role of market facilitator, it prompted a change toward a "subsidies to the demand" model that, together with increasing technical requisites, choked the OPVs out of existence (Carvajalino, 2019; Florián, 2019) and (Torres, 2019b). At the peak of its housing movement Colombia became an inspiration for other countries. Ironically, just as Mexico was copying the OPV model (Florián, 2011), in Colombia it was languishing quite irreversibly. Under the new policy model housing came to be exclusively characterized by new constructions of single-family cookie-cutter houses that channel mortgages and subsidies via large developers (Torres, 2019b), seriously sidelining upgrading, public housing, and rental alternatives. This episode reveals that the technification of slum upgrading practices in Bogotá is the counterpart of a latent political struggle.

4.3.2 The technical mechanics of formalization in Bogotá

The process of urban formalization, of how an informal accommodation can come to be fully compliant with the urban codes, involves a string of interrelated processes that are only coherent in theory but are rarely ordered in practice. In fact, formalization policy is itself the process of ex-post honing, of harmonizing the existing norms with the messy realities on the ground.

Formalization policy is an intricate entanglement of legal technicalities: obscure, seemingly contradictory, and dead boring. Committed to make sense of this regulatory filigree, I studied both national and city decrees, as well as zoning and business regulations, and interviewed over 40 local experts. The result of this research is the drawing in Figure 4.5. As with any other visualization, this one is a synthesis of the phenomena it describes. It is a map that helps transverse the complex nuts and bolts of Bogotá's urban law. But a cautionary note is necessary to read Figure 4.5.

The image of the staircase is as intentional as it is illusory. Formalization policy in Bogotá (and arguably in many other latitudes as well) upholds a series of discrete steps depending on the specific stage of urban development. But this is far from a streamlined process. While in the light of urban and civil law the path toward complete formalization intends this to be a straightforward process, in reality the steps involved are far from ordered. Hence, Figure 4.5 below offers a stylized view, but one necessary to understand the spirit of the law. My staircase portrays the nine operations in the process of evolving from an informal settlement to a formalized mixed-use building. The first three steps deal with *land* formalization, the next three with *building* formalization, and the last three with the *businesses* within. Also, the first half are processes that comprise what is commonly referred to as upgrading. The image of the stairs reflects what the spirit of the law intends: distinct steps gradually progressing from informality to formality. However, the image is grossly misleading because the formalization process is barely linear. There are plenty of incomplete steps, vicious cycles, and informalization rebounds, that make consistent progress hardly archivable. I will return to the issue of the deceptiveness of this stair-like mapping of the formalization policy on Chapter 5.

Complete formalization of houses like the ones described in Chapter 3 spans at least three realms, starting with the legalization of the land itself, followed by the habilitation (paving streets, completion of open public spaces, and provision of urban services), and then the incorporation of these new areas into the urban codes. The whole formalization of the settlement is a process between the local government and the community (whenever the urban developer is not present or accountable). Across Latin America, upgrading, regularization, and legalization are terms often used interchangeably (Fernandes, 2011), but as described, in Bogotá's punctilious urban law, this is more nuanced. Regularization is the process of ascribing public spaces for the city to manage while legalization refers to the titling of private properties. The law intends for legalization to be followed by regularization (Gonzalez, 2020). In practice, however, these three steps can get so entwined, that some government officials call regularization "a second legalization" (Uribe, 2019). The city has no option but to use regularization to legalize settlements that were already legalized, but re-informalized. Dealing with these informalization cycles poses regulatory challenges to cities. Bogotá deals with it by over-specifying the legal processes, that is,

140 *The politics of urban formalization in Bogotá*

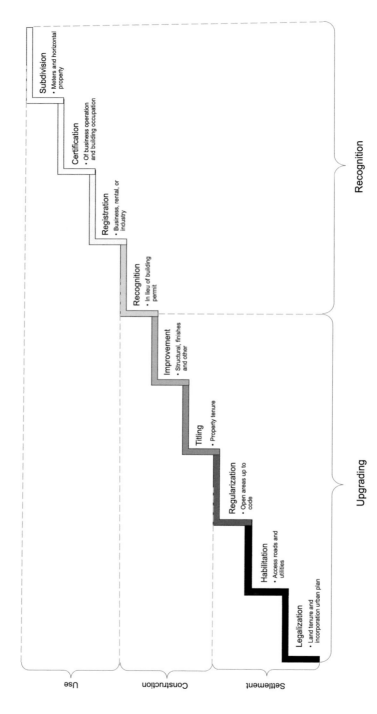

Figure 4.5 Visual map of urban formalization policy in Bogotá: Steps, phases, and realms (by the author).

making legalization and regularization, different processes. A notable detail of legalization in Bogotá is the fact that the 1990s legalization peak coincided not with the actual incorporations of informal properties, but of formal sites and services projects carried out by the city government in the two previous decades (Ceballos, 2005). This means historically, legalization has been most successful legalizing formal, not informal areas, an ironic contradiction.

After the settlement is regularized, the formalization of the buildings themselves can begin. This second stage of formalization has three consecutive steps. It starts with property titling, continues with structural and physical improvement works, and ends with the building permit asserting the construction complies with building and urban codes. To a large extent thanks to the persuasive optimism of Hernando de Soto, and the appropriation of his narrative by international finance institutions, titling is regularly confounded with urban formalization, even though it is only a sliver of the whole process. Whether this has to do with the pervasiveness of the legalistic approach to informality discussed in Chapter 2, with the neoliberal shrinkage of the state's footprint, or with the convenience of promising the transmutation of titles into wealth by mere stroke of a pen (Roy, 2005:14; Davis, 2005:82), and many others, having property title is far from achieving full formalization. As observed in Figure 4.5, titling is but a step halfway through the complete span of the process, and not even its crux, as will be discussed.

The property owner or possessor advances upgrading actions before the local government, with far less technical assistance than what CINVA's self-help forerunners envisioned to ensure a steady, smooth process. In fact, formalization efforts get increasingly daunting along this ladder. Without a doubt, the recognition step, that is, the legal act issued for buildings raised without a building permit, is the most cumbersome bottleneck. For instance, between 2016 and 2019 less than 6% of the recognition acts submissions were approved (CVP, 2020). Some background on the process of issuing building permits is important to understand the extent of the problem.

4.3.3 The impossible story of Carmen and the demiurge

Especially in a code-based planning scheme like Bogotá's, the mere deciphering of what the regulations for a specific plot are, is a process that requires expert know-how of the regulations, its constant complementary updates, and a skilled reading of scarce, creased, and color-less maps (see Figure 4.6). In an effort to decongest the building permit process in cities, Colombia introduced the figure of the Urban Curator in 1995. Much like notaries, curators are private individuals serving a public function. But unlike notaries, urban curators do much more than deter fraud by attesting signatures and taking affidavits. Their role is to interpret the city code, supervise if a building's drawings are compliant, and issue the corresponding permit. Curators must be certified architects or engineers and, as public servants, are subject to punctilious disciplinary scrutiny.

142 *The politics of urban formalization in Bogotá*

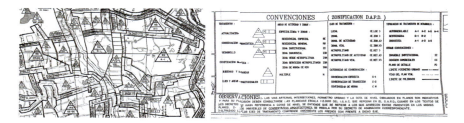

Figure 4.6 Snapshot of a section of Bogotá's 1990 zoning (left) and its map legend (right) (Accord 9, 1990).

Figure 4.7 Map legend to annex of Accord 7 of 1979. Land-use classification by activity areas (left) and Criteria for land-use classification in types and groups (right) (Escala 110:1981).

There are 11 modalities of building permits in the city: new construction, extension, adequation (i.e. change of use), modification (internal changes without added area), occupation, structural reinforcement, demolition (partial or total), enclosure, parking, modification of legalization drawings, and horizontal property; and the scope of issues covered for by building permits has only expanded over time (Bahamón, 2019). Curators interpret the law and ensure, for a fee, that building plans comply, on paper[11], with the

---

11 Supervising if the actual construction follows the permit is beyond their task and under the purview of the local police. This role of urban control is, to nobody's surprise, hardly ever exercised.

labyrinthic regulations. Urban curators are like demiurges[12] in a process that has 244 procedures that is, after more than 100 were removed thanks to a World Bank funded and De Soto inspired project (IFC, 2009).

If getting a building permit is cumbersome, for informal constructions the process of getting its equivalent, a recognition act, is nothing short of impossible. Over two decades have passed since the procedure was first regulated in 1997, but still, getting a recognition act is so difficult that even anecdotes about it are scarce. The story of Carmen is illuminating. Carmen wanted to change the leaking roof of her house (at a consolidated informal settlement in Ciudad Bolívar), for a typical concrete slab. She needed the recognition act in order to qualify for a microcredit to pay for it. Carmen, a domestic worker, asked her employee for help. A clever move since her employer was an architect with a Ph.D., part of Ward's Latin American Housing Network (LAHN, 2009), who, obviously, agreed to help at no cost. After a year and a half, five visits to a Curator's office (who was a friend of the architect's), a paid intern, and the involvement of a Swiss NGO dedicated to low-cost resilient construction; Carmen was told that the impromptu team had no option but to relinquish because no engineer was willing to sign off the paperwork. Plus, the papers laid out a structural upgrading that would cost more than the roofing, and the architectural plan included demolishing two rooms to guarantee code-compliant ventilation. "There is no way Carmen was ever going to do this" (Camargo, 2020).

This anecdote proves it is not only a matter of inconvenience (Urban Curator's offices are located far from informal settlements, and their fees hardly incentivize the trip), and building costs, but of unfeasible regulatory constraints. Community advocates have long pushed for the cost exemption of these procedures, a battle that was only won until 2017, with the creation of the "Curaduría Cero" (Urban Curatorship Zero), an interesting development that took years to set off the ground (Ramírez, 2019) and has yet to show its real impact.

Beyond the fact that the recognition process is taxing and time-consuming, the procedure is practically unachievable. Despite the need, conditions are not in place for a market of technical support services to develop, and in the absence of OPVs there is no one offering them. This missing market opens the door to much profiteering (i.e. "tramitadores") (Bahamón, 2019), which drains the scarce resources and formalization efforts from property owners. Many even question the relevance of the urbanistic requirements in these contexts (Gonzalez, 2020). For instance, is it feasible to expect a four-story informal building to demolish at least three rental rooms in order to have an open-air patio at the center of the plot? The realities on the ground make full compliance to the volumetric urban code more than difficult, unfeasible.

---

12 "In the Platonic school of philosophy, the Demiurge is a deity who fashions the physical world in the light of eternal ideas. In the Timaeus, Plato credits the Demiurge with taking preexisting materials of chaos and arranging them in accordance with the models of eternal forms" (Merriam-Webster, n.d.).

144 *The politics of urban formalization in Bogotá*

4.3.4 *After the physical, the economical: business formalization*

After the formalization of the settlement and the construction, the formalization path continues with a focus on the use or operation of the building. As shown in Figure 4.5, at least three steps are at stake here: the *registration* of the business, industry, or landlord, the *certification* that the operation of these specific uses is compliant with the regulations for those activities, and, finally, the *subdivision* of independent use units in the building. Subdivision entails both the separation of utility meters so that different households or businesses pay their bills separately and splitting the building in different apartments or shops via a horizontal property arrangement.

Uses can be informal when they do not follow the land-use urban code, when the businesses are not registered, and/or when they do not comply with the building or operation permits, or when they do not pass inspections. In the formalization process land-use plays the primary role of guaranteeing that incompatible uses are separated. Land-use restricts industries and businesses that pose nuisances to residential areas: toxic materials, insufficient ventilation, difficult disposal systems, or high noise levels (Nohn, 2011). This explains why a nuanced understanding of the intensity of mixed-use, like the ones portrayed in Chapter 3, is at the crux of the final steps in the formalization processes.

Contrary to the expectations, Bogotá's meticulous land-use coding system has been quite open to mixed-use from very early on. In the first place, the land-use classification understands there is a difference between the "vocational use" (the one intended in the master plan, called "destino" in the local technical lingo) and "actual use" (the one observed and recorded by the cadaster). In addition, zoning specifies the principal, complementary, and restricted uses. For instance, the 1964 zoning included 13 categories of the principal uses that "implied transgression of the CIAM monofunctional zoning principles. These mixed zones were applied to built areas where the mix of uses had already begun" (Salazar, 2017:100). Observing actual uses and incorporating these into the code encouraged the development complex use-coding techniques (see Figure 4.7). Coding complexity required a more robust legal scaffolding. And, with an expanded legal framework, the room for interpretation of the norms grew bigger, making the role of the Curator increasingly important. As explained earlier, the Curator's physical distance from the realities of the informal settlements makes the formalization process even more difficult. So, paradoxically, more awareness of actual mixed-use realities, and a mixed-use friendly coding system, turned out to be unwelcoming to formalization processes.

Despite the openness to mixed-use in the regulation, land-use codes remain an obstacle not only for urban formalization (building code compliance) but also for business formalization (firm growth). For instance, under the current regulation, there are three use types of residential areas: "net residential," "residential with limited areas for commerce and services," and "residential

The politics of urban formalization in Bogotá   145

with economic activity within the house." Areas in this last type are allowed to have industrial activities of light manufacturing or small businesses only if they do not have more than $60m^2$ (Decree 190, 2004, Art. 341) and only on the first floor (Ibid, Art 342). Also, in new areas designated as multiple use, the percentage of commercial uses cannot exceed 25% of the total area (Ibid, Art 351). These restrictions capping the size of "complementary uses" thwart the growth of businesses. In fact, after site visits to 3,760 informal businesses that were part of a city business formalization initiative in 2018, officers found that, despite receiving tailored technical and financial support, a third of them could not formalize. Among those, "the most common reason given was land-use noncompliance, as they are located in residential areas" (León, 2019). So, yes, Bogotá's code is keen to recognize mixed-use, but simultaneously it dwarfs the economic potential of home-based firms.

4.3.5 To subdivide is to formalize

The final step in the formalization stair is subdivision: splitting up independent household or business units within the same building. Of all the steps in the process, this one is the least explored in the literature and yet it is one with a considerable scope for action, particularly in areas of consolidated informal settlements and in mature site-and-services projects. Over the last decade, the share of horizontal property in residential buildings in Bogotá has increased up to a current 70% (SDP, 2019:55). Most of these are in new constructions of higher incomes (SDP, 2019:43). This comes as no surprise since process of partitioning buildings into independent units through horizontal property is not particularly straightforward nor cheap, as confirmed in 71% of my house interviews. To assess the cost burden of subdividing a building, I compiled information from different sources and estimated the minimum formalization costs for a typical 4-story residential informal building with a first-floor shop (see Table 4.1). The exercise reveals that in 2019, formalizing a subdivision in Bogotá costs almost 14 times a minimum monthly salary. Separating utility meters is a third of these, the professional services represent another third, and the last third is sunk into building permit (a task usually charged to the architect).

Subdivision remains an important frontier for formalization. As a senior officer in the Bogotá planning explains:

> The majority of the 1,700,000 residential plots in Bogota, are horizontal properties (i.e. condominiums). Because there are 2,600,000 households, we are aware there are many buildings that are not yet partitioned. (…) There is a tendency towards horizontal property. Non-horizontal property plots are concentrated in the south-west periphery, where horizontal property is still to reach.
>
> (Avendaño, 2019)

146   *The politics of urban formalization in Bogotá*

Table 4.1. Rough cost estimate of subdividing an informal mixed-used four-story building in Bogotá in 2019 (by the author)

Component	$ in COP	$ in USD	Cost in monthly minimum salaries
Building Permit Fixed fee	$ 185,000	$ 62	0.22
Building Permit for 300m^2 Residential	$ 965,000	$ 322	1.17
Building Permit for Commercial	$ 505,000	$ 168	0.61
Urban outline tax	$ 1,350,000	$ 450	1.63
Architect	$ 2,500,000	$ 833	3.02
Engineer	$ 1,500,000	$ 500	1.81
Approval of horizontal property drawings	$ 492,000	$ 164	0.59
Registration of horizontal property	$ 373,200	$ 124	0.45
Separation of electricity meters	$ 1,500,000	$ 500	1.81
Separation of water meters	$ 2,000,000	$ 667	2.42
TOTAL	**$ 11,370,200**	**$ 3,790**	**13.73**

Sources: (Dec. 1077, 2019; Res. 87, 2011; Res 6610, 2019). Professional fee estimates by informants.
Note: Estimates exclude demolition or construction costs and assume the building itself costs USD$20,000.

In fact, planning documents and cadaster studies increasingly welcome the categorization of "Non-Horizontal Property," as useful proxy to refer to informal housing (García, 2013:11; DTS-POT, 2019:47; Amaya, 2019), among many. This emerging conceptual development is particularly interesting when one considers, not what horizontal property arrangements bring to mind in common language, that is, noise complaints between neighbors or maintenance fees that are past due ("condemoniums," like condominiums are often called), but what horizontal property was originally designed to do. Legal scholars explain that horizontal property legislation evolved in parallel to urbanization with the primary objective of making housing more affordable. Horizontal property made it cheaper to get property by reducing investments in land, construction materials and labor, and enabling more individual houses to be constructed in less space in multistory buildings (Nader, 2002:16). In Colombia, the Law 182 of 1948, the basis of today's horizontal property legislation, was part of an arsenal of urban redevelopment tools deployed after the April 9th riots in Bogotá[13]. Beyond being a tool to combat housing shortage and affordability, scholars insist horizontal property regulation benefits all social classes by dynamizing the housing market and anticipating community issues (Pabón, 1990:13). I will return to the role subdivision beyond formalization at the end of this chapter.

13 The riots emerged after days after the assassination of a popular liberal politician, Jorge Eliécer Gaitán, who a couple of months earlier had led a silent protest of 100,000 people (a fourth of the city's population at the time) against political violence by the elites.

4.3.6 Upgrading, an impossible stair

The nine steps of formalization policy in Bogotá (Figure 4.5), that is: legalization, habilitation, and regularization (formalization of the settlement); titling, improvement, and recognition (formalization of the construction); and registration, certification, and subdivision (formalization of the use); can be grouped in two phases before and after the recognition step. More than a mere legal act that acknowledges the de facto existence of the building, recognition involves a change in the attitude of the formalization policy. Before it, the initial steps of the process entail what is known as upgrading, where neighborhoods and buildings achieve a level of physical development that raises their standards to levels more akin to those of the rest of the city. After upgrading, recognition continues delving into the life of the building by guaranteeing that the activities taking place within the building are clearly delimited and that each one observes the corresponding urban regulations. The recognition phase is as much about acknowledgment as it is about identification.

Notably, the last step of the formalization stair, subdivision, is very similar to the first step, legalization. Both are processes clearly establishing the domain of what is private. In this sense, formalization seems to resemble an impossible Penrose stair (Figure 4.8). Each flight of steps is reasonable in and of itself but taken as a whole the stair is problematic: the steps continually ascend counterclockwise (Ernst, 1992), without ever reaching an end. Like a mirage, full integration, full formalization is never reached.

Navigating through this arsenal of normative technicalities helped characterize the policy's fundamental intention, which is to *integrate* areas labeled as clandestine, marginal, peripheral, informal, subnormal, and incomplete;

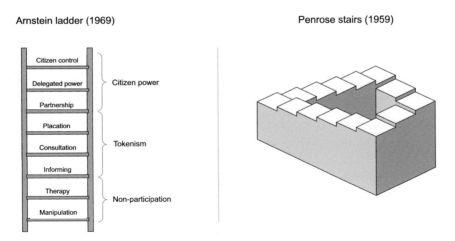

Figure 4.8 The formalization path from upgrading to recognition does not empower. Adapted from Arnstein (1969) and Penrose (1959) (by the author).

148 *The politics of urban formalization in Bogotá*

into the rest of the city. Via upgrading the purpose is to raise the quantity and quality of urban services in these areas to standards that even them out with the rest of the city. Via recognition, the purpose is to identify de facto realities and bring them into the purview of the regulations. Key in this integration purpose is the idea—or the illusion—of *inclusion*: these areas are left out of the city plans, programs, and policies, and formalization brings them in.

4.4 The actual purpose of formalization: practical outcomes of recognition

4.4.1 Formalization creates fiscal legibility

Few local informality scholars are as vocal as Torres in denouncing that the real outcome of upgrading programs has not been that of ensuring adequate housing but of "turning residents of informal settlements into fiscal subjects" (Torres, 2012:466). He notes that in practice, the most effective part of the upgrading policy is titling, where, by mere stroke of the pen (of a World Bank and IDB De Soto fantasy) low-income neighborhoods get access to the credit market. "However, it is not recognized that this type of political alternative needs sufficient technical and social support to work well. Without it, the outcome is increased costs of living in these parts of the city, bringing, among other consequences, the expulsion of the population and a greater deterioration of the housing stock" (Torres, 2012:466).

The integration professed by the formalization policy rather than social, economic, or physical becomes fiscal. Upgrading programs are only effective in guaranteeing the local government's "fiscal viability" (Torres, 2012). There are two avenues in which upgrading policy ensures fiscalization. The most obvious one is that after an informal property is titled, it becomes publicly legible and subject to property taxation. But there is another avenue through which upgrading informal settlements provides fiscal opportunities to the city government.

Settlements that legalize and regularize must comply with urban regulations regarding the share of parks and or community areas that they offer their residents (which between 1990 and 2000 increased from 17% to 25% of the net area (Torres, 2012:463)). These areas, called cessions (cesiones), are ceded to the city to be managed. Most of the times, informal neighborhoods are so consolidated that they do not have empty areas available, in that case cases, they must pay the city for them, so that the city can invest this money in providing these services back to this specific community, but this barely happens, and "only works on paper" (Gonzalez, 2020). Torres extensive research in Ciudad Bolívar shows that communities struggle collectively to gather these funds, and even if they do, the city fails to retribute them with local parks and community services. Cessions' funds are so scarce, that the city ends up using them to maintain the existing existent parks rather than to acquire new plots (Gonzalez, 2020).

"The formalization of neighborhoods of informal origin allows low-income population to be recognized as citizens with full rights. But in reality, these rights that are not necessarily reachable nor effective, so [recognition] ends up entailing, above all, more duties. Such duties are associated with the multiple costs of formally locating yourself in a neoliberal city" (Torres, 2012). So, as it currently stands, formalization is a better deal for the government than for informal settlements. Ultimately, formalization can only work when both parties contribute and benefit, that is, if there is a renegotiation of the urban social contract. The narrative of "renegotiating the social contract" became the guiding principle of the city's 2020–2024 development plan (López, 2019).

4.4.2 Stratification: naturalizations and disincentives

Colombia's novel stratification system was established in 1983 as a cross-subsidization system for utility bills. Only the middle class pay what the water and electricity services are worth. The two upper classes overpay so the three lower classes can pay less (Figure 4.9). The system proved very easy to implement and expanded the coverage of services. In fact, it grew to be so successful that "the legislative lexicon swiftly spread to other policy sectors" (SDP, 2016:22) and was adopted by other countries. However, in the early 2000s debate about the inefficiency and inequity of the stratification system, from economic and sociological perspectives, exploded. Critics denounce that far from a solidarity mechanism, it has become a poor targeting instrument, it promotes discriminatory practices, hinders social mobility, and it is a disincentive to the proper upkeep and maintenance of buildings and neighborhoods. While these critiques do not articulate their connection to formalization policy, their relationship is quite direct. Understanding the

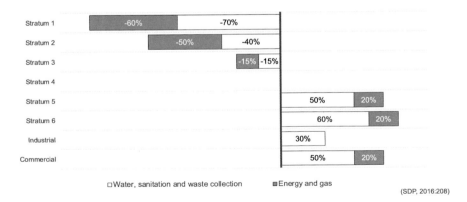

Figure 4.9 Cross-subsidization in Bogotá: Contributions and tariff reductions by strata (author based on SDP, 2016)

150 *The politics of urban formalization in Bogotá*

unintended outcomes if the stratification system helps to address the hiatus between the three different purposes of formalization policy: the intended, the actual, and the ideal.

A core problem of stratification is that it ceased to be a good proxy for the paying capacity of low-income residents (SDP, 2016:22). Economists lagged in identifying this issue, that a shop owner in Patio Bonito slum put so bluntly: "This is not a poor neighborhood, instead, this is where the rich come and hide their money" (DPU, 2006: Annex 5). Failing to detect paying capacity can betray the purpose of this instrument. If the system is incapable of detecting real paying capacity, it cannot guarantee subsidies and compensations are adequately progressive, so it fails to be equitable (SDP, 2016:22). At the time of the introduction of stratification, there was a significant backlash on property appraisals nationally (González, 2016) and Bogotá's cadaster was not nearly as updated as it is today. So, the system relied instead on an assessment of the physical characteristics of housing and its surroundings. This worked well for some time, until it did not.

What is being stratified is the building, not its residents. While this sounds appropriate, in practice stratification has become "a mechanism to geographically identify the poor" (Alzate 2006 in SDP, 2016:22). Moreover, economic stratification is now ingrained in the public imaginary (SDP, 2016:26) to such an extent that the word is used in common parlance to refer to types of people. For instance, a person from a higher class would point pejoratively to an unacceptable social behavior of someone of a lower class that he or she "showed the stratum." Not only is it a discrimination strategy, but it also naturalizes power hierarchies. Unfortunately, this comes very naturally to a former Spanish colony where the caste system was actively deployed: the "legacy of colonialism is stratification, a legitimized mentality of inequality" (Gouverneur, 2015:13). Further still, stratification not only naturalizes differences, but it seems to freeze them. For instance, between 2011 and 2014 the lower strata in Bogotá grew very slowly (on average 1.8%), the middle class shrank (by 2.2%), and the higher strata remained stable (SDP, 2016:25). Strata stagnate social mobility to the point that, to move up the social ladder, Bogotanians are forced to change to a differently stratified neighborhood (Uribe, 2008).

In theory, if upgrading programs were effective, buildings in lower strata (1, 2, and 3) would transition into the middle class (strata 4). A true formalization policy would "graduate" neighborhoods from upgrading to consolidation treatment and help move property owners out from subsidy recipients into full fee payers. While cross-subsidization is certainly a progressive taxation, it is not free from a moral hazard problem. Stratification of buildings, focused on the physical aspects and disconnected from the economic realities (formal and especially informal), incentivizes not upgrading, but urban decay. Stratification disincentivizes upgrading, property investments, and

The politics of urban formalization in Bogotá 151

general maintenance, if people are to retain the utility subsidies. The alternative approach is one where property taxation is an incentive to maintain buildings by discounting their costs from the owner's fiscal duties.

4.4.3 Subdivision, the key from residential to social mobility

One of the many truths hidden in plain sight regarding informal settlements is that their dwellers are also rentier capitalists. They have long been the primary providers of affordable housing, most of them rental units within existing houses. As was described in great detail in Chapter 3, it is not only additional residential units that these houses host, but also industries, shops, as well as recreational, care, and even religious services. Whatever services the city is not offering them, they assume themselves. Moreover, this is true not only of housing and urban services, but informal buildings also play the role of old age social insurance: "Housing is the pension of the poor" (Torres, 2019), is a widely used unattributed phrase. So, if "everything that is lacking from the social protection system is absorbed by housing" (Camargo, 2020), then it is necessary to think about what the ideal purpose of policies supporting informal settlements should be.

Identifying subdivision as the ultimate moment of upgrading and recognition (as my formalization stair shows (Figure 4.5)) is not something that the regulation does nor that the literature is currently instructing. However, I argue that it is an ideal purpose the formalization policy ought to have because subdivision facilitates upward social mobility. Camargo's research in consolidated informal settlements in Bogotá persuasive in this regard. With 400 surveys, 30 in depth interviews, and taking advantage of parallel studies being carried out simultaneously in 10 Latin American cities (LAHN, 2009), Camargo explains the link between residential and social mobility using an intergenerational life-course approach, or simply put, delving into grandparent's life stories.

Throughout the course of the life of these grandparents and their houses, residential improvement is hard-fought but significant. From wood shacks in the periphery that allowed their mere survival, houses were transformed into more centrally located multistory buildings producing rents that serve as unemployment insurance and that complement or supplement old age pensions. But with the passing of two or three decades, these grandparents' children, now adults with families of their own, are too often forced to stay at their parent's house despite their want for independence. Time shows that the survival miracle these houses allowed is a mixed blessing. Despite constant rents from shops or rented rooms, these houses are often tough to sell (Camargo, 2020). The two faces of informal productive housing go like this. On the one hand, as was proven econometrically, housing protects households against economic shocks *if and only if it is able to generate rent* (DNP,

152 *The politics of urban formalization in Bogotá*

2007:139). So, these houses represent a safety net for their owners. On the other hand, being unable to help the younger generations to further their upward social mobility, these houses are not working as springboards.

Subdivision into independent units via a formal horizontal property arrangement would dynamize the market for affordable housing options (as well as commercial and light industry) and help the grandchildren of these informal settlements further the social mobility that eluded their parents. Social mobility, let us remember, is related to the idea that one's prospects in life are better than those of one's parents. In this sense, being able to sell or easily rent a part of inherited real estate is instrumental for social mobility. Helping these productive houses become not only safety nets but springboards should be the objective of a joint urban formalization and social protection policy. Two decades ago, when the World Bank issued its first social protection strategy with this same name: *From Safety net to Springboard*, it already foreshadowed the importance of "expanding the rights to own assets, especially of productive assets like land and housing via revised cadasters" (WB, 2001:36). Subdivision, as the latter step in a formalization process of upgrading and recognition, would allow just that.

4.4.4 *The incomplete shift away from code-based planning*

Lauded by national and international scholars (Doebele, 1998), the Law 388 of 1997 represented a seismic change in urban planning in Colombia. In principle, established specific urban development tools designed to implement the constitutional mandate of the "social function of land," tools that are inseparable from the law's essence (Maldonado, 2006:13). Besides making mandatory the issuance of municipal master plans (*Planes de Ordenamiento Territorial, POT*), the new tools in this law allowed cities to recapture the value added to urban land via urbanization, helping local governments finance prioritized projects (like transport infrastructure) and upgrade legalized informal settlements. Planning saw a shift away from plot-by-plot code-based planning to flexible regulations for public-private partnerships in mid-sized urban developments (*planes parciales* of least 10 hectares). Unfortunately, more than two decades later, these innovative tools are far from being widely implemented, and when they are, they bypass developers in informal settlements, who continue to be tied to the strictures of old codes. In other words, "the problem is who are the rules written for" (Parra, 2019).

In terms of housing policy, this law had a paradoxical effect as it was introduced in tandem with a Chilean-inspired neoliberal turn in housing policy, away from any direct public intervention. Critique to this model is commonplace in urban studies literature, showing examples of urban developers that, fueled by subsidies, produce large housing projects disconnected from employment centers and of poor quality (eloquently described as the "houses without people" phenomena [Ziccardi, 2020]). However, less discussed and perhaps more promising is the critique that fact that this neoliberal turn espoused housing policy to economic policy (i.e. growth) and divorced it from social policy (i.e. protection) (Maldonado, 2008:59). Research on the social protection uses of housing in informal settlements, like the examples described in Chapter 3, bring evidence of the intimate link between informal housing and social protection. Acknowledging and operating in this nexus may open up a new policy space but would demand that the shift from code-based to partnership-based planning includes both formal and informal urban developers. Moreover, this link reveals housing is, more than a market product, a productive asset that complements income and hence protects families from crises (economic, health, or natural).

4.5 Beyond recognition

4.5.1 Cosmetic upgrading and false recognition

Critiques to upgrading frequently gravitate around the argument that, while in principle programs claim to be integrated and give equal standing to social, economic, and physical components of the intervention, in practice this is hardly ever the case [Torres, 2012; López, 2017], to name a few local experts). During the implementation, the infrastructure component overpowers all the others in budgetary terms (between 50 and 75% as estimated by the World Bank [WB, 2017]) and in managerial weight. Ceballos goes further assuring that even the physical interventions are quite insignificant, usually "too

Figure 4.10 The Butterfly (La Mariposa) HabitArte upgrading program in Usaquén (SDHT, 2019).

154 *The politics of urban formalization in Bogotá*

shallow and without real impact on the conditions of habitability and health" (Ceballos, 2019). To illuminate this genre of thin upgrading interventions there is no better example than that of the "world's biggest butterfly" (SDH, 2019). The project, part of a city-wide program included much-needed water and sanitation works, sidewalks, improvements to the local school, and the painting of 2,800 façades in slums at Usaquén in Bogotá (Figure 4.10).

While the project circulates globally as a transfer-worthy success story[14], the community submitted a right to petition questioning the city's "unjustified emphasis on painting of the façades, sidelining improvements in sewage and roads" (Tabares, 2020). Community leader Janeth Duarte argued that "the many years of neglect to the area are not resolved with a 'macro-mural.' The budget should be executed in full" (Tabares, 2020). Art-based interventions can definitely be powerful detonators of social appropriation and positive urban transformation. In fact, they have been proven quite successful in Bogotá, especially when the initiative comes from within the community (as was the case of the Juan XXIII experience with youth gangs, which inspired the butterfly [Camargo, 2020]). But not any kind art-based intervention will do.

The butterfly only reveals itself to the outside spectator. Legible from a distance, especially from a top down, helicopter perspective. Outsiders can distinguish the shape and have a calming sense of understanding of these informal settlements that would otherwise be cognitively removed. Such beautification is awkwardly othering. This is undoubtedly a case of recognition: viewers can recognize the contours of a butterfly, but this is recognition that stops at identification. It is one-sided, narrow, and falls short to what true recognition entails. These slums are brought to visibility only to invisibilize them under a colorful (even clownish[15]) coat that strips them for their power to speak back, challenging whatever the upgrading delivers.

4.5.2 *True recognition: remuneration and redistribution*

To fully grasp the difference between true and false recognition, I recur to two strategies: first an example of an authentic formalization policy deployed in Bogotá (not about housing but about waste management), and later, some background references about the philosophical underpinnings of the concept of recognition.

Waste-pickers, locally referred to as "recyclers," have long been part of the urban landscape in Bogotá. Even with their shabby and smelly horse-drawn

---

14 Guangzhou International Award for Urban Innovation, University of Berlin, ETZ-Zurich, and others.

15 In his starkly illuminating analysis of the way the higher classes regard the lower classes, Miller's *Anatomy of Disgust* explains: "Clownish or invisible is what the contemptible are when they do not constitute a threat" (Miller, 1997:238).

carts (frequent up to 2014 when they were finally banned), and despite their important environmental contribution to the chain of waste management (adding sorting and recycling steps before final disposal into landfills), they were largely disregarded and invisible. It took countless legal battles, dodging anonymous threats,[16] and a strong national association to get their claims to be understood. In 2011, Colombian Constitutional Court (CC-275, 2011) forced national and local governments into more decisive action (similar to what happened in the realm of slum upgrading in 2016 (CC-373, 2016)). Today, 12,000 organized waste-pickers, out of the 18,000 working in Bogotá, receive a monthly payment between US$100 and US$170 from the city government for the two services they deliver: collection and recycling (Parra, 2019). Bogotá was the forerunner in this process, and today other 80 municipalities have waste-pickers' organizations, and 25 of them receive regular payments. The path unlocked by the informal recyclers from an initial situation of invisibility, to finally receiving payment for the urban services they offer, is perhaps a prototype of what formalization policy of informal settlements, constructions, and especially their use, could look like.

The first lesson is that, for the recyclers, formalization is not inclusion. Despite inclusion being lauded as the doctrine of the formalization policy, informal recyclers understood well that inclusion is far from beneficial for them, in other words, inclusion is not equality. "[W]e've distanced ourselves from the word *inclusion*. As if they were outside. No, they have always been inside, but they haven't been recognized" (Parra, 2019). Recyclers prefer the word recognition, which in common parlance also has the meaning of economic remuneration. The city has to pay someone (usually either a public, private or mixed firm) to collect, sort, and recycle waste. These services are paid for by all citizens, as a percentage of the water utility bills. Nonetheless, recyclers have long offered sanitation and environmental public services without being paid for it by the city, cashing only for the materials they collect. But recyclers in effect reduce the waste poured into a landfill, and this translates into city budget savings. The Colombian National Association of Recyclers made the legal case that informal recyclers should have preferential treatment as service providers, and the Constitutional Court agreed. The payback to recyclers should cover, according to the Court's decision *support* for their consolidation as an organization. Because the payments are made to a cooperative, with a redistributive objective, the Court's decision opened ground third model of service provision, apart from discussions of more or

---

16 Federico Parra (WIEGO's Latin American Coordinator for the waste-pickers' sector) reported receiving systematic "anonymous" death threats, directly related to business interests in recycling, when working for a progressive city administration. "Sadly, this is a commonly deployed strategy in our country: to deal with dissent by elimination" (Parra, 2019).

less market and or government. The lesson is that remuneration is key for recognition, but so is redistribution.

The beauty of the Colombian model of formalization of waste-pickers is that it is labor intensive (unlike the Chilean model) and that it relies on citizens paying a fee and having, especially in small municipalities or in certain neighborhoods, a direct personal relationship with their local recycler (Parra, 2019). This became evident when the city put forward an at-the-source sorting campaign asking to "Put recyclables in white bags *for the recyclers.*" Adding these three words had a tremendous effect: "People started thinking about them, who are they? They started seeing them as different from the garbage piles and their makeshift push carts. [And at the same time,] It also made the recyclers think of themselves as service providers" (Parra, 2019). When recognition includes remuneration, it goes beyond mere identification, it dignifies the work being done. In fact, as Parra recounts, this formalization policy has had a tremendous effect: second-generation recyclers. The sons and daughters of informal recyclers started to see a possible future in this activity as social promoters, technicians, and environmentalists, something unthinkable when the organization began.

For informal workers, the remuneration that comes with their recognition as service providers has a profound effect in the way they perceive themselves. Parra recalls that when the Popayán association started using their bright yellow uniforms, workers stopped calling themselves "recyclers" or "collectors" and started saying "service providers." More important still, they stopped calling the payment a "subsidy," or, as one of them used to say: "I no longer receive my suicide" (Parra, 2019). In this case, the alliteration of the Spanish words "subsidy" (*subsidio*) and "suicide" (*suicidio*) is no elaborate pun, but an actual conflation of their meanings. This should come as no surprise to a population that is used to hiding or disowning its assets in order to enjoy the benefits of the national welfare system (SISBEN). When poverty is a prerequisite to access government services, ensuring one does not lose a subsidy is much like taking, little by little, one's own life.

4.5.3 Notes on the philosophy of recognition

Hegel saw recognition as a necessary condition for the development of the spirit. Without recognition, the collective consciousness of a society, that is, the spirit's progress, gets blocked and cannot continue its path of self-knowledge. The *Phenomenology of the Spirit (1807)* details how the spirit is in a constant process of self-knowledge toward realization, of becoming-its-own-self. Outside philosophy we hardly encounter reflections on the spirit, and in fact the word used by Hegel, the German word *geist*, is at the same time spirit, mind, intellect, and ghost[17]. To our discussion about recognition

---

17 Or specter, as Marx, a left-wing Hegelian, famously put it.

of informal housing/work arrangements, the philosophical baggage of the concept of recognition is useful at least in two regards.

First, the mutuality of recognition. Recognition goes a step further than neighboring, yet narrower, concepts like "identification" and "acknowledgment" because "it implies a positive valuation" (Ricoeur, 2005:16) in (Iser, 2019). When recognizing the other, one holds a positive attitude toward an identifiable feature that the other one has. Misrecognition can be dangerous for those who suffer from it. "[T]hose who fail to experience adequate recognition, i.e., those who are depicted by the surrounding others or the societal norms and values in a one-sided or negative way, will find it much harder to embrace themselves and their projects as valuable (...) Misrecognition thereby hinders or destroys persons' successful relationship to their selves" (Iser, 2019). Of course, the process of recognition entails having a subject of recognition (the recognizer) and an object (the recognized). But what is truly important is that recognition can only happen if it is mutual. Recognition is a double-sided cognition. "Within the *Phenomenology* this idea is first and foremost a thesis about how we can gain self-consciousness as autonomous agents, namely only by interacting with other autonomous subjects" (Iser, 2019). Beyond interest in the other, beyond respect for the other, only empathy with other persons allows us to take over their perspective" (Cavell, 1969 in Iser, 2019). So, if according to Hegel, we can only advance in our own self-knowledge development through a process of mutual recognition, then failing to recognize, failing to value the other prevents us from becoming our true selves. Going back to our subject, a city that does not recognize its informal settlements, constructions, and businesses, fails to develop and reach its own potential.

Second, recognition is in a necessary parallel with redistribution. Social justice theorists and feminists, especially since the 1990s resonated strongly with Hegel's recognition and its potential for identity and emancipation (Sennett, 2003; Appiah, 1992; Young, 1990), and (Fanon, 1952), to name a few. However, optimistic descriptions of recognition have been challenged for being conservative, freezing others at their present state under the present rules. "The concern is that because the need for recognition renders persons utterly dependent on the dominating societal norms it may undermine the identity of any critic. Thus, some worry that struggles for recognition may lead to conformism and a strengthening of ideological formations" (Iser, 2019). Fraser has been particularly vocal in this regard. Concerned with the fact that in a post-socialist world the language of distribution has evaporated from the grammar of political contestation (Fraser, 2000:108), she emphatically sees redistribution at the other side of the same coin as recognition; none can do the work alone (Fraser, 2000:109).

Rather than shifting emphasis away from recognition (as Fraser's critics point out), the parallel with redistribution emanates from the definition of recognition itself. Fraser explains recognition is not to be reduced to a question over identity, but rather it should be viewed as an issue of *status*. This

158 *The politics of urban formalization in Bogotá*

view is particularly useful in the context of highly stratified urban fabric like Bogotá. In this light, misrecognition is nothing else but an institutionalized status subordination (Fraser, 2000:113). So, to be misrecognized "is not simply to be thought ill of, looked down upon, [invisibilized], or devalued in others' attitudes, beliefs, [regulations], or representations. It is rather to be denied the status of a full partner in social interaction" (Fraser, 2000:119). Fraser's status model of recognition clarifies what the objective of recognition should be: "establishing participatory parity as a normative standard" (Fraser, 2000:119). Recognition is not necessarily an end in itself, not even if taken jointly with redistribution. Instead, recognition is the means to achieve equal participation in public life. Learning from Fraser and going back to our case in point, we can say that only at the top of the urban formalization stair (Figure 4.5), can informal settlements, houses, and businesses, participate as equals in the construction of the city itself.

References

Accord 7 of 1979. (1979). *Bogota Development Plan: "Por el cual se define el Plan General de Desarrollo integrado y se adoptan políticas y normas sobre el uso de la tierra en el Distrito Especial de Bogota*, Bogota City Council, Bogota. https://jbb.gov.co/documentos/juridica/antiguo/acuerdos_ambientales/Acuerdo_007_1979.pdf

Accord 6 of 1990. (1990). *Bogota Physical Development Plan: "Por medio del cual se adopta el Estatuto para el Ordenamiento Físico del Distrito Especial de Bogota, y se dictan otras disposiciones"*, Bogota City Council, Bogota. https://www.alcaldiabogota.gov.co/sisjur/normas/Norma1.jsp?i=540&dt=S

Acebedo, Luis Fernando. (2003). "El CINVA y su entorno espacial y político", *Revista Mimesis* 24, pp. 59–89.

Appadurai, Arjun. (2004). "The Capacity to Aspire: Culture and the Terms of Recognition", In Rao, V. and Walton, M. (eds.) *Culture and Public Action*, Stanford University Press, Palo Alto, CA, pp. 59–84.

Arnstein, Sherry. (1969). "A Ladder of Citizen Participation", *Journal of the American Planning Association*, 35:4, pp. 216–224.

Avendaño, Antonio. (2019). *Personal interview with officer at Bogota's Planning Secretariat*, July 15.

Beuf, Alice. (2011). "Nuevas centralidades y acceso a la ciudad en las periferias Bogotanas", *Bulletin de l'Institut Français d'Études Andines*, 40:1, pp. 147–178.

Camargo, Angélica. (2017). "Prácticas residenciales y movilidad social en barrios populares", PhD dissertation, Universidad Externado de Colombia. https://bdigital.uexternado.edu.co/entities/publication/ce0b2dc2-cfdb-4ab2-babe-97b1ae6721de

Camargo, Angélica. (2019). "Vivienda y estrategias familiares de vida en barrios populares consolidados en Bogotá", *Revista INVI, Santiago*, 35:98, pp. 101–125.

Camargo, Angélica. (2020). *Interview with local social housing expert*, May 26.

Carvajalino, Hernando. (2019). *Personal interview*, July 14.

CC – Constitutional Court. (2011). Auto 275: Special Treatment of Minorities in the Provision of Public Sanitation Services. https://www.corteconstitucional.gov.co/relatoria/autos/2011/a275-11.htm

CC – Constitutional Court. (2016). Auto 373: Guidelines and Criteria to Raise the Unconstitutional State of Things Regarding Forced Displacement. https://www.corteconstitucional.gov.co/relatoria/autos/2016/A373-16.htm

Ceballos, Olga. (2005). *La legislación urbanística para la producción de vivienda de bajo costo. La experiencia de Bogota*, Scripta Nova, Revista Electrónica de Geografía y Ciencias Sociales, Universidad de Barcelona, IX, 194:25. https://www.ub.edu/geocrit/sn/sn-194-25.htm

CEDE – Centro de Estudios de Desarrollo Económico. (2003). *Estimación del efecto de Metrovivienda sobre el bienestar de la población de Bogota,* Metrovivienda – Universidad de los Andes, Ediciones Uniandes, Bogota.

Crane, Jacob L. and McCabe, Robert E. (1950). "Programmes in Aid of Family Housebuilding: 'Aided Self-help Housing'", *International Labour Review*, 61, pp. 1–18.

Currie, Launchlin, Reuan, Hernando, Villate, Eduardo, Garcia, Manuel, Rother, Hans, Ternet, Anthony, Tellez, Miguel, Cortes, Adolfo, and Schwartz, Howard. (1962). *Alternativas para el desarrollo urbano de Bogota D.E.*, Estudios e informes de una ciudad en Marcha, Editorial Andes, Bogota.

CVP – Caja de Vivienda Popular. (2020). "Informe de gestión y resultados 2019", Caja de la Vivienda Popular, Alcaldía Mayor de Bogotá, Bogota.

Davidoff, Paul. (1965). "Advocacy and Pluralism in Planning", *Journal of the American Institute of Planners*, 31:4, pp. 331–338.

Davis, Mike. (2006). *Planet of Slums*, Verso, London.

Decree 190 of 2004, Alcaldía Mayor de Bogota, June 22, 2004, Bogota. https://www.alcaldiabogota.gov.co/sisjur/normas/Norma1.jsp?i=13935&dt=S

Decree 476 of 2015, Alcaldía Mayor de Bogota, November 19, 2015, Bogota, http://sisjur.bogotajuridica.gov.co

DNP – Departamento Nacional de Planeación. (2007). *Las condiciones habitacionales de los hogares y su relación con la pobreza*, Misión para el diseño de una estrategia para la reducción de la pobreza y la desigualdad (MERPD), DNP-ECLAC-IDB-UNDP-World Bank, consultant: Jorge E. Torres, Bogota.

Doebele, William A. (1998). "The Recovery of 'Socially Created' Land Values in Colombia", Land Lines, Lincoln Land Institute, July 1998, Web.

DPU – Department Planning Unit of the University College London. (2006), "Costs of formality and informality in the market for land and housing", *Colombia: Housing and Land for the Urban Poor. Case studies of Bogota-Soacha-Mosquera and Medellín,* report for Cities Alliance, World Bank, Departamento Nacional de Planeación, and Ministerio de Ambiente Vivienda y Desarrollo Territorial.

DTS-POT – Documento Técnico de Soporte del Plan de Ordenamiento Territorial. (2019). "Análisis de ordenamiento y gestión del suelo de la demanda de vivienda esperada", Secretaria de Planeación Distrital, document 3, annex 1, Web.

Ernst, Bruno. (1992). *The Eye Beguiled: Optical Illusions*, Benedikt Taschen, Kohn.

Eyheralde, René. (1953). *El concepto del desarrollo progresivo en el diseño de la vivienda*, Técnica #1, Centro Interamericano de Vivienda, CINVA, Bogota.

Fernandes, Edesio. (2011). *Regularization of Informal Settlements in Latin America, Policy Focus Report*, Lincoln Institute of Land Policy, Cambridge, pp. 18–25.

Florián, Alejandro. (1991). "Fedevivienda: The National Federation of Self-help Community Housing Organizations", *Environment and Urbanization*, 3:2, pp. 87–91.

160 *The politics of urban formalization in Bogotá*

Florián, Alejandro. (2019). *Personal interview,* January 28.

Fraser, Nancy. (2010). "Rethinking Recognition", *New Left Review,* 3, May 1, 2000, pp. 107–120.

Fraser, Nancy. (2003). "Social Justice in the Age of Identity Politics: Redistribution, Recognition, and Participation", In Fraser, N. and Honneth, A. (eds) *Redistribution or Recognition? A Political-Philosophical Exchange,* Verso, New York, pp. 7–109.

Freire, Mila; Lima, Ricardo; Cira, Dean; Ferguson, Bruce; Kessides, Christine; Mota, Jose Aroudo; Motta, Diana. (2007). Land and Urban Policies for Poverty Reduction: Proceedings of the Third International Urban Research Symposium Held in Brasilia, April 2005, Volume 2. World Bank, Brasilia. © World Bank. https://openknowledge.worldbank.org/handle/10986/21557 License: CC BY 3.0 IGO.

García, Wilson. (2013). "Dinámica de las construcciones por usos en la Localidad Kennedy 2002-2012", Unidad Administrativa de Catastro Distrital – UACD, Bogota. https://www.catastrobogota.gov.co/sites/default/files/archivos/kennedy. pdf

González, Jorge Iván. (2014). "No mas estratificación", Diario La Republica, August 1. https://www.larepublica.co/analisis/jorge-ivan-gonzalez-506394/no-mas-estratificacion-2152081

González, Lina Maria. (2020). Personal interview with expert in legalization and upgrading, May 5, 2020, and personal email communication, October 9.

Gutiérrez, Francisco. (1998). "El Clientelismo y sus enredos. Caso 1. El Barrio La Meca y el movimiento forerista (vida, pasión y muerte de Rafael Forero Fetecua)". In *La ciudad representada: Política y conflicto en Bogota,* Tercer Mundo Editores – IEPRI, Bogota, pp. 55–120, Web excerpt.

Hanna, Mar. (2017). "A Lot of What Is Known about Pirates Is Not True, and a Lot of What Is True Is Not Known", *Humanities,* 38:1, National Endowment for the Arts. https://www.neh.gov/humanities/2017/winter/feature/lot-what-known-about-pirates-not-true-and-lot-what-true-not-known

Harris, Richard. (2003). "A Double Irony: The Originality and Influence of John F.C. Turner", *Habitat International,* 27:2, pp. 245–269.

HfH – Habitat for Humanity Colombia and CENAC – Centro de Estudios Nacionales de la Construcción y el Desarrollo Regional. (2014). *Documento Ciudadela Sucre: Componente socioeconómico y demanda efectiva de mejoramiento de vivienda,* Bogota.

IFC – International Finance Corporation. (2009). "Trámite Fácil, Construcción Positiva", Secretaria Distrital del Hábitat, Ventanilla Única de Construcción, PowerPoint presentation. https://slideplayer.es/slide/3583414/

Iser, Mattias. (2019). "Recognition". In Edward N. Zalta (ed.) *The Stanford Encyclopedia of Philosophy,* Summer 2019 Edition. https://plato.stanford.edu/entries/recognition/

LAHN – Latin American Housing Network. (2009). *Third Generation (3G) Housing Policies in Consolidated Low-income Settlements,* University of Texas, Web.

López, Claudia. (2019). "Plan de Desarrollo Distrital 2020-2024: Un nuevo contrato social y ambiental para el siglo XXI", draft pending City Council approval.

López, Walter. (2017). "La recomposición social y urbana del territorio como alternativa a los programas de mejoramiento barrial. Caso de estudio: Bogota", Doctoral dissertation, Universidad Tecnologica de La Habana, Habana.

León, Diana. (2020). Personal interview with officer at Secretaria de Desarrollo Económico de Bogota, August 1.

López, Walter. (2019). Personal interview, August 1.

Maldonado, et al. (2006). *Planes parciales, gestión asociada y mecanismos de distribución equitativa de cargas y beneficios en el sistema urbanístico colombiano*, Lincoln Institute of Land Policy, Panamericana, Bogota.

Maldonado, María Mercedes. (2008). "La Ley 388 de 1997 en Colombia: Algunos puntos de tensión en el proceso de su implementación", ACE Arquitectura Ciudad y Entorno, 3:7, Universitat Politècnica de Catalunya, Barcelona.

Mejía, Germán. (1991). "Los itinerarios de la transformación urbana Bogota: 1820–1910", Anuario Colombiano de Historia Social y de la Cultura, 24, Universidad Nacional de Colombia, Bogota.

Mejía, Germán. (2008). "Santafé. De ciudad fundada a ciudad construida". In Lucena, Manuel (ed) *Urbanismo y Vida Urbana en Iberoamérica Colonial*, Alcaldía Mayor de Bogota, Bogota.

Merriam-Webster. (n.d). "Demiurge." *Merriam-Webster.com Dictionary*, https://www.merriam-webster.com/dictionary/demiurge. Accessed 1 May, 2020.

Miller, William. (1997). *The Anatomy of Disgust*, Harvard University Press, Cambridge, MA.

Mosquera, Gilma. (1984). "El movimiento de los destechados colombianos en la década de los años 70", Revista Mexicana de Sociología, Universidad Nacional Autónoma de México, 46:4, October–December 1984, pp. 127–144.

Nader, Lina Margarita. (2002). "Análisis Jurídico de la Propiedad Horizontal en Colombia", LLB thesis, Universidad Javeriana, Bogota.

Naranjo, Maria Elvira. (2017). "Colonos, comunistas, alarifes y fundadores en Colombia: una historia de la Central Nacional Provivienda CENAPROV (1959-2016)", PhD Dissertation in Political Studies and International Affairs, Universidad Nacional de Colombia, Bogota.

Nohn, Matthias (2011). "Mixed-Use Zoning and Home-Based Production in India", WIEGO Technical Brief (Urban Policies) No. 3, WIEGO, Boston.

Offner, Amy C. (2019). *Sorting Out the Mixed Economy: The Rise and Fall of Welfare and Developmental States in the Americas*, Princeton University Press, Princeton, NJ.

Oram, Nigel. (1965). *Towns in Africa*, Oxford University Press, London.

Pabón, Ciro. (1990). *La propiedad de inmuebles divididos por pisos o departamentos: Teoría y práctica de la propiedad horizontal*, Ediciones Librería del Profesional, Bogota.

Penrose, Lionel Sharples and Penrose, Roger (1958). "Impossible objects: A special type of visual illusion". *British Journal of Psychology*. 49, pp. 31–33.

Ramírez, Ricardo. (2019). Personal *interview with expert in recognition processes*, February 12.

Revista Escala 110. (1981), *Ordenamiento del espacio urbano*, Escala Editores, Bogota.

Rivera, Jorge Alberto. (2001). *El CINVA, un modelo de cooperación técnica. 1951-1972*, Master thesis in history, Universidad Nacional de Colombia, Bogota.

Rodríguez, Maria Alejandra. (2012). "El que peca y reza empata: Vida y obra del urbanizador y político Rafael Forero Fetecua", Journalism Thesis, Pontificia Universidad Javeriana.

Roy, Ananya. (2005). "Urban Informality: Toward an Epistemology of Planning", *Journal of the American Planning Association*, 71:2, pp. 147–158.

162 *The politics of urban formalization in Bogotá*

Samper, et al. (1971). *Estudio de normas mínimas de urbanización, servicios públicos y servicios comunitarios*, ICT – Instituto de Crédito Territorial, DAPD – Departamento Administrativo de Planeación Distrital, and DNP – Departamento Nacional de Planeación, Bogota.

SDHT – Secretaría Distrital de Hábitat. (2019). "La Mariposa abrió sus alas para llenar de color siete barrios y ser un nuevo símbolo de Bogota", *News*, September 10. bit.ly/3Z2bbKu

SDP – Secretaría Distrital de Planeación. (2016). "La estratificación en Bogotá: Impacto social y alternativas para asignar subsidios impacto social y alternativas para asignar subsidios", Bogota. https://www.sdp.gov.co/sites/default/files/estratificacionbogota2016.pdf

SDP – Secretaría Distrital de Planeación. (2019). "La propiedad horizontal residencial en Bogota vista desde sus equipamientos comunales", Bogota. https://www.sdp.gov.co/sites/default/files/ph_equipamientos.pdf

Smolka, Martin (2003). "Informality, Urban Poverty and Land Market Prices", *Landlines*, 15:1, pp. 4–7, Lincoln Institute of Land Policy, Cambridge, MA.

Stevenson, Rafael. (1979). "Housing programs and policies in Bogota: a historical/descriptive analysis". World Bank City Study Research Project RPO 671-47.

SCA – Sociedad Colombiana de Arquitectos- Regional Bogotá Cundinamarca. (2011). "Apuntes para una hoja de ruta de la Comisión Hábitat", Blog entry July 19, http://comisionhabitatsca.blogspot.com/

Suache, Jenny. (2019). "Inicia construcción de espacios culturales de lujo en pilonas de TransMiCable", Bogota.gov.co.

Tabares, Laura Marcela. (2020). "La Mariposa de Usaquén, en peligro de extinción", *Plaza Capital-digital news outlet-*, Universidad del Rosario, February 27. https://plazacapital.co/esquinas/4170-la-mariposa-de-usaquen-en-peligro-de-extincion

Torres, Alfonso. (2013). *La ciudad en la sombra: Barrios y luchas populares en Bogotá 1950-1977*, Universidad Piloto de Colombia, Bogota.

Torres, Carlos, Atanassova, Carlos, and Rincón John Jairo. (2009). "¿Es posible pasar de la ciudad informal a la ciudad formal? Aproximación a algunos problemas urbanos y a las estrategias de intervención estatal desde la perspectiva del mejoramiento integral de barrios, MIB", In *Procesos urbanos informales y territorio: Ensayos en torno a la construcción de sociedad, territorio y ciudad*, Universidad Nacional de Colombia, Bogotá.

Torres, Carlos. (2007). "La ciudad informal colombiana", *Revista Bitácora*, 11:1, Universidad Nacional de Colombia, pp. 53–93.

Torres, Carlos. (2012). "Legalización de barrios: acción de mejora o mecanismo de viabilización fiscal de la ciudad dual", *Bulletin de l'Institut français d'*études andines, 41:3, pp. 441–471, https://doi.org/10.4000/bifea.304

Torres, Jorge E. (2019a). *Personal interview*, February 12.

Torres, Jorge E. (2019b). "Colombia: The singularity of housing policy in urban development", In *Urban Policy in Latin America: Towards the Sustainable Development Goals?* Routledge, Oxford.

Uribe, Alfredo. (2019). Personal interview with Officer at the Habitat Secretariat, March 12.

Uribe, Consuelo. (2008). "Estratificación social en Bogotá: de la política pública a la dinámica de la segregación social", *Universitas Humanística*, 65, pp. 139–171.

WB – World Bank. (2001). *Social Protection Sector Strategy: From Safety Net to Springboard*, World Bank Group, The Human Development Network, Washington, DC.

WB – World Bank Group (2017). "Upgrading Urban Informal Settlements (facilitated online course)", Open Learning Campus, January–April. https://olc.worldbank.org/

Yunda, Guillermo. (2019). Personal interview, May 20.

Ziccardi, Alicia. (2020). "Mexico. From Habitat II to Habitat III: Assessment of the Commitments Undertaken", In Cohen, Michael, Carrozosa, Maria, and Gutman, Margarita (eds) *Urban Policy in Latin America: Towards the Sustainable Development Goals?* Routledge, Oxford.

5 Space–use intensity and urban formalization in African cities

5.1 Background of the study

5.1.1 Note on the research setup

The replication study summarized in this chapter was possible thanks to a collaboration between the Friedrich-Ebert-Stiftung (FES) and The New School on the Just City initiative, which included five working papers and a set of policy advocacy convenings between 2021 and 2023. FES manifested interest in the "space-use intensity" approach for its potential to develop and operationalize of the "just city" concept, which is concerned with putting the "urban invisibles" at the center of urban development (FES, 2020). This gave place to the paper: "Urban Informality and the Making of African Cities," of my authorship, published by the FES Kenya Office in 2022. The contents of this chapter are based on that work, about which some background is relevant.

As a recent doctoral graduate, the opportunity to replicate my Bogotá study in various African cities was an exceptional opportunity to test the validity of the concept across different physical, cultural, and socioeconomic conditions, and to assess whether the methodology to document it could be easily transferred to others and applied to diverse local conditions. Moreover, the alignment of my own approach with the policy advocacy agenda of FES, gave me freedom to compare earlier findings in a way that proved fertile for both parties. My approach relates quite closely with the "just city" narrative, because both claim the "urban invisibles" at the center. My work contributes a mode of assessing the extent and the type of "urban invisibility" that the just city mandate claims must be addressed.

The cities selected to be part of this research (Kampala, Dar es Salaam, and Dakar) were defined in conjunction with FES Country Office Directors (Rolf Paasch in Uganda, Elisabeth Bollrich in Tanzania, and Thomas Maetigg in Senegal), who opted in to participate in the study and offered decisive assistance to ensure the research could be carried out remotely in a short span of time (between July 2021 and December 2021). Country offices in Kampala, Dar es Salaam, and Dakar deployed their support in three ways. Shortlisting

DOI: 10.4324/9781003297727-5

Space-use intensity and urban formalization in African cities   165

the local experts to be interviewed in each city, offering extensive translation services in the case of work in Senegal, and most importantly, hiring local researchers to conduct the field research under my guidance. The training, supervision, and debriefing sessions with the teams of local researchers were one of my most rewarding research experiences ever. I am extremely grateful for the professionalism and enthusiasm of Teddy Kisembo and Hafisa Namuli in Uganda, Imma Kapinga and Antidy Kamawala in Tanzania, and Amadou Ndiaye and his team in Senegal; without their input this project would not have been successful.

5.1.2 Note on urban informality in Africa

Datasets released by the International Labor Organization (ILO) reveal that informal employment represents 61.5% of the world's employment and 85.8% of jobs in Africa (ILO, 2018). In terms of the built environment, experts concur that urban informality accounts for at least 60% to 80% of the existing urban fabric of developing countries (Chen et al., 2018). African urban experts seem to concur that at least 70% of urban land is occupied by informal settlements (Komu, 2022) and that 98% of housing is self-built (Limbumba, 2022). In addition, Africa underwent its urban transition in 2015 and it is projected to have the fastest urban growth rate in the world over the next three decades, most of it unplanned (OECD, 2020). These statistics are undeniable. Urban informality is the predominant mode of city-making today.

It is impossible to miss the vibrancy of informality in African cities: street vendors are central to food security, informal transport modes keep the city moving, home-based workers offer care services that ensure economic activity. This realization comes in tandem with increasing statistical clarity about the uncomfortably large scope of the urban informal economy and its contribution to the continent's GDP. Despite this reality, positive framings of informality in policymaking are rather new. Only recently have governments adhered to supporting informality rather than to fighting it (ILO, 2015; Kiaga et al., 2020). Sidelining these new approaches, prejudices against urban informality abound within governments, academia, and in the streets.

All the while and despite its problems, informality makes cities function and raises people's well-being. In fact, without informal contributions in the form of income (informal employment), housing (informal housing and informal settlements or slums), and community services (informal care arrangements, informal water provision, informal waste recycling activities, and so on), people would be worse off. Informal service providers guarantee the flow of goods and services that formal conduits do not reach, and in this sense, informality helps cities function. Because African cities *do* function in a way that is not easily legible to urban managers and that is different from what planners assume and expect.

Against this backdrop, the COVID-19 pandemic forced the world to recognize that residential space is an essential part of the public health infrastructure and that homes are a fundamental component of the work infrastructure, during the crisis and beyond. Now, let us acknowledge that, while working from home is a new experience for many, it has long been an indispensable strategy for those living in self-built homes in informal settlements. This means that learning about the way informal settlements offer income opportunities and services should be a worthwhile endeavor for any urban researcher and manager.

If urban informality is not a deviation from the norm but the norm itself, our understanding of it, and consequently, the way it is treated by policy, must change radically. Unfortunately, when it comes to the design of locally relevant urban policy options, the scope of imagination is not only narrow, but dated prejudices about what informality is and how to curb it, persistently reemerge. Calls to rethink social protection measures and to enhance the productivity of the urban informal sector are only starting to be listened to and phrased (Guven and Karlen, 2020). And, while it is increasingly clear that social protection measures ought to be tailored to the way urban informality operates (WIEGO, 2020), the way these measures actually look like is hardly progressive or innovative. More must be done to arrive at more fitting measures to support urban informality.

This chapter reveals that across the informal settlements studied in Uganda, Tanzania, and Senegal, residential spaces host a wide range of economic activities and community services. Space-use intensity in consolidated informal settlements demonstrates that houses are much more than just houses and that informal settlements are more than just residential areas; they are foremost economic sites of production. Here, housing and employment cannot be differentiated. These neighborhoods and their residents internalize the services they do not receive through formal channels. In other words, social protections and urban services are being co-produced by the citizens. People are contributing much more to making life in the city possible than their municipal governments. Rather than labeling this state of affairs as good or bad, the point here is to acknowledge the extent of these activities, so policy is able to fine-tune itself to these realities, and hence be more effective and more just.

5.2 House interviews in Kampala, Dar es Salaam, and Dakar

As explained in greater detail in Chapter 3, the method used to capture space-use intensity data is called the house interview, which aims to interrogate, not residents, but the house itself. The interviewer, if allowed, tours each room in the house taking impromptu photographs of every space. The method uses semi-structured interviews, rough drawings, and photographs, to interview each space within the house. The objective is to compile a complete tally of different uses (range) and users (granularity) in the space. The complete count of observed uses is then compared with whatever information that is locally available about the recognized uses of the space (land-use documents, cadaster, or other sources). Each local researcher selected the houses to interview based on two simple criteria. First, ease of access (rapport guaranteed), and second, that houses were deemed locally as "typical" or "average" located in neighborhoods that were not the poorest nor the richest, but middle-to-low income, and in consolidated informal settlements (defined by Ward, 2015 as old peripheries).

In what follows, the text will walk the reader into three of the 12 houses interviewed as part of this study, one in each city: Kampala, Dar es Salaam, and Dakar.

5.2.1 Agnes's house in Kampala

North of Lake Victoria sits Kampala, former seat of the Buganda Kingdom and capital of Uganda. The metropolitan area has roughly 200 square kilometers and is home to 3.5 million people. Kampala spreads throughout 24 low flat-topped hills surrounded by wetland valleys that are mostly encroached upon. Administratively, it is divided into five divisions and a hundred parishes.

This is Agnes's house in Masanafu, Lubia parish, Rubaga division (Figure 5.1). She has been living here for over a decade with her three children and her father, whom she takes care of. Agnes runs a loaning business and describes herself as a businesswoman. For the local government, hers is a residential unit. However, our research identified 11 additional uses happening alongside her living quarters.

In front of her house facing the street, there is a food stall. Next to it some banana trees that she uses for her own consumption and also to sell in the stall (Figure 5.2). In the shaded veranda, there is an open space where her

Figure 5.1 Agnes' house in Rubaga, Kampala (Kissembo and Namuli, 2021).

community group regularly meets. In addition, Agnes runs a shoe shop and exhibits different models here. In the front, she keeps a handful of chickens.

At the back of her house, Agnes got installed a water tap (Figure 5.3). Until recently, she used to sell water to neighbors, but stopped doing so because that business is no longer good. She also has a large space dedicated to store and dry solid waste, which is then used in to produce briquettes (compressed combustible made of biomass, a substitute to charcoal). She stores the briquette machine at her house, so from time to time neighbors gather at her place to produce them, either to use themselves, store, or to sell.

The visual summary of the observed uses in Agnes house is shown in Figure 5.4 and discussed in Section 5.3.

Figure 5.2 Some uses in the front of Agnes's home: vegetable and cooking stoves stall (left), shoe shop (center), and briquettes for sale (right) (Kissembo and Namuli, 2021).

Figure 5.3 Some uses in the back: briquettes machine (left), water tap (center), and toilet stalls (right) (Kissembo and Namuli, 2021).

Space-use intensity and urban formalization in African cities 169

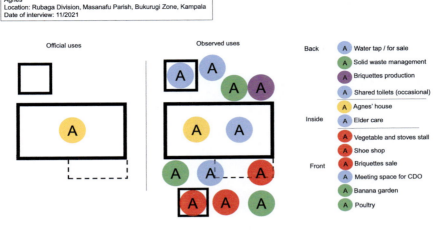

Figure 5.4 Visual record of observed uses in Agnes' house (Kapinga, 2021).

5.2.2 Neema's house in Dar es Salaam

Dar es Salaam, Tanzania's largest and fastest growing city, is situated on the Swahili coast of the Indian Ocean. The metropolitan area has roughly 1,400 square kilometers and is home today to seven million people, three-quarters of whom live in informal settlements. Administratively, Dar es Salaam is divided into five districts subdivided into wards.

This is Neema's house in the Ubungo district of Dar es Salaam (Figure 5.5). Neema shares her room with a friend. The house has five other rented rooms. Neema prepares *samosas* and other pastries, mixes peppered spices, and makes soaps, which she sells on the streets. She also uses the space outside of her room in the backyard to host weekly traditional ceremonies and dances from her tribe. These are lively and well-attended event, in which the whole neighborhood gets involved. Neema earns some money when hosting these ceremonies. In both streets of this corner house, there are commercial activities. Neema's *samosa* shop is next to one that sells fried chips. There is also a vegetable stall, a grocery shop, a cooking gas refill station, and a nail polishing shop (Figure 5.6). On the other street, there is a sports betting shop with some slot machines. Other tenants of the house use the shared outside space to raise chickens, dye *batiki* cloth, recycle metal parts, and make juice, all of which are later sold.

Neema's house story is far from exceptional. The 2016 World Bank's *Measuring Living Standards in Cities Survey*, which is statistically representative of both formal and informal areas, revealed that 80% of Dar es Salaam's households live in one or two rooms (Panman, 2021:237). Furthermore,

Figure 5.5 Neema's room in Ubungo, Dar es Salaam (Kapinga, 2021).

Figure 5.6 Neema making spices next to stored metal (left), shops from tenants (center), sports betting stall (right) (Kapinga, 2021).

evidence here presented estimates that 89.7% of the activities taking place in consolidated informal settlements in Dar es Salaam remain invisible to the city government, and yet they provide indispensable urban services, goods, and social protections that make life in the city possible.

The visual summary of the observed uses in Neema's house is shown in Figure 5.7 and discussed in Section 5.3.

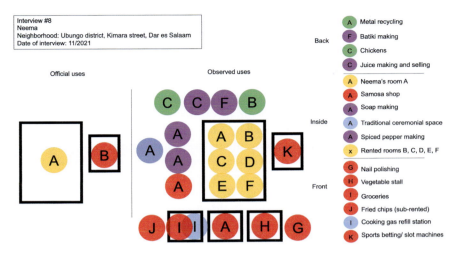

Figure 5.7 Visual record of observed uses in Neema's house.

Figure 5.8 Traoré's house in Grand Yoff (Ndiaye, 2021).

5.2.3 Traoré's house in Dakar

Senegal's capital Dakar is situated on the Cap-Vert peninsula on the Atlantic coast. The metropolitan area has roughly 550 square kilometers and is home to 4 million people, of which at least 40% live in informal settlements. Administratively, the department of Dakar is divided into four arrondissements and 19 communes d'arrondissements, composed of banlieues.

This is Traoré's house in Grand Yoff (Figure 5.8). Traoré is the third of four children. He and his siblings lost their father in 2005. Ten years ago, they began building on what were then bare barracks. Facing the street there are three shops: a hairdressing salon, a multiservice shop, and an imports shop selling second-hand appliances. Next to it is the entrance to the house. Rents from the shops bring Traoré an income of US$386. All shops have independent meters but share the bathroom inside the house.

The house has four rooms, one for Traoré's family of four and the others for his brothers and their respective families. A total of 15 people live permanently in this house. The corridor connecting the rooms and the shared kitchen is used as a guesthouse for incoming migrants from the south of Senegal. This is also the room used by a famous footballer, whenever he is in town (Figure 5.9). In this corridor, guests keep their belongings and boil tea to share. The stairs to the upper floor are in the kitchen, which Traore says is problematic because it gives direct access, and no rain protection, to the most private part of the house.

The real business of the family is sheep farming (Figure 5.10). The 50 purebred sheep they own are kept in three enclosures on the rooftop. The sheep were given by the government to Traoré and his brothers after their

Figure 5.9 Traoré's family room of four (left), the corridor/guesthouse (center), and the open-air stairs in the kitchen (right) (Ndiaye, 2021).

Figure 5.10 Sheep enclosures (left), food containers and drying clothes (center), sheep's waste recycling (right) (Ndiaye, 2021).

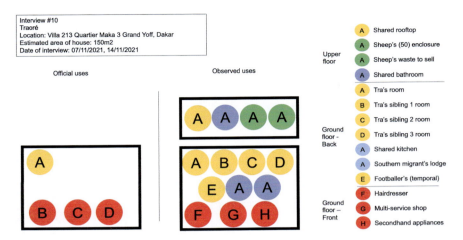

Figure 5.11 Visual record of observed uses in Traoré's house.

father's passing. This business brings in an average of US$8,570 per year and is especially profitable during festivities. In fact, the family wishes to construct a third floor to construct more sheep enclosures and expand the business. The rooftop is also used to dry clothes, keep the sheep's food, and recycle their waste, which is sold as fertilizer.

The visual summary of the observed uses in Traoré's house is shown in Figure 5.11 and discussed in Section 5.3.

5.3 Space-use intensity findings across African cities

As detailed in Chapter 3, following Jane Jacobs' (1969) ideas about mixed-use, "space-use intensity" addresses two key variables in spaces that multi-task: (1) *granularity* (the internal parts within an observed unit) and (2) *range* (a variety of types of uses). Or, in simpler terms, (1) different *users* within a house (independent households or independent businesses) and 2) different *uses* within a house (residential, commercial, industrial/manufacturing, services, and "green"— recycling or urban agriculture). The purpose of space-use intensity data is to compile a detailed count of the discrete uses and users within the studied houses, a simple but comprehensive tally.

Each house interview is documented with a visual record. The schematic layout of the plot is drawn in a plan view. Each use receives a color: yellow for residential, red for commercial, blue for urban or social services, purple for industrial or manufacturing, and green for recycling, urban agriculture, or livestock. Each colored circle has a letter representing different users. For each independent household or independent business, a new letter is added. The full story of all the observed uses can be read in the legend. Each visual

174 *Space-use intensity and urban formalization in African cities*

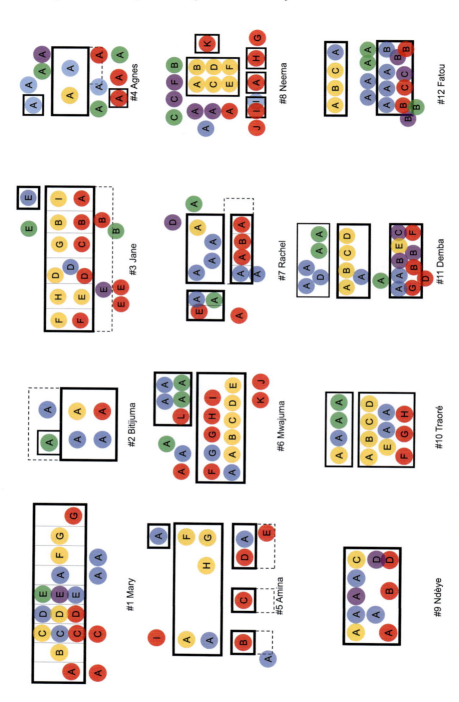

Figure 5.12 Visual summary of the 12 house interviews in African cities.

record includes a diagram that locates whatever the local government records (business permits, building licenses, land-use maps, and cadaster data) acknowledges that happens in this house. Figure 5.12 shows a summary of the 12 house interviews (four in each city) carried out in the Africa study. The original study in Bogotá collected 19 interviews (Figure 3.30).

After completing a visual record for each house interview, a complete list of space-use intensity variables can be extracted from them (Table 5.1). These numbers are obtained by reading the visual diagrams, ultimately by counting the number of colors and letters detailed in the legends of each diagram. A more comprehensive analysis could engage with greater detail in area measurements, density calculations, visits at different schedules (Kapinga, 2021), and more precise official information on each site. For the current exercise, the two key variables analyzed were: "use-units" that reflect granularity (number of independent households or business units per house, represented with letters) and "use-types" that reflect range (categories of uses often found on land-use maps: residential, commercial, services, industrial, etc., represented with colors). Before getting into the analysis of these two variables, a few comments are pertinent about the methodology itself and the process of interacting with the three groups of local researchers in Uganda, Tanzania, and Senegal.

First, it is fair to conclude that the methodology deployed was successfully adapted and applied across the different cities. Local researchers, all of whom were experienced, explicitly mentioned that they found it a useful, engaging, and novel way of looking into these settings. Notably, because the emphasis is placed on the house rather than on a single interviewee, researchers can collect data from neighbors and different family members for a more rounded and thorough perspective (Kisembo, 2021). More importantly, the input from local researchers strengthened the process, because in clarifying and supporting each data point in a group debriefing meeting, implicit bias can be identified and corrected via a collegial triangulation.

The second comment on the methodology is that it revealed that the very idea of what is a house varies widely. Of course, as a unit of analysis, a house is universal and is never devoid of meaning. But what a house entails in each context may differ considerably. To some, a house is a single room rented out within a larger structure. To others, it is a structure with several partitions and no windows, kitchen, or bathroom. It can also be a larger building with several rooms for members of various nuclear families and even guests, in other cases, it is a plot with ample spaces for crops and livestock. In this exercise, local researchers exercised their discretion in selecting the houses to be surveyed, within two firm criteria for selection. The first criterion was the ease of access, that is, that enough rapport with the interviewee was assured within the tight timeline of the project. The second was that houses were reflective of a "typical" living arrangement in their city, not poor not rich, not fully formal nor fully informal. In other words, "consolidated informal

176　*Space-use intensity and urban formalization in African cities*

settlements" (Ward, 2015), where the shades of gray between the formal and informal could be appreciated.

The third conclusion about the methodology is that the use categories (residential, commercial, services, industrial, and green) were relatively straightforward to identify. Two specific points could be revised to fit better the type of evidence that this data contributes. One, "storage" uses should be recorded, as often warehousing areas are indispensable for carrying out businesses elsewhere (the methodology only records those linked to recycling). The other point of improvement is a more precise definition of what the "services" entails.

It is important to differentiate service uses that are commercial (for example, an office that sells micro insurance) from services that offer public goods (be their facilities or amenities) to the community (for example, toilets, water, and spaces for community meetings). This distinction could be crucial for urban planning purposes and should be improved upon on future iterations of this research.

Lastly, having the same type of data from the original study in Bogotá, Colombia (Chapter 3), allowed for interesting comparisons. A crucial one is

Table 5.1 List of space-use intensity variables from house interviews comparing averages across cities

Space-use intensity variables	*Dar es Salaam*	*Kampala*	*Dakar*	*Bogotá*	*Total*
	n = 4	*n = 4*	*n = 4*	*n = 19*	*n = 31*
Observed use-units (letters)	9.3	4.5	5.5	4.2	5.9
Observed uses (colors)	4.3	4.5	4.8	3.6	4.3
Total count of uses observed	17.8	14.5	15.8	7.7	13.9
Residential	4.3	3.5	4.0	3.6	3.8
Services	4.3	3.8	4.5	0.9	3.4
Commercial	6.3	4.5	3.3	1.5	3.9
Industrial	1.3	0.8	2.0	1.1	1.3
Green	1.8	2.0	2.0	0.6	1.6
Non-economic	8.5	7.3	8.5	4.5	7.2
Economic	9.3	7.3	7.3	3.2	6.7
Total count of recognized uses[a]	1.8	2.5	3.0	1.4	2.2
Invisible uses	15.3	12.0	12.8	6.3	11.6
% Residential	23.9%	21.3%	25.8%	46.3%	29.3%
% Economic	52.1%	47.9%	45.8%	41.6%	46.9%
% Services	23.9%	30.8%	28.3%	12.1%	23.8%
% Visible	10.3%	16.3%	19.9%	18.5%	16.2%
% invisible[b]	89.7%	83.8%	80.1%	81.5%	83.8%

[a] These numbers are estimated, as the investigation on cadaster information is incomplete.
[b] Calculated using the total count of official uses, as per local government plans or databases.

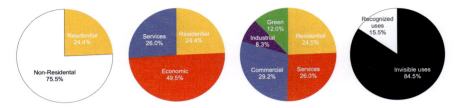

Figure 5.13 Space-use intensity data from house interviews in Kampala, Dar es Salaam, and Dakar (Carrizosa, 2022).

that the diagrams used to map the uses visually had to be plan views rather than cross sections, due to the fact that urban development in these African cities is less dense and more sprawled (Bhanjee and Zhan, 2018). This fact speaks of a potential for vertical development in African cities that is yet to be tapped (Baziwe, 2021). Consolidated urban areas are in general less compact, and hence they hold more potential than their Latin American counterparts for densification. Another interesting comparative insight is that less vertical consolidation is associated with more granularity (a larger number of use-units cohabitating within the same building or property).

As shown in Table 5.1, houses hold much more than one single household, and much more than residential uses alone. In fact, residential uses in the described houses are less than 24% of the total uses observed. In other words, the residential use is merely a quarter of what is happening in these houses. The economic uses within the houses, that is, either commercial, manufacturing of any kind, recycling and urban agriculture, represent almost half of what happens inside these houses: 46.9%. Finally, services, meaning community areas, urban services like water or sanitation, or commercial services like repair shows, account for 23.8% of the uses within these houses. This is a high percentage compared to previous findings from houses in consolidated informal settlements in Bogotá, Colombia, where services only account for 3%. Data for African cities is shown in Figure 5.13.

It is worth noting that this research is qualitative despite its quantitative outcome. With this small sample, which is not statistically representative but qualitatively, we are able to estimate the extent of what local governments are ignoring. Based on our research in these three cities, we estimate that 84.5% of the activities are being ignored. In other words, one could say that 84% of African cities are yet to be recognized, understood, and supported.

These findings reveal that informal settlements cannot be thought of as residential areas, because doing so would render invisible too much work, services, capacities, challenges, and possibilities. For policy to be smarter at dealing with urban informality and support it better, a more detailed knowledge of what happens in informal settlements is indispensable.

The intense use of residential spaces proves that houses in Africa are for much more than sleeping, in fact, their residential use is less than a fourth of

178 Space-use intensity and urban formalization in African cities

what they accommodate inside. In houses, people work offer community services, maintain businesses, and save for the future. Houses serve as employment, as social protection, and as service providers. In consolidated informal settlements, residents provide for themselves and their communities whatever is not provided to them by the city governments. Informal neighborhoods and their residents internalize the services they do not receive through formal channels. In other words, social protections and urban services are being co-produced by the citizens. People are contributing much more to making life in the city possible than their municipal governments. Rather than labeling this state of affairs as good or bad, the point here is to acknowledge the extent of these activities, so that policy can be fine-tuned to these realities and be more effective and just. For policy to get smarter at supporting people, experts need to recognize that a house in an informal settlement is much more than a place of residence. The next section delves into this.

5.4 African insights on formalization

This final section channels the voices of ten African experts collected in online interviews between November 2021 and May 2022.[1] The interviews were arranged by FES representatives in Uganda, Tanzania, and Senegal as part of the Just City in Africa project, led by Bastian Schultz from FES' Kenya Office and the Tanzania Housing Working Group, spearheaded by Elisabeth Bollrich from FES' Tanzania Office.

The experts who shared their views are: Oumar Cissé, Executive Director, Institut Africain de Gestion Urbaine and Chair of the African Network of Urban Management Institutions (ANUMI) in Senegal; Gaston Kikuki, Director of Vikundi vya Biashara Ndogo (VIBINDO) Association of informal traders of Tanzania; Tumsifu Jonas Nnkya, Former Director of Housing, Ministry of Lands, Housing and Human Settlement Development, retired professor Ardhi University in Tanzania; Albert Nyiti, Assistant Research Fellow at the Institute of Human Settlements Studies (IHSS), Ardhi University, and housing specialist from The Just City Working Group in Tanzania; Dave Khayangayanga, Acting Director of Housing, Ministry of Land, Housing and Urban Development of Uganda; Sarah Nandudu, Vice-Chairperson of the National Slum Dwellers Federation of Uganda; Amin Tamale Kiggundu, Head of Department of Architecture and Physical Planning, Makerere University in Uganda; Dorothy Baziwe, Executive Director, Shelters and Settlements Alternatives (SSA) Uganda Human settlements Network; Felician Komu, real estate expert and Chief Editor of The African Real Estate Society (AfRES) Research Journal in Tanzania; and Tatu M. Limbumba, Senior researcher Ardhi University in Tanzania.

---

1 All personal interviews are cited in the text using the interviewee last name and year when it was made. Further details of each interview are listed as part of the bibliography.

All these experts are public officials, community leaders, or academics actively involved in formalization policies, both urban (that is, of housing and settlements) as well as of businesses (be they shops, rentals, trades, or manufacturing of any kind) in their own cities, and often beyond. Their perspectives are presented in two blocks. First are comments about the conceptual *framing* of informality followed by ideas about best to *deal* with it.

5.4.1 Framing informality

5.4.1.1 Informality is mixed with formality and appears everywhere

In line with the continuum school of thought on informality (Chapter 2), African experts acknowledge that informality does not exist in direct opposition to, nor is isolated from, formality. Rather, both are part of a gradient, a mix. Strongly committed to Southern knowledge-production, Nyiti is quite observant of the informality in the formal, and the numerous gradients and mixtures between the two:

> In the interphase between the formal and the informal there are a lot of layers and interaction between these layers that are easy to miss, unless one is very careful. There are so many forms of informality in the formal. This complicates the way we should be labeling them, because many unplanned settlements are not informal settlements any longer as they've been regularized. And many formal settlements develop informally so they become unplanned.
>
> (Nyiti, 2021)

Nyiti details three types of urbanization: "formal but unplanned" (formal with informal origin), "informal but regularized" (informal formalized), and "planned but informalized" (formal but informalized). Navigating these mixtures is crucial, and sadly, it does not happen enough: "these layers, these realities, are not documented, so we are indeed missing a lot" (Nyiti, 2021). The lack of documentation, clarity, visibility, and legibility about these realities is problematic. It is a kind of blindness, as will be later explained.

Complementarity between formal and informal urban areas is seldom exploited by policy, yet it is as old as urbanization itself (Mumford, 1961) and accentuated in bigger cities (Sassen, 2002). Nnkya (2021) goes further and assures that the "mix actually helps regularization policy." Mixed-income settlements accelerate formalization by providing more diverse economic environments, as higher-income neighborhoods demand locally available products and services that can be offered by lower-income residents. The mix, then, promotes local markets.

On the same topic and with incisive precision Nandudu, a seasoned Ugandan community leader, explains this same phenomenon in Kampala: "we have big developments, but they also need cleaners. These cleaners cannot afford to go there from very far. This is why we need the informal in the formal" (Nandudu, 2021). Later, she adds:

> We need housing typologies that can accommodate different categories of people as we transit from informality to the formal. She calls this type of mixture "inclusive formality", and explains that without it, "people will just sell what they have made in the city and go back to the village. This is bad, this means people would lose it all."
>
> (Nandudu, 2021)

The fact that informality does not exist in direct opposition to, nor is isolated from, formality, is in Africa an easier grasp. Informality has long been "a victim of excessive dichotomy," states Cissé, who insists dualism should be replaced with "trialism," discriminating two types of informality (Cissé, Gueye and Sy, 2005), one more beneficial than the other. He takes this argument further, stating not only that there are types of informality but also grades of formality. For this Senegalese expert, urban formality is informalizing, it is changing so that: "the formal is becoming less formal" (Cissé, 2021).

According to Limbumba, the desegregating mixture of formality and informality is post-colonial. Tanzanian informal settlements—*uswahilini*—used to be quite distinct from formal ones—*uzunguni*—which were planned, were occupied by Europeans, and had larger plots. At first, and in many people's imaginaries, *uzunguni* did not informalize. But currently, informal subdivisions within formal *uzunguni* settlements are more and more common. She gives the example of Oyster Bay, initially owned by the government, then it passed the property to residents, who have been subdividing the plots (Limbumba, 2022). Subdivision is one of the most important processes in the formalization continuum, as I will address later.

5.4.1.2 When the problem is not informality but formality

Tanzania's former Director of Housing and Urban Development Ministry and retired professor bluntly claims: "our interventions in informal settlements do not work" (Nnkya, 2021). Indeed, stories about formalization projects, programs, or policies that, while well-intentioned, betray their own purpose abound. Even though their unjust outcomes get engraved in the minds and hearts of those aware or old enough to remember, the same type of initiatives resurges again later, with slightly different guises.

The Namuwongo slum upgrading project in Kampala is well remembered by many. Initially, it was deemed a success for being able to erect 135 new houses in a former slum. But the residents found themselves incapable of adjusting to the requirements of a formal settlement, like paying utility bills, garbage fees, and the like, so most sold their rights and went back to encroaching someplace else, creating a new slum elsewhere (Baziwe, 2021). Another example of the problems with formality is when formal businesses

Space-use intensity and urban formalization in African cities   181

deliberately informalize recently formalized areas. Baziwe sees this frequently happening in open areas or public spaces in upgraded informal settlements that fought to get schools and community spaces, but which are taken up by corrupt private investors, entrenching new cycles of urban informality. Speculators see some of these areas as development opportunities and purchase the land from those who do not own it, so they can claim ownership (Baziwe, 2021). This sort of ill-intentioned, perverse re-informalization is bound to happen more in settlements and communities that are more consolidated, and which have struggled for their urban services the most.

Kiggundu sees this as an example of how formalization that includes only physical upgrading and overlooks local economic development, ends up being "planned eviction" (Kiggundu, 2021). Leader of local, national, and international community savings groups (BAMU, NSDFU, and Slum Dwellers International (SDI)), Sara Nandudu explains: "if there's no affordability, we are simply doing a very polite eviction ... if houses are too expensive, people cannot afford to live there and this leads to automatic self-eviction" (Nandudu, 2021). Cases like this abound; hard-fought and well-intentioned but incomplete, and hence destined for failure. Clearly, if the urban invisibles are not understood and seen, planning, even if well-meaning and sound, will bypass them.

Similar experiences have happened in business formalization. For example, Kikuwi got involved with VIBINDO in 1998, when Dar, "as a result of its new city master plan, started persecuting informal traders, beating harassing, confiscating their goods" (Kikuwi, 2021). The informal businesspeople got organized, not so much to fight back, but to guarantee representation. Twenty years later, the government issued the Blueprint law (GoT, 2018), removing 200 regulations to facilitate formalization: e-registration of businesses, national e-card, and the like. However, "its impact is very minimum ...worse than that, de-formalization is what they actually do. The government is encouraging more informality" (Kikuwi, 2021). Not the outcome these De Soto advocates expected.

5.4.1.3 Missed innovations, either forgotten or overlooked

Urban informality has long been in the face of the governments, academics, and the community leaders in Africa and across the South. Plenty of innovations—theoretical, practical, and legislative—have been deployed. Sadly, the topic seems to suffer from a Sisyphean fate, inventing and reinventing innovations that get forgotten or erased by prejudices, or by incomplete understandings. For instance, half a century ago:

In 1972, Tanzania issued a national law recognizing progressive development. It acknowledged that informal settlements are there because of our policy failures, failures of the system to deliver housing and services. 1972, that is even before ILO coined the term informal sector, even before Vancouver, before UN-Habitat existed, Tanzania recognized these settlements and argued they should not be eradicated but supported.

(Nnkya, 2021)

Nnkya explains that this 1972 policy meant a paradigm shift, reversing the more punitive 1960s law that advocated for slum clearance. With it, Tanzania understood informal settlements as valuable investments; the 1972 policy meant political recognition of informal settlements. In 1978, it also inspired the architecture and planning programs at Ardhi University to gear its curriculum to respond to this law. Ardhi incorporated lessons on upgrading and taught students how to physically improve the settlements. Even though the curriculum did not expose planners and architects to business and tenure topics (which were only reflected in urban laws in 1995), this was completely innovative at the time (Nnkya, 2021). This disciplinary focus is still innovative, and sadly, uncommon.

In fact, reflecting on the history of housing policy in Tanzania, Nyiti is not optimistic. He explains that the first independence policies of the 60s strove to help the poor and to make housing central. While good-intentioned, resources were scarce, so the state-led housing provision efforts resulted in few houses being built and much slum clearance (Nyiti, 2021). Later, the housing policy shifted to embrace sites and services projects where the government provided land and access roads, but people built their own houses: "we were told you need to own your own house" (Nyiti, 2021). While this might have provided a solution to the scarcity of resources and weak government capacity, it had an excessive emphasis on home ownership that only works for some. He concludes: "the government is not being fully responsible for the mess they've created: the government is not helping the people get from point A to point B" (Nyiti, 2021). In fact, it is best to come to terms with the notion that the legacy of sites and services[2] programs is not one of failure, but one of incomplete success (Owens et al., 2018).

Another example of missed innovations or potential is mentioned by Kiggundu, the head of the Architecture and Physical Planning Department at Makerere University. He critiques the way decision-makers not only misunderstand informality but also forget and scorn African traditional values, simply because they do not conform with Western paradigms. Kiggundu argues that it is non-sensical for local governments to disregard the contributions to maintain the urban infrastructure of communities, inspired in traditional practices. An example is Kiganda's "bulungi bwansi" practice of "community service," which instills in people a love to care for their place,

---

2 Housing alternative championed by the World Bank in the 1970s as an effective slum prevention policy. The model (deployed by Latin America's CINVA in the late 1950s), proposed "the delivery of incremental housing for the poor through the provision of small-serviced plots, sometimes with a core unit" (Owens et al., 2018:260).

Space-use intensity and urban formalization in African cities   183

their nation, and their kingdom. Bulungi bwansi encourages communities to get together to fix a pothole in a road, or clear the bushes, and these types of activities. However, the local government does not allow it.

> The KCCA [Kampala Capital City Authority] argues citizens cannot construct nor fix roads, because they do not know how to do it well. Denying this impulse to collaborate, denying people's dynamism is absurd, when in fact the government does not have the capacity to respond everywhere.
>
> (Kiggundu, 2021)

In a similar vein, Ndezi and others highlight the theoretical potential of the maisha bora" or "good life" principle, which they compare to UN-Habitat's Prosperity Index. Maisha bora is indeed quite powerful as a more rooted theoretical construct that can synthesize and efficiently communicate complex and interrelated urban topics. Interestingly, Ndezi's research has shown that *maisha bora* prioritizes livelihoods, among the many issues (Ndezi et al., 2020). Taking traditional concepts more seriously could help in making policies that adequately address the most daring challenges, like designing workable urban financing models. "We need to be more imaginative and more inclusive. Informality needs to be thought of as an opportunity for city revenue" (Kiggundu, 2021). A scholarly and pragmatic attitude that does not overlook but incorporates traditional knowledge, values, and everyday practices, is a more sensible approach. Recognizing the inputs, and not just the drawbacks of informality, is simply a more reasonable baseline for public action.

Incorporating grounded types of knowledge has proven difficult. On this point Nandudu explained the hurdles faced by SDI self-enumeration data collected from more than 7,700 slums worldwide. "We have done a lot of enumerations, but local governments are taking a lot of time to accept them. Their bureaucratic systems do not recognize ours...they feel community data is not authentic" (Nandudu, 2021). Khayangayanga confirms this and explains that at first

> local governments claimed the data was informal, not standardized. But then there was a process with the Ugandan Bureau of Statistics and the World Bank, after which there is some appreciation for this data, especially since SDI collects data more regularly than what the governments are able to do.
>
> (Khayangayanga, 2021)

However, despite some acceptance gained, the actual use of this data by the local government is very narrow. "Now it is mainly used to identify local community projects" (Khayangayanga, 2021), this is a gross underutilization of a highly detailed and actionable data resource.

5.4.1.4 Blindness that goes both ways

In his 2007 book, *Why Planning Does Not Work*, Nnkya denounces the "professional blindness" of planners. In this ethnography land-use planning (or anti-planning) he argues that planners fail to see the opportunities for inclusive planning that become available with community input. He contrasts this blindness with the job of land surveyors, who walk the land and see more, and make an effort to translate into lines on paper what they see on the ground. The book shows how it was a residents' regularization plan that was executed (thanks to a court ruling) while the local government sat, irrelevant, in their office (Nnkya, 2007). This "fable" of planning blindness and assumed irrelevance is, sadly, widespread. It should be a call to open eyes.

The extent of professional blindness to what happens in the city is widespread. Professional or technical knowledge is restricted to the small percentage of the city that is not informal, which at most is 30% of the city (Nnkya, 2014) (Cissé, 2005). Accordingly, the rules are designed for that meager 30%, and outside of it, they have no impact. For instance, in Uganda, the Registration of Titles Act (amended in 2020), the Building Control Act (2013), and Condominium Property Act (2001) exist only for the formal real estate (Baziwe, 2021). The rules overlook (and are overlooked) by informal urban developers.

Nandudu believes urban regulations should never disregard those that in effect are making the city—the people themselves. In terms of businesses, it is the same: "rules are designed for formal employment, they have no meaning in the informal sector" (Kikuwi, 2021). This is why Kikuwi argues that rules should be designed by those who know the issue at stake best; and adds: "businesspeople know their trade better than everyone. And people who spend their time reading and writing do not" (Kikuwi, 2021). Even those in the government acknowledge that: "we need to use different lenses to understand these realities" (Khayangayanga, 2021).

To be fair, the blindness goes both ways. People living and working in informal systems know very little of about formal systems. As explained, this partly has to do with the fact that formal and informal are so mixed, so that "those living in it do not see the difference between formal and informal" (Nnkya, 2021).

At the same time, a more disconcerting idea was raised by long-time Makerere academic Kiggundu:

> All we see here is informality, informality, informality. We need to see something different at work. We need model cities within the developing world. Like the small green city of Putrajaya in Malaysia, funded in the 70s. We need to see how a functioning city looks like.
>
> (Kiggundu, 2021)

It is important to confront directly and seriously this kind of "worldling" impulse (Ong, 2011). How does one respond to African aspirations that emulate global models of sustainable cities? Disregarding these impulses can surely lead to the irrelevance of Just City campaigns, relegated to only persuade those who are already convinced.

5.4.1.5 Mindset issues

Urban informality has stigma attached to it that obstructs learning from it. The idea of taking advantage of it, of making the most of its potential, remains problematic for both technicians and welfarists alike. There is much learning, and some unlearning to be done. Kiggundu advocates for the

> need to introduce short courses on slum upgrading and informality to benefit city managers, planners, private sector and NGOs ... [we need to] train new change agents and leaders in city planning and management... even at the parliament, because it is them who decide on the national budget.
>
> (Kiggundu, 2021)

In a similar vein, Kikuwi explained that: "the biggest challenge to recognition is the mindset from the authorities. They see informality as a nuisance, as stubborn. They can't think outside the box, they don't see there is no box! 97% of businesses in Tanzania are informal" (Kikuwi, 2021).

Kiggundu goes further to claim that: "we need new types of leaders... more imaginative, more talented, more flexible" (Kiggundu, 2021). But he is not confident this is easy, because:

> Schools have not changed much in the last 60 years. Teachers are mostly trained in Europe, and they come back wanting to implement what they learned there here, which is impossible... what people like me studied in Western schools does not work here.
>
> (Idem: 2021)

"The things that matter in African cities are not prioritized in Western schools...the conventional planning system does not recognize informality, yet the reality is mostly informal" (Idem, 2021). Southern urban planning, while active and promising (AAPS, 2021), is not seen as mature enough, not even within the continent. Knowledge production and theory building remain anchored in colonial structures that see Africa as an immense repository of data to be cropped and extracted from, at best, with assistance from local universities (Pieterse, 2015).

5.4.1.6 Housing policy needs to re-align with the majority

The center of the housing policy at the national leaves appears to be misaligned with the real needs and possibilities of the urban majorities. Focusing on formal mortgages and refinancing of new constructions dismisses the fact only "2.7% of the urban households can afford the cheapest newly built house" (CAHT, 2021:13). This means there is a mismatch between the solutions being offered and the problems that abound. This housing policy, focused on formal solutions, disregards the real needs and possibilities of the majority. The core of the challenge is misplaced setting aside the fact that 90% of residents do not have trunk sanitation infrastructure (Ndezi, 2022) to prioritize the financing of new buildings. If 70% of the urban areas are informal (Komu, 2022) (as is the income of its residents), then why focus the policy primarily on the formal minority? When 98% of the housing stock is self-built (Limbumba, 2022), this is the city. A city already there, that needs support. Given this reality, housing policy ought to look very different.

The form of housing policy that Africa needs may contrast with conventional expectations. Necessarily, for housing policy to be effective and just, it needs to firmly center itself in the needs of the majority: it should not shy away from embracing informality. Upgrading efforts need to be bolder, the servicing of informal settlements needs to be more widespread and more generous. Aligning the center of housing policy with the informal reality should not be seen as unbecoming or unambitious. Coming to grips with the reality is not aspiring to less but having the courage to appreciate the heroic minutiae city-making efforts of the people and accept them as part of the national urban identity.

5.4.2 Housing policy needs alternate housing vocabularies: nyumba(ni) and (ma)kazi

As a unit of analysis, a "house" is universal and is never devoid of meaning. But what a house entails in each context may differ considerably. To some, a house is a single room rented out within a larger structure. To others, it is a structure with several partitions and no windows, kitchen, or bathroom. It can also be a larger building with several rooms for members of various nuclear families and even guests. In other cases, it is a plot with ample spaces for agricultural crops and livestock. Also, Swahili speakers often disregard the difference between housing and settlement, using the words *nyumba* and *makazi* interchangeably (Nyiti, 2022). More importantly still, work and residential

Figure 5.14 Swahili word for settlement is more closely related to the word work than to the house.

uses are indistinguishable, as the very word for neighborhood, *makazi*, shares the root word *kazi* (Figure 5.14). Commercial activities are also merged with residential in Swahili: "a typical 'commercial building' 'nyumba ya biashara' which directly translates to 'commercial housing' in English" (Nyiti, 2022). Perhaps more effective working vocabularies can come from grounded realities and its research. As Limbumba argues, concepts like space-use intensity can broaden urban planning and management because "traditional housing statistics can only get us so far" (Limbumba, 2022). This reflection on language is quite profound and ought to be addressed with all its philological rigor. For now, I will just echo the comments of Obeng-Odoom (2021), who claims the need to expand the taxonomies to think housing beyond the common disciplinary traditions and conventional theories of value.

5.4.3 Dealing with informality

5.4.3.1 What is the current purpose of formalization?

This question was the centerpiece of conversations with African experts. As a rule, most initially gave a single straightforward answer: "to widen the tax base, that's it, nothing else" (Kikuwi, 2021). All of them had much more to say about this, and to many, it was very clear that formalization has different purposes for different stakeholders.

Baziwe was most thorough in addressing the multiplicity of perspectives. She detailed six perspectives. "For the city government, formalization means order," she said. For the slum dwellers, formalization means paying taxes that they don't want "because they don't feel taxes tie back to a way of supporting their businesses grow … [taxes are not] being reflected in the development that they are getting" (Baziwe, 2021). For civil society organizations, formalization means having more services for the community. For policymakers, it means having "functional investments," that is, safeguarding the investments done by and for the high-income urban development areas, while guaranteeing the small-scale businesses that service them. For real estate private developers, formalization works the most, because it attracts more middle- and high-income businesses to an area. But for informal real estate actors, formalization is the worse, because it closes their scope, as their business thrives in unclear tenure systems (Baziwe, 2021).

Nyiti concurred with this faceted view, saying that for the government, formalization's purpose "is to have an accountable central system, to be able to know what there is" (Nyiti, 2021). For slumdwellers, he added, formalization is the way to have the security of tenure, which is a positive thing for them, since it enables accessing a "bundle of rights." He said that for academics, formalization is missed opportunity. "It means we are not curing the problem. Because as we regularize, more people move to the outskirts" (Nyiti, 2021). He's not only concerned with uncontrolled urban sprawl, but with the fact that urban planning is not done from a Southern perspective, giving tools directly to the people who are really making the city.

Nyiti also explained that for the local government guaranteeing access roads is an important requirement for formalization. He argued that the "regularization project, the Urasimaji Wa Makazi Holela[3] is some sort of baptism where town planners [give existence to these houses on the maps] while land surveyors [do it with beacons on the ground]" (Nyiti, 2021).

With two decades of experience as a Ugandan housing policy officer, Khayangayanga argues there are three main purposes of formalization from the government's perspective. With regard to business, to widen the tax bracket (curiously, he did not mention this in relation to property taxes (Mirondo, 2021)). With regard to housing and settlements' formalization, to provide urban infrastructure. Lastly, another purpose is to combat urban crime better. Here, he mentioned that the National Identification System helps tracking down unlawful activities (Khayangayanga, 2021).

From Kiggundu's perspective, there are at least three types of purposes. One is physical upgrading or modernization. He regards upgrading as beneficial because public investments (be they new roads, or modern markets) are followed by people's voluntary improvements. The second type are simply organizational mergers like the associations of matatus and boda boda drivers promoted recently by the Ministry of Transport (a model to be followed in other urban subsectors) (Kiggundu, 2021). The last type mentioned were the updates to urban physical standards. Kiggundu gave the example of the re-zoning of the upscale neighborhood of Kololo to reflect recent small-scale commercial developments. Tellingly, the example shows that if this can be done for higher-income areas, it can be done in lower-income areas as well.

Sara Nandudu concluded that there was nothing wrong with the policies, especially since she's appreciative of the fact that KCCA officers have expressed interest in partnering with communities to improve the settlements.

> I think this purpose is good, however the question is how is it going to be done. We may have to do away with the slums or informality, but the people must not be done away with. The how is the question.
>
> (Nandudu, 2021)

Insights like this make it evident that there was more agreement on what the policies should do, but less clarity and consistency in how to put them to work. And, as was mentioned before, how not to betray formalization's very purpose when enacting the specific policies.

---

3 Urasimaji Wa Makazi Holela, the Swahili name for Dar es Salaam's most important regularization policy (geared towards road accessibility) is automatically translated as "Arbitrary Settlement Bureaucracy" (Google Translate, 2021), a sort of omen for its uselessness.

5.4.3.2 What should be the purpose of formalization?

Many experts concur with the realization that formalization should not be a purpose in and of itself, and that as a policy intention, it is simply wrong. Furthermore, the idea that the goal of formalization is integration is incomplete. As many experts have noted, the integration alone, and legibility of informality into government structures, is far from a desired endpoint.

Cissé, who is not only a wide-ranging expert on urban informality (with research in solid waste management, urban agriculture, and flooding in informal settlements, among other issues) but is also recently interested in Senegalese city politics, explained:

> The issue is not to formalize; this is not the way to produce the city. The formal production is failing to produce a system with equity and diversity. Informal actors have the capacity and have proven to be successful providers of sustainable solutions. If you formalize, the risk is that you'll lose this capacity; and governments do not have capacity to spare, their capacity is already very limited... There is simply too much opportunity here to ignore.
>
> (Cissé, 2021)

One of the most detailed statements about what should be the purpose of formalization policy came from Kikuwi, leader of the VIBINDO Society, a member-based organization of informal manufacturers, traders, and service providers. Kikuwi argued that "the purpose of formalization should not be to formalize, the purpose should be transformation … transformation from informal to formal" (Kikuwi, 2021). "There are two components to transformation," he stated.

> One is recognition. We need to understand better who workers and businesses are in terms of gender, age, sector, and why they work in what they do...the second component is incentives: conducive working spaces, finance, social protection, skills' training, appropriate technologies, and marketing.
>
> (Kikuwi, 2021)

Such a two-pronged approach to formalization, with recognition and supportive components, is fundamental. Cissé concurred with this when he stated: "recognition might not be enough: the objective should also be to support" (Cissé, 2021). Khayangayanga talked about a "supportive infrastructure," that goes beyond physical and legal support, and also considers information systems that can be useful for regular citizens.

Since there can be no real formalization without recognition, and since recognition cannot happen without more accurate knowledge of informality, legibility-enhancing efforts are fundamental. These can include censuses, cadasters, and enumerations, among others. Legibility that can lead to recognition can be attained through different channels. For instance, recent research in Dar es Salaam provides substantial evidence that informal institutional arrangements are "surprisingly effective in securing ownership and addressing transaction costs" (Panman, 2021:230). Up to "75% of informal owner–occupiers say they are not at all concerned that someone may take their property away from them without their permission" (Panman, 2021:233). Leaders from the lowest level of government—subwards or *mitaa* (streets)— serve as witnesses to transactions. Ward tribunals effectively resolve conflicts, making the informal system more functioning than its formal alternative. If the effectiveness of this system were better recognized and taken advantage of, formalization processes would be streamlined. Another noteworthy example is the online platform MyDalali.co.tz that registers informal real estate brokers (*dalalis*) serving as a control for their integrity, mapping crowdsourced real estate information, and facilitating transactions with potential clients. An example of a legibility-enhancing effort in the path toward the formalization of the *dalali* business.

Indeed, to see formalization simply as integration of informal activities into the official structures will hardly ever be regarded by citizens as beneficial. Many authors have discussed the evils of "pernicious assimilation" that drains the livelihoods out of informal practices and gives little back (Kamete, 2018). In other words, "there is no right without on obligation … the government has no right without servicing its people" (Kikuwi, 2021).

From Nandudu's perspective, the link between housing and livelihoods is what makes formalization work well. "Housing makes formalization affordable," she stated, adding:

> Housing determines the type of informality you have. Housing is key to transform formality into formality. [Formal] housing should respond to economic factors that can allow people to have a business at home. This is important because it's important that people can afford moving from informality to formality.

(Nandudu, 2021)

Her perspective goes to the core of the problem with formalization and hence to determining what working formalization policies should be like. If formalizing and remaining formal has a cost, then it should envision a way by which people can afford these costs and thus reap the mutual benefits of transformation. Formalization without incentives, without a supportive structure, is nothing else than a mirage.

5.4.4 Can formalization of horizontal property make taxation fair?

Despite the understandable political controversy, substantial public investments across the South inevitably require increased collection by either "widening" or "deepening" the tax base. Thus, the important question to ask is how knowledge of space-use intensity relates to taxation. Specifically, how to guarantee it is fair and viable while preventing it from being exploitative.

It is broadly recognized that African cities need to capture the benefits of its accelerated urbanization and reinvest this value for the common good. Among the fiscal policy options, expert urban development economists deem that "property taxes are fairer and more efficient than other types of taxes" (Collier et al., 2018:2). Further, they argue that land and property taxes represent "the largest source of untapped municipal revenue" (Collier et al., 2018:4).

Komu (2022) explains how Tanzania had been making good progress at this:

> Arusha was performing exemplary well, collecting as much as $1 million USD. But when the national government realized this potential, it nationalized it. Everything changed in 2016. The system became charged via the electricity bill for anyone with a meter, not property owners. So, this is not a property tax, and obviously not local revenue!

Tanzania's levying of property taxes through electricity bills has rightly been deemed both innovative and exploitative (Makakala, 2021). Indeed, it has elements of both. On one side, the system widens collection by fragmenting the client base, which means cheaper bills that are likelier to be paid. But on the other hand, it is unfair that while the tax is tied to urban buildings, the revenue stream flows away from the city government, which should be using it to service precisely those areas that are more intensely used. Intensely used areas should be paying more taxes (even if in minuscule fragments) but at the same time they should be receiving corresponding municipal investments and maintenance.

Another way to approach property taxation that widens collection while becoming cheaper (hence likelier to be paid), is to promote horizontal property subdivisions. In fact, horizontal property laws were invented to encourage affordability and ease transactions. Horizontal property arrangements, that is, formal subdivisions, can become a partner and not a rival of urban formalization. Limbumba acknowledges that the upgrading of informal settlements often triggers subdivisions, and laments this as a contradiction— formalization triggers more informalization (Limbumba, 2022). However, subdivisions also mean that the city is becoming more compact, denser, and more walkable, all of which are tenets of sustainable urban development. What is important is that subdivisions are as legible as possible. This entails giving *mtaa* leaders, who are close to the issues, mandate to enact urban control when there are serious health hazards (Limbumba, 2022).

Discussing taxation is always politically unpleasant. It can only stop receiving so much backlash if residents and governments understand that taxes are the cost people pay for the provision of good public goods and services. If people see high-quality goods and services, taxes would be seen as worthy.

192 *Space-use intensity and urban formalization in African cities*

For example, the bar here is quite low in Tanzania. A recent FES survey of more than 2,000 households in formal and informal settlements in Dar es Salaam revealed that: "only about one in ten participants expected the government to provide them with the service because they paid tax" (FES, 2021:38), of course, the lower the income the less people expect (79%), and women expect even less than men (FES, 2021:40). Perhaps we can read this low baseline optimistically. If municipal governments give quality infrastructures to those that less expect to receive them, the social contract will become stronger and healthier.

5.4.5 Policy should include people's co-production of urban services, goods, and social protections

A co-production approach to urban goods, services, and social protections would reconceptualize public provision, not as a matter of "the-state-does-it-all," or "the-private-sector-does-it-best," but as one that welcomes regular citizens, especially those who are majoritarian subjects and objects of government action. Numerous examples of synergistic collaboration between public and informal stakeholders to improve service provision have been documented across different sectors (Meagher, 2013), such as waste management (Nzeadibe, 2013; Parra, 2020), water and sanitation (Ahlers et al., 2014), housing and urban planning (Watson, 2014), and social protection (Tokman, 2007; Steiler, 2018).

Informal housing arrangements play a social protection role for many people. Houses with intense uses, especially economic uses, offer protection for their residents in times of need, acting exactly as social insurance (as a source of life insurance in times of death, severance or unemployment payments, and the like). It does take some degree of intellectual flexibility to understand that social protections can take many forms and that some of those forms can be spatialized, even photographed, if one dares to look close enough. But at the same time, *using their spaces as social protection* is just a natural way of getting by in the city, and in fact, the notion that housing is used as a pension, and old-age security and fundamental patrimony to leave one's offspring, is connatural to urban development, a widespread practice of the poor (Torres in Carrizosa, 2021) and the well-off too.

Co-production understands, pragmatically, that when addressing joint state and market failures, partnerships are the key to achieve effective, on the ground, scalable success. This is one of the reasons why for local governments it is indispensable to recognize informal activities—not to erase informality, but to lay the true baseline from which to build a more just system, to lay bare people's assets, however fragile, fractioned, or seemingly disorganized they look on the surface. The intense economic and urban services activities happening in consolidated informal settlements should not only be recognized but also supported. Attaining just cities in Africa requires supporting social

infrastructure, co-production can simply mean devolution of responsibility, so it becomes exploitative, and hence an opportunity for redistribution is missed (Chen, 2006). Without a creative, spatialized, and unbridled support structure to help informal service provision of goods, services, and social protections to perform better.

References

AAPS – African Association of Planning Schools. (2021). *Urban Africa in the 21st Century: Current Issues and Future Prospects of Urban Governance and Planning*, 5th AAPS – Conference, November 18–20.

Ahlers, Rhodante, Cleaver, Frances, Rusca, Maria, and Schwartz, Klaas. (2014). "Informal Space in the Urban Waterscape: Disaggregation and Co-production of Water Services", *Water Alternatives*, 7:1, pp. 1–14.

Baziwe, Dorothy. (2021). Personal interview, November 17.

Bhanjee, Sheliza and Zhan, Charlie H. (2018). "Maping Latest Patterns of Urban Sprawl in Dar es Salaam, Tanzania", *Papers in Applied Geography*, 4(3), pp. 292–304. https://doi.org/ 10.1080/23754931.2018.1471413

Carrizosa, Maria. (2022). *Urban Informality and the Making of African Cities*, Friedrich-Ebert-Stiftung, Nairobi.

Chen, Martha A. (2006). "Rethinking the Informal Economy: Linkages With the Formal Economy and the Formal Regulatory Environment", In Guha-Khasnobis, B., Kanbur, R. and Ostrom, E. (eds) *Linking the Formal and Informal Economy: Concepts and Policies*, Oxford University Press, Oxford. https://doi.org/10.1093/0199204 764.003.0005

Chen, Martha A., Harvey, Jenna, Kihato, Caroline Wanjiku, and Skinner, Caroline. (2018). *Inclusive public spaces for informal livelihoods: a discussion paper for urban planners and policy makers.* Prepared by WIEGO for the Cities Alliance Joint Work Programme for Equitable Economic Growth in Cities, p. 17. WIEGO Limited, Manchester.

Cissé, Oumar, Gueye, Ndeye Fatou D. and Sy, Moussa. (2005). "Institutional and Legal Aspects of Urban Agriculture in French Speaking West Africa: From Marginalization to Legitimization", *Environment and Urbanization*, 17:1, pp. 143–154.

Cissé, Oumar. (2021). Personal interview, November 8, 2021.

Collier, Paul, Glaeser, Edward, Venables, Tony, Blake, Michael, and Manwaring, Priya. (2018). "Land and property taxes for municipal finance", Cities that Work, International Growth Center, LSE and Oxford University, UK Aid.

De Soto, Hernando. (2000). *The Mystery of Capital: Why Capitalism Triumphs in the West and Fails Everywhere Else*, Basic Books, New York, NY.

FES. (2020). Towards the Just City in Kenya, Friedrich Ebert Stiftung Kenya, Nairobi, http://library.fes.de/pdf-files/bueros/kenia/17107.pdf

FES. (2021). "Towards a Socially Just Urbanization in Tanzania", research report on Tanzania's General Urbanization and Migration Survey, White Paper.

Government of Tanzania – GoT. (2018). Blueprint for Regulatory Reforms to Improve the Business Environment, Ministry of Industry, Trade and Investment, Government of Tanzania, Dodoma.

Guven, Melis and Karlen, Raphaela. (2020). Supporting Africa's Urban Informal Sector: Coordinated Policies with Social Protection at the Core. Africa Can End Poverty, World Bank Blog. October 29, 2021, https:// blogs.worldbank.org/africacan/supporting-africas-urban-informal-sector-coordinated-policies-social-protection-core

Perry, Guillermo, Maloney, William, Arias, Omar, Fajnzylber, Pablo, Mason, Andrew, Saavdra-Chanduvi, Jaime. (2007). *Informality: Exit and Exclusion*, World Bank, Washington, DC.

ILO. (2015). *Transition from the Informal to the Formal Economy Recommendation, 2015 (No. 204)*, International Labour Organization, Geneva.

ILO. (2018). *Women and Men in the Informal Economy: A Statistical Picture* (3rd ed.), p. 24. International Labour Organization, Geneva.

ILO. (2020). *Report on Employment in Africa (Re-Africa) Tackling the Youth Employment Challenge*, pp. 1–2. International Labour Organization, Geneva.

Jacobs, Jane. (1969). *The Economy of Cities*. Random House, New York. https://doi.org/10.1002/ ncr.4100580916

Joshi, Anunradha and Moore, Mick. (2004). "Institutionalised Co-production: Unorthodox Public Service Delivery in Challenging Environments", *The Journal of Development Studies*, 40:4, pp. 31–49. https://doi.org/10.1080/00220380410001 673184

Kamete, Amin. Y. (2018). "Pernicious Assimilation: Reframing the Integration of the Urban Informal Economy in Southern Africa", *Urban Geography*, 39:2, pp. 167–189. https://doi.org/10.1080/02723638.2017.1298219

KCCA. (2012). *Updating Kampala Structure Plan and upgrading the Kampala GIS Unit, Draft Final Report*, Kampala Capital City Authority, Kampala.

Khayangayanga, Dave. (2021). Personal interview, December 8.

Kapinga, Imma. (2021). Debriefing meeting with local researchers, Urban informality and the just city in Africa, FES – TNS, December 3.

Kiaga, Annamarie and Leung, Vicky. (2020). The Transition from the Informal to the Formal Economy in Africa, Global Employment Policy Review Background Paper #2, International Labor Organization (ILO), Geneva.

Kiggundu, Amin Tamale. (2021). Personal interview, November 17.

Kikuwi, Gaston. (2021). Personal interview, November 9.

Kironde, Lusugga. (2021). "Focusing on Housing Could Catapult Tanzania Into Higher Development Levels", *The Citizen Newspaper*, July 8, https://www.thecitizen.co.tz/tanzania/news/business/focusing-on-housing-could-catapult-tanzania-into-higher-development-levels-3466056

Kisekka, C. (2019). Buganda Subjects Urged to Promote Community Service among Youngster, Uganda Radio Network, https://ugandaradionetwork.net/story/buganda-subjects-urged-to-promote-community-service-among-youngsters-

Kisembo, Teddy. (2021). Debriefing Meeting With Local Researchers. Urban Informality and the Just City in Africa, FES – TNS, December 3.

Komu, Felician. (2022). Conversation With Members of the FES-Tanzania Housing Group, Personal interview, May 4.

Limbumba, Tatu Mtwangi (2022). Conversation with members of the FES-Tanzania Housing Group, Personal interview, May 4.

Makakala, Charles. (2021). "Tanzania: Taxation Decisions That Reflect Desperation, Innovation." *The Citizen*, 2 September 2021, https://allafrica.com/stories/202109020823.htm

Meagher, Kate. (2013). Unlocking the Informal Economy: A Literature Review on Linkages Between Formal and Informal Economies in Developing Countries. WIEGO Working Paper #27, April.

Mirondo, Rosemary. (2021). TRA starts collecting property tax via Luku today, *The Citizen News*.

Mumford, Lewis. (1961). *The City in History: Its Origins, Its Transformations, and Its Prospects*, Harcourt Brace Jovanovich, New York.

Nandudu, Sarah. (2021). Personal interview, November 24.

Ndezi, Tim, Woodcraft, Saffron, Osuteye, Emmanuel, and Makoba, Festo D. (2020). "Pathways to the 'Good Life': Co-producing Prosperity Research in Informal Settlements in Tanzania", *Urban Planning*, 5:3, pp. 288–302.

Ndiaye, Amadou. (2021). Final Report from House Interviews in Dakar, Urban Informality and the Just City in Africa, FES – TNS, Personal communication, December 6.

Nnkya, T. J. (2007). *Why Planning Does Not Work: Land Use Planning and Residents' Rights in Tanzania*, Mkuki Na Nyota Publishers, Dar es Salaam.

Nnkya, Tumsifu Jonas. (2014). *Financing Affordable Housing in Tanzania: Policy, Initiatives, Challenges and Opportunities*, Presentation to the 6th Global Housing Finance Conference, Washington, DC. May 29, http://center4affordablehousing. org/wp-content/uploads/2019/01/Session6.2_TumfisuNnkya.pdf

Nnkya, Tumsifu Jonas. (2021). Personal interview, November 10.

Nyiti, Albert. (2021). Personal interview, November 29.

Nzeadibe, Thaddeus C. (2013). "Informal Waste Management in Africa: Perspectives and Lessons from Nigerian Garbage Geographies", *Geography Compass*, 7, pp. 729–744.

Obeng-Odoom, Franklin. (2021). "Urban Housing Analysis and Theories of Value", *Cities*, https://doi.org/10.1016/j.cities.2022.103714

OECD. (2020). *Africa's Urbanisation Dynamics 2020: Africapolis, Mapping a New Urban Geography*. West African Studies, p. 4. OECD, Paris. https://www.oecd-ilibrary. org/development/africa-s-urbanisation-dynamics-2020_b6bccb81-en

Ong, Aihwa. (2011). "Introducing Worlding Cities, or the Art of Being Global", In Roy, Ananya and Ong, Aihwa (eds) *Worlding Cities: Asian Experiments and the Art of Being Global*, Blackwell Publishing, Oxford, pp. 1–28

Ostrom, Elinor., Guha-Khasnobis, Basudeb. and Kanbur, Ravi. (2006). "Beyond Formality and Informality. Linking the Formal and Informal Economy: Concepts and Policies". https://doi.org/10.1093/0199204764.003.0001

Owens, Kathryn, Gulyani, Sumila, and Rizvi, Andrea. (2018). "Success When We Deemed It Failure? Revisiting Sites and Services Projects in Mumbai and Chennai 20 Years Later", *World Development*, Elsevier, pp. 260–272, https://doi. org/10.1016/j.worlddev.2018.01.021

Panman, Alexandra. (2021). "How Effective Are Informal Property Rights in Cities? Reexamining the Relationship Between Informality and Housing Quality in Dar es Salaam", *Oxford Development Studies*, 49:3, pp. 230–244.

Parra, Federico. (2020). "The Struggle of Waste Pickers in Colombia: From Being Considered Trash, to Being Recognised as Workers", *Anti-Trafficking Review*, 15: pp. 122–136. https://doi.org/10.14197/atr.201220157

Pieterse, Edgar. (2015). "Epistemological Practices of Southern Urbanism", In Ding, W., Graafland, G. and Lu, A. (eds) *Cities in Transition II Power, Environment, Society*, Nai010 Publishers, Rotterdam, pp. 311–325.

196 *Space-use intensity and urban formalization in African cities*

Rakodi, Carole. and Lloyd-Jones, Tony. (2002). *Urban Livelihoods: A People-centred Approach to Reducing Poverty*, p. 3, Earthscan Publications Ltd, London.

Republic of Uganda – RoU. (2001). Condominium Property Act, Uganda Gazette, 12:904. February 23, UPPC, Entebbe.

Republic of Uganda – RoU. (2013). Building Control Act, October 2.

Republic of Uganda – RoU. (2020). Physical Planning Amendment Act, January 10.

Roy, Ananya. (2005). "Urban Informality: Toward an epistemology of planning", *Journal of the American Planning Association*, 71:2, pp. 147–158. Chicago, IL: American Planning Association.

Roy, Ananya. (2009). "Why India Cannot Plan Its Cities: Informality, Insurgence and the Idiom of Urbanization", *Planning Theory*, 8:1, pp. 76–87. https://doi.org/10.1177/1473095208099299

Sassen, Saskia. (2002). *Global Cities and Diasporic Networks: Microsites in global civil society. Global Civil Society 2002*. Chap. 9, pp. 217–238, Oxford University Press, London.

Steiler, Ilona. (2018). "What's in a Word? The Conceptual Politics of 'Informal' Street Trade in Dar es Salaam", *Journal of Urban Research*, pp. 17–18. https://doi.org/10.4000/articulo.3376

Tokman, Victor E. (2007). Modernizing the informal sector. DESA Working Paper No 42. United Nations Department of Economic and Social Affairs, New York.

Varley, Ann. (2012). "Postcolonialising Informality?" Environment and Planning D: Society and Space, University City London, Print Vanek, Joan, (1974), "Time Spent in House Work", Scientific American, November 1974.

Ward, Peter. (2015). "Housing Rehab for Consolidated Informal Settlements: A New Policy Agenda for 2016 UN-Habitat III", *Habitat International*, 50:2, pp. 337–384. https://doi.org/10.1016/j.habitatint.2015.08.021

Watson, Vanessa. (2014). "Co-production and Collaboration in Planning – The Difference", *Planning Theory & Practice*, 15(1), 62–76. https://doi.org/10.1080/14649357.2013.866266

WIEGO. (2021). Social Protection Glossary. Women in Informal Employment Globalizing and Organizing, https://www.wiego.org/ resources/social-protection-glossary

6 Conclusions. Abling intensity

Extraction, porosity, and the recognition continuum

The three previous chapters dove into the intricacies of the use of space in cities in the South. How people in consolidated informal settlements extract the most of their houses, how the complexities of policy in regulations hinder formalization, and how local experts make sense of the fallacies of formalization. This concluding chapter leaves the colored local minutiae and exposes its conceptual underpinnings by presenting some metaphors that resonate within and between the empirical and the theoretical findings.

The first one is that *space is porous and that informal practices saturate those pores*, so that people extract value (often monetized, but not always) out of seemingly barren places, as if "squeezing water out of a rock". This procedure is not necessarily painstaking nor unreasonable but is more historically and geographically common than what is usually accepted. Moreover, it is quite different from what traditional cadastral surveys account for space-use. By tallying the uses observed in the filled-up pores of houses in consolidated informal settlements, one finds *how much more* is there than what is assumed or apparent. More than twice the activities found in residential buildings in Bogotá are economic, rather than domestic, and a third of the activities in the African sample are urban or community services. These facts compel a different definition of what these neighborhoods actually are: beyond residential they are sites of production, accumulation, recycling, urban services, and social protection.

The second lesson is that counting more of something enables, or empowers, a larger share of it, while not accounting for it is disabling. Not counting is crippling. This means that when the intensity of space-use is not accounted for, large swaths of our cities are systematically being disabled, they are incapacitated rather than enabled. Counting and accounting for economic spatial practices that are regularly ignored or invisibilized severs the real capacities of our cities. This research—I hope to show—is not a cry against injustice nor a celebration of resourcefulness. Instead, it is an exercise of responsible optimism. I claim that more nuanced accounts of urban life have an enabling power. I dare for scholarly research that is responsible enough to care about the world unselfishly, applying intelligence and sensibility to enhance the agency and accountability of those less privileged.

DOI: 10.4324/9781003297727-6

198   *Conclusions*

6.1 Visual research: data excavation from photographs and conceptual maps

Qualitative and quantitative research methods are thought to be at opposite ends of a spectrum (Creswell, 2014:32). Researchers are generally either good wordsmiths or capable statisticians. Likewise, consumers of one type of knowledge regularly fall prey to this tunnel vision. In the methodological spectrum words seem to lie on one end and numbers at the other end. Mixed methods research designs sequence qualitative and quantitative phases, but seldomly blend these two. My research is a bit different; it defies these siloes. It is qualitative in its general approach and in its instruments of data collection and analysis, but unlike most qualitative research, my aim is not to ascribe and interpret socially embedded meanings. Instead, my research is intentionally pragmatic. The conclusion of my methodological journey can be summarized in simple numbers. The numbers I have arrived at are both a synthesis and an invitation to action. First, I will describe the process of extracting numbers out of qualitative observations, and then, I will explain how this synthesis is in itself an invocation.

I call "data excavation" the layered process through which my "house interviews", as opposed to "resident interviews", allowed me to *unearth* evidence about space-use that could be tallied. Counting here was not an immediate act where numbers followed one another, but one where each point was progressively discerned and carefully arrived at. Each number was discovered. Like an archeologist at an excavation site, treasures were found by brushing away dust, uncovering layers of awareness. Sediments to be removed were varied. Some refer to what people intentionally hid from me, like the reasons why Alba washes young men's clothes. Others were unintentional silences, like activities so quotidian that people engage in them inadvertently. And others still refer to economic activities that do not seem economic because they are non-monetary, like recycling. Especially stubborn were the sediments I brought myself to the interview, with my want-to-learn-from-you attitude and frequent paraphrasing during the interviews. In this case, my words muffled the findings and dirtied the very pieces of evidence I wanted to observe. This only got better once I internalized the topics I wanted to touch upon during my visits; but purposefully forgot the—carefully crafted—interview questions. In this sense, the word "interview" is somehow misleading here because talking often stood in the way of other markings. What proved to be most useful in removing these sediments were the images and photographs.

I took photographs of every space of every house I was allowed in. Of course, just asking permission to photograph ordinary life was awkward, so I played it down by being deliberately quick and acting with carelessness. When, a month after the visits, I focused on reading the photographs, I realized that the more impromptu the photographs were, the richer they were, bearing witness to deeper layers of data. This is very obvious, for instance, when comparing the photographs from Teresa versus Rosa's rooms. In Teresa's house, where the house visit was completely unplanned, there were t-shirts

Conclusions 199

and vests with logos of community and government institutions scattered near her desk, revealing her parallel and conflicting work allegiances, which she never disclosed in conversation. On the other hand, when I visited Rosa's home, every room was so spotlessly tidied, it felt emptied out, without hints or trace of extra uses. I knew photographs would be important, but I had not imagined they were going to prove so instrumental, nor *by how much*. Even photos of the outside were revealing. For instance, the façade of Alba's house has a gas ventilation inlet that does not correspond with the kitchen nor bathroom inside, so rather than serving any real safety purpose, it is a mock-up gesture to comply with the regulations. Inadvertently, the photographs silently helped me capture the information I was too full of words to absorb during the visits.

Data excavation is the process of revealing data in sequenced layers, progressively adding depth and accuracy. The first level of data retrieval is the register of the actual use of plots, a task any conventional cadaster does and maintains. More proactive cadasters monitor consumption of data from utility companies as well as real estate advertisements (Bogotá uses both to periodically update its records), and this is a second level of data retrieval. A third level are on-foot recognition brigades, something very few cadasters have the institutional bandwidth or resources to do (Bogotá stopped its city-wide recognition brigades in 2004 [Amaya, 2019]). Beyond this level, data extraction happens via surveys or interviews that generally do not feed into official cadasters, not even the official ones. The depth of surveys and interviews increases substantially with home visits at different schedules and by cross-questioning multiple residents or neighbors. For example, the self-enumerations carried out by slum dwellers in Mumbai (at different times of the day and week and by cross-referencing community members) revealed the extent of undercounting of official data was 1:4 (Beukesm, 2015:6). In my research in both Latin America and Africa, the extent of undercounting of use-units uncovered by my house interviews was 1:2.68. Further, continuing the data excavation process with the detailed reading of the photographs, the undercounting rate my sample revealed was 1:2.94. An almost one to three rate is certainly not negligible, considering that Bogotá's land-use plan is particularly open to mixed use,[1] that it has a particularly diligent cadaster, and that in the African cities business formalization efforts have a deep reach.

---

1 The pandemic opened up the world to mixed use by calling into question the separation between home and work. It became evident to all how kitchen tables, garages, verandas, and bedside desks, where instrumental to keep the world running. Of course, this is not new, in fact, it is the separation between home and work that represents a historical anomaly. The 19th cottage industries worked like this, so does the peasant economy. More recently, in 1992, for example, 50% of all US firms operated from home generating almost $500 billion annually (Gonzalez and Gray, 2020). Abstruse standards (like mandating extra parking spaces, or only allowing clock repair and millinery services) make this intensification of space a widespread informal practice in the United States. Recently recognized as a policy problem, the Housing Supply Action Plan rewards jurisdictions that eliminate single-use zoning laws (The White House, 2022).

200   *Conclusions*

In presenting this data excavation ratio (1:2.94), my interest goes beyond illuminating blind spots in the official data. Undercounting is an important, yet unsurprising fact. Cadaster information will always lag behind the real use dynamics, and in this sense, full legibility, that is, 1:1 registers are not only an ever elusive ideal (Borges, 1960), but often times an undesirable one, as many "adverse incorporation" critics denounce (Meager, 2013:63). Increasing the legibility of the informal to the gaze of the state, is not always beneficial. Indeed, critical social studies tend to see invisibility as a "weapon of the weak", part of the arsenal in the tools of resistance. However, advocating for legibility, as my research unmistakably does, is not the same as standing against the uncounted as long as the aim of legibility is clear, fair, and "abling" as I will explain later on. James C. Scott acknowledged this is one point on which he is most misinterpreted: "Legibility is morally neutral… legibility is a capacity and, as such, is not morally worthy or unworthy in and of itself. It depends on the *purpose* for which it is used" (Scott, 2010). Arguing that legibility is morally neutral is a tough sell, especially in progressive circles. However, the important point made here by this progressive scholar is to break the automatic association of legibility as "bad", intrusive, or adverse. My emphasis on counting intends to do just that, rather than labeling legibility along a good-bad moral axis, I "describe evaluatively" (Fergusson, 2007:79) that is, simply put, I *count how much* space-use intensity I observed.

At this point, it is interesting to compare the data extraction capabilities of my space-use methodology with that of the aforementioned recent experiments with image-based time-use surveys (what is known as photo-elicitation). Researchers at the Centre for Time Use Research (host of the Multinational Time Use Study, the largest collection of comparative and historical time-use national data) explain that there are important data reliability issues when asking people direct questions about their daily activities. They reference "recall bias": "respondents may be unaware of the total amounts of time devoted to specific activities" (Gershuny, 2019:1), as well as "social desirability bias": "attempts to enact particular sorts of normatively sanctioned identities" (Gershuny et al., 2017:2). To overcome these biases, they have experimented with image-based surveys.

As explained in Chapter 2, in experimental image-based time-use surveys, photographs increase the likelihood of overcoming the mentioned biases and help capture a wider (or deeper[2]) range of activities. "The image-reconstructed day captured more than one and a half times as many activities compared with those reported in the self-report diary, with generally lower

---

2 "Robinson and Godbey (1997) conceptualize multitasking as the 'deepening' of time, although it may be more useful to consider the broadening of time, such that time is seen as a horizontal, non-linear entity, rather than a vertical, linear entity" (Kenyon, 2008:887). It might be fair to say that while temporal multitasking is better conceptualized as a broadening of time, spatial multitasking is better conceptualized as a deepening of space.

mean durations of activity bouts" (Gershuny et al., 2015:9). So, whereas image-based time-use surveys can add 1.5 more activities to a day, my image-based house interviews add almost thrice as much (2.94) activities to a house. While these methodologies are only experimental, tested on voluntary subjects, with no statistical representativity, and without reliability measures, both show promising avenues for valid data extraction. Furthermore, my research hints the scope for extraction is considerably larger in space-use than in time-use studies, a fact that calls attention to the importance of multimodal research.

Remaining open to multiple modes of research proved as relevant as remaining open to multiple voices within one's research itself. This was most evident tracing back one of the three language puns I came across with (the other phonetic mix-ups being "sacrifice" for "certify," and "suicide" for "subsidy"). When Lucy, talking about her economizing strategies said proudly said she was an economist, she was not misusing the word, nor being ignorant. She was actually revealing a powerful yet, heterodox, hidden truth about the economy, not about economics. This completely resonates with Ellerman's[3] account of Jane Jacobs: "a one-person antithesis to orthodox economics (...) [she] studied economies, rather than economics" (Ellerman, 2005:76–77). Lucy, the heterodox informal economist went further on to tell me how to value extraction works in her informal savings and loans: "I had two million; I spent three, and I'm left with two" she softly said while proudly smiling.

My research experience taught me that data extraction can also take place from visual mapping. I want to take a moment to reflect not on the cross-sectional diagrams of uses within the houses (which are also maps), but on the conceptual visualizations I produced as part of the policy analysis in Chapter 4: Figures 4.2, 4.3, and 4.5. Navigating the arid maze of decrees and obscure regulations was proving a Sisyphean task before drawing these visual maps. This time, visualization was not only an instrumental step in the document analysis, but it became an inflection point: only after feeling confident with these conceptual maps, and after testing their accuracy with local experts, did I find enough confidence to begin to write. Having a map to transverse the confounding territory of regulations proved reassuring and helped make sense of an otherwise unintelligible landscape.

In all three cases, the images map discrete policies on a continuum between informal (in black and located on the left-hand side of the drawings) and

Figure 6.1 Visualization of the continuum between informal and formal.

---

3 Philosopher, economist, and mathematician interested in workplace and property theory, who worked as an Advisor to Stiglitz at the World Bank.

formal (in white and on the right-hand side) (Figure 6.1). This deceivingly simple orientation is quite meditated and purposeful, it has a meaning that is not always evident in the regulations. Every element mapped in my figures is strategically positioned: localization in the drawing adds a level of knowledge. It is not simply a matter of collecting similar phenomena in a drawing, but of organizing it, rendering visible their relationships. For instance, Figure 4.2 shows that there are different procedures to be followed by different types of settlements, and at the same time it explains there is a hierarchy of settlements. In this hierarchy both aspects are important: the sequence (vertical paths) and also the notion that squatting invasions and subsidized public housing are ultimately different types of the same kind of element: settlements (horizontal positioning).

In Figure 4.3, the importance of placing the urban treatments along the formal-informal continuum is crucial in revealing the easiness of transitions between the different treatments. It shows that areas subject to upgrading are cognitively and normatively distant from those of conservation. This visualization is successful in showing how difficult it is for urban policy to consider that areas of upgrading can have a heritage value and may one day be considered monuments to the self-help efforts of the communities that built them. It also clarifies why urban plans tend to focus on the lighter right-hand-side treatments and are increasingly difficult for the darker left-hand-side treatments. Placing the treatments in a formal-informal continuum is a simple

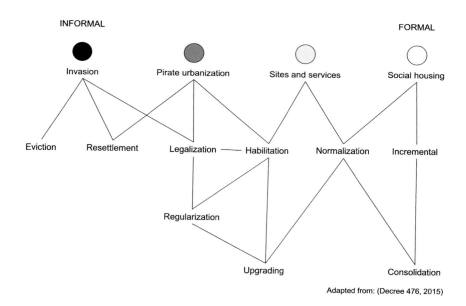

Figure 4.2 Map of formalization paths for different types of settlements. Adapted from (Decree 476, 2015).

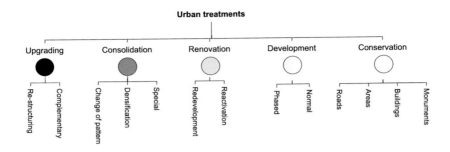

Figure 4.3 Map of formalization paths for different types of settlements. Adapted from (Decree 476, 2015).

cognitive devise that helps explain that policies are not supposed to freeze neighborhoods but ease left to right transitions, promoting changes from informal to formal. Dynamism between urban treatments depends on both knowledge of street-level realities and regular monitoring of what treatments are assigned to which districts.

Figure 4.5 is perhaps the most central to my argument because of what it reveals and also because of what it hides. This visual takes the transition from informal to formal, from black to white and left to right, a step forward by adding a vertical axis. The vertical view adds an additional dimension to the policy analysis: phases of formalization that span different and yet contiguous policy sectors from the bottom to the top of the stair. Formalization of plots and buildings (what is usually known as urban formalization) is placed in a continuum with business formalization (which includes employment formalization). Simply by positioning different types of formalization one after the other, I show that what is currently disarrayed collection of policies, are actually phases of one and the same process of formalization. They all have the same objective, formalization, even though they are relatively unaware of each other. City officers working in formalization at the economic development (León, 2019), planning (Botero, 2020), as well as in Curadurías (building regulation experts) (Bahamón, 2019), bluntly confessed this is the case.

Unifying formalization policies on upgrading (carried out by Caja de Vivienda Popular and Secretaría Distrital de Hábitat), recognition (Secretaría de Planeación Distrital and Curadurias), popular entrepreneurship (Instituto de Promoción de la Economía Solidaria), and business formalization (Secretaría de Desarrollo Económico), can help this specific policy area gain the conceptual consistency, efficacy, and budgetary leverage, it has lacked (Carrizosa, 2010). This visual formalization map connects urban and business

204   Conclusions

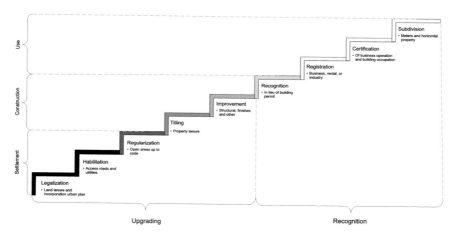

Figure 4.5 Visual map of urban formalization policy in Bogotá: Steps, phases, and realms.

regulations improving the understanding of formalization policy in Bogotá, and perhaps beyond.

The apparent simplicity of these maps is both an achievement of conceptual clarity and synthesis that contributes to the policy analysis. This is important because once something has been rationalized, it cannot be forgotten. However, at the same time it is also a problematic representation that fixates a specific view while muddling others. Acknowledging both facts is important. I will follow the geographer Denis Cosgrove here, to illustrate this point:

> Acts of mapping are creative, sometimes anxious, moments in coming to knowledge of the world… Their apparent stability and aesthetics of closure and finality dissolve with but a little reflection into recognition of their partiality and provisionally, their embodiment of intention, their imaginative and creative capacities, their mythical qualities, their appeal to reverie, their ability to record and stimulate anxiety, their silences and powers of deception. At the same time their spaces of representation can appear liberating, their dimensionality freeing the reader from both the controlling linearity of narrative description and the confining perspective of photographic or painted images.
> (Cosgrove, 1999:2) -or of ethnographic accounts, I would add-

As explained in Chapter 4, the image of the stair is utterly deceiving because it gives the wrong impression that these normative steps flawlessly transform informal spaces and practices into formal ones. A set of stairs is meant to take you up. But the reality is messier, far from linear, always disordered. The

Conclusions 205

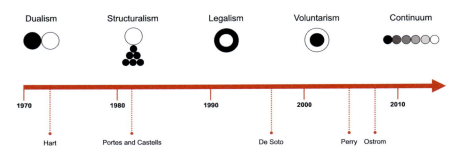

Figure 2.8 Chronological overview of the schools of thought on informality.

streamlined image of the rising stairs reflects the *purpose* of formalization policy in the first place, not its actuality. This visual policy map allows to make sense of the intentions, it helps arrive at a cohesive understanding of otherwise inchoate norms and previously disconnected sectors (i.e. urban and economic). But it fails to illuminate what could be a radically different policy purpose. This means that my formalization visualizations in Chapter 4 are better described as synthetic and descriptive communicative pieces than as tools to unearth invisible evidence, like the ones resulting from the house interviews in Chapter 3.

Yet another type of communicative visuals are the icons I designed in Chapter 2 to show the different relationships that the informal and the formal realms have in each of the main five schools of thought. These icons, shown in Figure 2.8 along a timeline, help the reader grasp structural differences in the way informality has been understood. In every case, a black circle represents the informal and a white circle represents the formal. The icons wordlessly communicate that these realms have relative sizes and that they have different types of relationships (specular, above/below, within/surrounding, or gradient). I regularly use these icons as teaching tools, helping students navigate this extremely convoluted conceptual landscape. Furthermore, as I confront new literature that claims to be innovative, or as I unpack old texts, designing these visual icons (Figure 6.2) helps discern what are really new ways of thinking from mere cosmetic changes.

The degree of distrust for visual research tools and methods is largely unwarranted compared to their potential to "enhance the richness of data by discovering additional layers of meaning, adding validity and depth, and creating knowledge. They add to traditional methods by capturing more detail and a different kind of data than verbal and written methods" (Glaw et al., 2017). Visual research will only gain more traction in the decades to come as disciplinary boundaries continue to bend mixing siloed approaches. The use

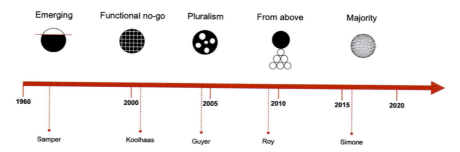

Figure 6.2 Alternative thinking on urban informality.

and literacy of visual research is also growing as the size of data repositories explodes and as transdisciplinary efforts bring in non-expert views into the core of knowledge building. I hope my approach and research can contribute to the larger task of legitimizing visual thinking as inseparable from traditional qualitative methodological approaches.

6.2 Porosity and value creation: counting more than the sum of its parts

Susy shares her house's bathroom with a soap shop, so she interacts quite often with the owners of this business. Just by mingling, she got a side job selling the cleaning products her neighbors make on their shared rooftop. This is a perfect example of how, through time and in the same space, the interaction between uses creates value and creates something out of nothing. Susy's side gig shows "the mysterious vitality of diversity" (Jacobs, 1980:113), it shows, in a nano scale, how economic growth first happens, and how it ignites. Intensity of use is creative in a way division of labor is not, Jacobs explained when refuting Smith. To be more precise, it is by agglomerations of diversity that division of labor can come into being, something that Smith blatantly ignored (Jacobs, 2003). Diverse use ecosystems create value, they "increase the well-being and viability of actors in reciprocally beneficial service exchanges" (Gummerus, 2013). It is fair to say that value creation is beneficial and productive.

By mere friction, the value that is created out of nothing, bit by bit, adds up. Therefore, recognizing the origins of value creation entails, quite simply, counting. Without counting, without accounting, value still exists, but it is unseen. Real recognition needs to go beyond identification and account for value creation. Recognition that does not count is incomplete. By counting, recognition raises what is being identified. It reveals things add up. Counting is political, it is an act of recognition. Recognition dignifies what it observes, and helps seeing things more whole. My research attempted to do just this.

The power of simple frequency counts should not be underestimated. As detailed in Chapter 3 and Chapter 5, the data excavated through observation, conversation, and careful reading of photographs was tallied to reveal the extent of space-use intensification throughout the 31 houses interviewed in Bogotá, Kampala, Dar es Salaam, and Dakar. I found that no house is just a house, and that invariably, these houses are being used beyond their 100 percent. Let me explore this idea. The total count of residential uses in my sample is merely 28% of the total uses, making non-residential uses majoritarian, 72%. Even before the pandemic, the domestic are the most porous of spaces. Their interstices fill with a plethora of economic uses and social services (manufacturing, recycling, caring, making, vending, storing, cropping, breeding livestock, servicing of public utilities, and worship). My data reveals that, simply put, houses are not what we think they are. They are not only houses. To think of them as mere houses, is to not understand them at all.

Furthermore, the Latin America sample showed that 81.5% of the activities remain invisible to the cadaster. Non-residential uses in houses are more than half, 54%, and of those, 97% are economical. This very high percentage speaks volumes about people's needs and priorities. Now, in the African sample, 84% of the uses remain invisible to the authorities. Residential uses within houses are less than a quarter, 24%. Interestingly, the share of urban services that houses hold is, 29%, which reveals the extent to which people have no option but to privatize and internalize government roles that are missing.

Despite the fact that both the planning instruments and the cadaster welcome and acknowledge the mixed-use nature of neighborhoods of progressive development, the extent of the space-use intensification acknowledged is far from accurate. In the Bogotá sample, the cadaster's account of use-units is just 34% of the total, and in terms of use-types, it is 39% of the total. Invisible, unrecognized uses are more than 60%. How should such invisibilization or misrecognition be interpreted? And conversely, what is the meaning of such vibrancy of intensification? What is the purpose of recognizing space-use intensity and how does it relate to formalization?

The concept of porosity emerged as an accurate and powerful means to interpret space-use intensity phenomena. Porosity helps explain the existence and capacity of the spaces within, helps assess the extent of residual voids (that are not empty, so are better called pores), and their role as pockets storing productivity, minute stock. Porosity can accurately describe what cannot be seen at plain sight.

Houses in neighborhoods of progressive development extract the most out of them. People commonly mention a good house is one which one can "take out from", to the extent that "*sacarle a la casa*" is a broadly understood

208   *Conclusions*

idiom for taking economic advantage of the pores of the house, making room within, squeezing it while maintaining it. Everyone wants a house that one can take out from, subdividing up or within. A better house is one that one can take out from more. For instance, a house on a commercial street can hold commercial subspaces in addition to residential or productive ones. A house in a corner can have more pores than one in the middle of the street. This is quite clear when comparing Lucy and Susy's houses. This fill-up of pores translates into more economic activity via small businesses, rental housing, and construction. In fact, in Bogotá (and these statistics are not distant from the ones in other Latin American cities (Moreno, 2008)), at least 40% of the cement purchased in the city is consumed in these neighborhoods, and in the same vein, 40% of the city's housing demand is met here as well (Torres, 2019a). The dynamism is undeniable, yet it is also elusive.

With sparkling eyes revealing the excitement that an outsider could be interested in such sunken technical subtleties, an experienced mid-level cadastral statistician explained to me that wherever there is a cluster of high use-units, as is the case of Patio Bonito, on-site recognition is requested (Amaya, 2019). Not always is on-foot recognition possible, he continued, but it does not make it any less necessary. A high number of use-units, or in porosity's terms, filled in pores, show more activity than what comes into view. Amaya suggests these numbers can help construct an alternative overcrowding index, or one to flag the need for urban services by locale. These are both promising, unexplored avenues. What has been advanced is to use the scores of use-units as a justification to raise property values. Torres points out that as a rule of thumb, Bogotá's property taxes for housing used to be in the order of a month of rent. However, when in the most recent adjustment, they were raised to about three months of rent, people voiced their discontent, of course, but payments did not falter (Torres, 2019a). "What does this really tell us?", he asks. This renders clear that the use-unit construct lacks a supporting theory, hence the difficulty of interpreting it or letting the idea enter the public academic arsenal.

As pores saturate, houses take in, absorb the many services that dwellers do not find publicly. Any service that is not met by the city, is satisfied this way. Absorbing urban responsibilities, these houses clog their inner pores, become more productive and more intense. Intensification takes advantage of spatial porosity, occupying residual voids, stifling every pocket of air. Space-use intensification frees oneself from depending on public services but asphyxiates the private realm. Unlike other types of violent choking, the porosity fill-up of these houses is yet unspoken for. Speaking for intensification or about it is marred with controversy, in part because while forbidding, it is also beneficial and even promising. Intensification takes out air but adds value, increasing carrying capacity, and supporting life. As spaces saturate, not only are they more vibrant, but they also start playing social protection roles, and filling the gaps left by absent or insufficient public urban services. Though not in spatial but only in social terms, Ostrom recognized this role in the 1990s, under the term "coproduction". Ostrom praised the potential of "coproduction of many goods and services normally considered to be public goods by government agencies and citizens organized into polycentric systems ... for achieving higher levels of welfare in developing countries, particularly for those who are poor" (Ostrom, 1996:1082). Specially in the face of the disappointing results of efforts of improving the capacity of public officials or contradictions in citizen participation (Ibid). I will return to the issue of coproduction of social protections and urban services later on in this chapter when discussing what the aim of formalization policies should be, in Section 6.4.

Before leaving the reflection on porosity I invite the reader to consider the image of a rotting carcass. While the automatic reaction to it is one of smelly disgust, the process of decomposition is central to the life cycle. As the carcasses decompose, worms hatch within the remains and bacteria covers the bones, providing critical sustenance crucial for the overall health of the ecosystem. In this sense, the carcass becomes a powerful analogy of informality for the post-industrialist philosopher Berardi: "capitalism is dead, and we are living inside its corpse, frantically looking for a way out of the rotting putridity" (Berardi, 2017:163). The intense space-use of informal houses in consolidated informal neighborhoods I have described is showing how life thrives within and between disregarded spatial interstices. People are inhabiting the carcass, filling up every pore until the structure that holds it all disappears or changes meaning. This is exactly what Koolhaas described of the way Lagos uses its crumbling infrastructure: "road embankments, the underside of private flyovers, railway tracks, and the city's multiple shorelines have been colonized by a host of secondary industries and services" (Koolhaas, 2001:674). Every void gets filled with economic activity used to its highest potential. This means not that infrastructure is unimportant and informality takes over completely, as there are no pores to be filled if there is no underlying structure to start with. Instead, infrastructure is that unto which urban life clings so it can thrive.

6.3 Imposed disability: the violence of remaining stratified and unrequited

I did not expect this research to arrive at a discussion on violence. In fact, I tried to avoid it. For example, when visiting Alba's house in Caracoli, stories about paramilitary gangs, girl trafficking, beheadings, and social cleansing (vigilante killings) were in the air (revert to Figure 3.28). I listened, observed, and took notes, but decidedly stepped away from those conversations. I was not looking for violence in my research, but I found it. The violence I am calling out is very different from the overt physical violence that, sadly,

210 Conclusions

my country is most known for.[4] Never outspoken, I had to uncover the aggressions before calling them out. I came to realize that what I was describing was a type of violence late in the research process, re-reading my own words. In Chapter 4 on formalization policy, violence is concealed under the mantle of the law. In chapters documenting space-use intensification, oppression is more hidden and more subtle still, though it is no less severe.

As was shown, the state of affairs in Bogotá is one where formalization of a mixed-use house in a neighborhood of progressive development is practically unachievable. Full formalization exists only as a mirage, an idealized status that eludes everyday realities. And as explained, the openness of the code itself clashes with the procedural impossibility to comply with it. The illusion of formalization becomes a form of permanent subjugation: silencing dynamic uses, interactions, and economies that provide work (as well as its associated social protections) and housing (as well as its associated urban services) for many. What makes the policy more disturbing still is that exclusion is bureaucratized and repression is technified. And when violence is sanitized it easily becomes excusable.

Intricate legal antics, allegedly a-political, reproduce a systemic classism that is hostile to those residing in informal systems. Most often, oppressive technicalities are born out of well-intended concerns, when efforts to close the gap between everyday dynamics and government's plans unintendedly backfire. Other times, legal technicisms are bluntly deployed as a smokescreen to depolitize public policy or programs. The housing movement in Colombia was a casualty of this depolitization, as was shown in Chapter 4. To be more precise, these are tactics of "repolitization" rather than "depolitization", because throwing a mantle of technical regulations is another way of annihilating political adversaries, tilting the balance to the benefit of those inside the norms.

For example, in 1992 this covert class warfare was evidenced in the differential treatment of two politicians who participated in the distribution of 3.8 million dollars[5] of city funds: Forero Fetecua, the pirate urbanizer turned congressman, and Vargas Lleras[6], then a councilmember born into the powerful family of two former presidents (El Tiempo, 1992a). The pirate's case scaled up to the Supreme Court, and he got jailed some 20 months

---

4 For over 50 years, Colombia has suffered the longest armed internal conflict in the Western hemisphere, accounting for at least 220,000 deaths, close to 2,000 massacres, 5.7 million internally displaced persons, and 25,000 forced disappearances (GMH, 2016). It is also home of three of the five worst serial killers in the world, including the grim World Guinness Record Garavito, who straightforwardly admitted raping and murdering 138 boys, of more than 300 cases under investigation (Morgans and Rodriguez, 2020).

5 The amount publicized in the press was $1,400,000 Colombian pesos of 1992 (El Tiempo, 1992b), adjusted by inflation and converted to 2019 USD.

6 It is noticeable that these men are commonly referred to including their second last name, which is not the norm in Colombia. "Fetecua" is a denigrated indigenous word and "Lleras" is the last name of two former Presidents.

Conclusions   211

after. Meanwhile, Vargas Lleras' case was treated with secrecy (Rodriguez, 2012:75), and even though his involvement was admitted (El Tiempo, 1992b), evidence against him was quickly deemed inconclusive. The case sunk into oblivion, leaving undisturbed his political career as Senator, Minister of the Interior and of Housing, Vice-President, and Presidential candidate. By the same token, Lemos, a former Vice-President asked quite rhetorically: "why are votes mobilized to elect Forero Fetecua bad, but votes to elect President Barco good?" (El Tiempo, 2006). Beyond this particular example, let us agree that class-based partiality is a form of covert violence.

But perhaps more central to my research is another form of veiled violence: invisibility. When people, groups, or phenomena are not seen, silencing and contempt pervade each other, so that invisibility leads to disrespect. "...[I]nvisible is what the contemptible are ..." (Miller, 1997:235). Of course, one cannot respect what one does not see. Similarly, not seeing what is evidently there is disrespectful, it is a form of indirect violence. Inflicting violence is easier on unknown subjects, othered, belittled, or presumed marginal rather than on what is familiar. This is why bringing back from invisibility is a powerful tool for dignification. The case of waste pickers, recounted in Chapter 4, is illuminating. Waste pickers in Colombia were for many years referred to with the insensitive misnomer "disposables" ("desechables"), as if they were indistinguishable from the trash they were collecting. One of the many remarkable consequences of the formalization process they underwent, was the fact that people started calling them "recyclers", a name that literally describes their work. Moreover, the official documents and their contracts referred to them as "service operators", a radical shift out from invisibility into recognizing not only their work, but also their role in urban public service provision. I will argue later that such a profound dignification could not have happened without them being paid for their services. Afterall, any recognition payment acknowledges a previous act of violence.

Recyclers had long performed this public service. However, without recognition, anyone remains invisible and undignified (Honneth in Iser, 2019). Their work efforts, and their contribution to urban sustainability, were not matched by the public. Not only is this state of affairs unfair, but it also keeps their agency and freedom away from them, it is a form of erasure. Let me elaborate on this point by saying that unrecognized is much like unrequited love. An etymological digression on the meaning of "unrequitted" is perhaps most useful here:

"The "quite" in "requite" is a now obsolete English verb meaning "to set free, discharge, or repay." ("Quite" is also related to the English verb "quit," the oldest meanings of which include "to pay up" and "to set free.") "Quiten," the Middle English source of "quite," can be traced back through Anglo-French to Latin *quietus* ("quiet" or "at rest"), a word which is also an ancestor of the English word *quiet*" (Merriam-Webster, n.d.).

Unrequited work is more than invisibilizing, it is annihilating. The violence of not being recognized does not stop from being quiet. It builds up,

212   *Conclusions*

reinforced by other layers of "epistemic violence" (Spivak, 1988:283) that I described earlier in relation to the centers of knowledge production. As an unfair status quo lingers, this type of violence builds up. The invisibility remains, cementing in time a posture of staying put. Informal, incapable of being granted a coherent form, invisible, silenced, quieted, incapable of "speaking back" (Spivak, 1988). Silencing disables, it removes from the public understanding of the *abilities* of informality. It is a form of ablism, a discrimination or prejudice against tracts of the city that are considered disabled, less abled, less urban. However, while quieted the informal continues holding on, living, growing, and filling up its pores. Intensifying its economic capacities and its social protection abilities.

6.4 Formalization: rather than integration, a recognition continuum

It is not a cynical conclusion to state that the problem with informality is formalization. Formalization has fallen short not because of undeniable implementation shortcomings but because it has been wrongfully understood. Formalization has never had an appropriate purpose because it has always been one-sided. Ostrom pinned this problem down when she argued that formalization is regularly counterproductive when it crowds out functional informal arrangements (Ostrom et al., 2006:18). Formalization, that is, more reach of government, is not necessarily always a good thing. More often, formalization that "helps" actually harms despite its intent (Ostrom et al., 2006:2). In the same vein, informalization is not necessarily bad. As Ostrom's research implies, it is *description* rather than *prescription* what is necessary to modulate the right level of formalization that works for each case. Beneficial policy interventions are not those that aim for full formalization, but those that strike the right balance of rules and informal practices. The notion that formalization is always desired is incorrect.

Without doubt, the most interesting question I asked my interviewees was: "what should be the purpose of the formalization policy?". To the residents, the question was simply empty. The very word formalization has no specific meaning. The answers I got were not fully fleshed, but it was absolutely evident that the question struck a deep chord with the experts. Eyes sparkled, people moved in their seats, and struggled to throw an answer immediately, only to find out they were uncertain about how to put into words their feelings that something is disturbingly wrong. Most strikingly was the hard-felt awareness, against the mainstream local and global narratives about upgrading, that *formalization is not integration.*

When I asked: "what should be the objective of formalization?" to Carlos Torres, author of the book *Informal City in Colombia*, he said: "well, definitely it should *not* be to incorporate into the formal" (Torres, 2019). He explained in his deep veteran voice that when formalization finally comes to a very few, it invariably does so with more collective and individual fiscal burdens than improvements in the quality or quantity of urban services received, putting into question its worth. While arguing that formalization only results in increased fiscalization sounds like an ideologized, almost automatic response, it is still true that integration cannot only mean, one-sidedly, to be included in the fiscal base. If so, the relationship between the people and the state, the social contract goes sour.

Ramírez' answer, or rather, his disproof of my question was illuminating. Doggedly dedicated for decades to the topic of recognition, in particular to the conundrum of structural reinforcement of informal constructions, Ramírez was energetic and short on patience when he argued:

I'm disappointed with architects. They still believe it is necessary to formalize informal settlements, when the sheer size of the phenomenon, and the incapacity of the formal market and of government institutions make it impossible (...) I'm fed up with academia. They keep saying nothing is known and nothing can be done in upgrading when the reality is that so much has been advanced already. I'm aware the feeling is mutual. Academia and us practitioners, we despise each other (Ramírez, 2019).

This disillusionment is reasonable and in fact quite widespread in broader debates on informality, as was shown in Chapter 2. Practitioners and academics forget each other's struggles and accomplishments all too frequently. As if maintaining informality hidden behind a curtain of "complexity" was a naturalized and unfixable status quo. Not because integration is well intentioned is it beneficial, in fact, because it looks sympathetic it is all the more dangerous. In order to shake these cemented, ideologized ideas, and move the discussion forward, reimagining formalization is necessary. It is crucial to part with the automatic association between formalization and inclusion on two grounds. First, the language of inclusion is othering and second, it is immobilizing. Speaking about the violent integration of the indigenous cultures during the colonization, Saramago, a theopoetic writer, explained:

Integration is often assumed to be a magic word, but the word itself is not enough to produce magic. Integration, to be authentic, must be an inter-integration. I become part of you, and you become part of me. However, this is not what we think about when we say "integration" ... integration [usually] means that "they" are incorporated into the dominant values.

(Saramago, 2007)

The purpose of formalization should not be, as is generally believed, to incorporate these neighborhoods, these workers, or these businesses into the rest of the city. Such a purpose is impossible because they are the majority of the city already. "Inclusion" policies label people, areas, and processes as marginal and fixes them into a constant condition of exclusion despite their predominance and their constant state of change and progression. Furthermore, the

214   *Conclusions*

integration purpose is impossible as long as the formal counterparts are not at the table too. It is no wonder that formalization continues to fail in delivering its equalizing promise. As long as the process is one-sided, its purpose is incomplete. Formal and informal are the idealized, non-existent extremes of a continuum (Figure 6.1). Recognition, the fulcrum of formalization, operates in this two-way continuum and must always be a bidirectional process. Intriguingly, in Spanish the word recognize, *reconocer*, is a palindrome, it reads both ways.

The notion of "continuum" comes from the adjective "continuous" which describes phenomena "held together" or "marked by uninterrupted extension in space, time or sequence" (Merriam-Webster, n.d.). A continuum is an unbreakable set, without distinct spaces between the values. In mathematics, for instance, "continuous" is the opposite of "discrete." In the lexicon I have introduced, a continuum is "non-porous" or "intense." A continuum is a "*coherent whole* characterized as a *progression* of values or elements varying by minute degrees" (Ibid, n.d.) (*emphasis* added). This definition is particularly useful to the field of urban informality because it brings into light two essential characteristics that have been brought up earlier: *progressive* development (a subject extensively documented in the two previous chapters), and the *wholeness* (or oneness as I rather call it) of what that cities are and should aim to be. Both these characteristics, *progressiveness* and *wholeness*, are not only fundamental, but they also constitute a radically different approach. One that once fully understood, cannot be forgotten: once informality is seen as a continuum, it cannot be unseen.

Informal settlements and buildings are in a constant state of progressive development. In fact, formal ones too. All buildings, neighborhoods, and cities themselves, as dynamic systems, are in permanent transformation. Urban change is constant, cycles of improvement and decay are connatural to the urban existence. As explained in Chapter 4, "progressive development" is a broader concept than the watered-down terms "site-and-services" and "self-help". The notion of "progressive development" links spaces to time, embracing permanent change as a dynamic, foundational fact. Neighborhoods of progressive development are not finished, they are being, they are constantly becoming. Such emphasis on time helps break away with the ingrained condescending look toward urban informality, one that has been amplified and reproduced unchecked by the spurious identification between poverty[7] and informality that was discussed in Chapter 2. In this sense, Samper's *Minimum Rules* legacy was revolutionary because it blurred the line that divides informal and formal, rich and poor. Samper carefully traced this line in a specific

---

7 It is worth noting that none of my interviewees self-identified as poor. This is even true of a woman who lives in an un-serviced wooden shack by a non-paved road and feeds on discarded foodstuffs she collects outside the vegetable market. When she told me that her blender got stolen, she showed not only moral indignation with the thieves in her neighborhood, but also a proud awareness of being more well-off than others.

threshold that made such distinction irrelevant. In fact, this is such a radical proposition, that it has been hard to believe it is real. It is hard for both experts and the regular public to accept that Bogotá has long deployed regulations that ignore the distinction between the formal and the informal. In Samper's theory of progressive and productive city-making, tracing that line, and adjusting it as the city evolves, is the key. This is exactly what Ostrom et al argued should be the purpose of policy, to aim for "just right" levels of intervention so that formalization does not crowd out functional informal arrangements.

The second characteristic of the continuum, that of wholeness or oneness, refers to the fact that a continuum is full, cohesive, and dense; always one instead of a set of elements that can be discerned separately. Discrete phenomena along a continuum are more than a disarrayed group, and more than the ordered sum of its parts. They are held together in one whole, a unity. The city is one. Adopting the language of the continuum to think formal-informal dyad, invites to think and to deal with range. Formal and informal positions have less relevance than formalization and informalization movements, and their pace and strength. Understanding formalization in the framework of a recognition continuum helps redefine its purpose and it clarifies that this aim is ever changing. What changes is the moment a building or settlement is in, but all moments are part of the city. All directions take part in urban development, those of improvement and those of decay. Those of addition as well as those of subdivision. The city is one, the role of policy is not to negate some urban statuses but to recognize and manage all movements enabling the whole.

Policies designed as a recognition continuum understand the issues they manage as a whole, as one, even though they entail different and even opposite operations. A good example of a recognition continuum is a taxation system that goes in two directions allowing those who earn a lot to pay more and those who earn too little to be paid. In a continuum like this, the aim of the policy is to modulate the breakpoint between contribution (tax paid) and retribution (benefit received). Colombia's tax system and Bogotá's property tax system are one-sided, meaning only those above a certain threshold of income and above a certain property value, must pay. No one receives as part of this same system. One-sided systems like these disconnect social benefits from taxation, and by ignoring the progression between one and the other, they miss important opportunities. Recent debates in new fiscal sociology about taxing the informal sector, argue that a continuum approach clarifies the relationship between the people and the local government and has the potential to reinstate the social contract (Rogan, 2019). Overlooking the two-sidedness of the recognition continuum easily leads to predation, as more often than not, informal workers already pay relatively high piecemeal *local* taxes (Meager and Lindell, 2013). On the other side, one-sided systems also run the risk of overlooking informal and yet full active partners of urban development.

216   *Conclusions*

Adopting a recognition continuum to address urban formalization is also a means of connecting different policy action realms that, when separated, increase the chances of contradicting each other or at least miss opportunities to reinforce actions. An interesting yet contested example of such connections is reverse mortgages, financial products that make housing serve as a pension. Unlike the case of Lucy, Susy, or so many other of my interviewees that use their house as a pension, the bank is the one that ultimately profits, not the residents' families. Reverse mortgages allow seniors who own their house to receive monthly payments from a bank for as long as they live in return for the property title after the owner passes away. Homeowners in consolidated informal settlements may reap the harvest of their efforts in building the house at the expense of their children's capacity to build up intergenerational wealth. Delving into the advantages and disadvantages of the reverse mortgage is not the point here. Instead, I insist on the importance of acknowledging informal housing and informal work as *one* activity in order to connect and expand policy options that would otherwise remain ignored.

How would such a policy look like? Reimagining urban formalization policy in a recognition continuum opens up opportunities that seemed quite distant before. Firstly, it would account for urban services provided both formally and informally and connect those with social protections offered to those that need them, as part of a single coproduced system. The groundwork for such a system has already been set forth by feminist economics. As recounted in Chapter 2, by fine-tuning time-use surveys, feminist economics of care has not only called for invisible economies (unpaid work that is undercounted and uncounted) to be accounted macroeconomically, it has also gotten into the task of correcting conceptual inaccuracies (Hirway, 2015:6). Similar to a unitary tax/benefit system, in a unitary system of urban services and social protections people would get paid for the urban services they provide to the community, and they would get paid so they can benefit themselves and also improve on the services. This is not a foreign idea in sustainable building practices, for example, where bidirectional meters measure the flow of energy consumed, as well as the one fed back into the grid. Direct payments like cash transfers are but one option in the universe of alternatives, others can include social security benefits, employment-related measures, benefits on-kind, or market incentives (Razavi, 2007:35), depending on the direction and intensity of the urban services flow.

★ ★ ★

The blueprint for this unitary system is a task beyond the present endeavor, but it is undoubtedly one that this research has illuminated. As the approach presented here matures with iteration studies, new literature, and valuable feedback, I remain decided to inquire into ways in which social protection policies can be spatialized, and housing policies come to grips with the fact that housing is not about houses.

This reflection on the intensity of residential space in informal settlements provides evidence that the pores of our living spaces are filled, not empty. It teaches us that it is important that we recognize that our cities are full, full of our—future—selves. These insights explained that our intensity is a capacity, and knowing it can enable more of us, not less. Recognizing ourselves, our neighborhoods, communities, and cities, is likely the only avenue for us to become fully ourselves.

References

Amaya, Aureliano. (2019). Personal interview, July 15, 2019, Bogota.

Berardi, Franco. (2017). *Futurability: The Age of Impotence and the Horizon of Possibility*, Verso, New York.

Beukesm, Anni. (2015). *Making the Invisible Visible Generating Data on 'Slums' at Local, City and Global Scales*, Slum Dwellers International and the International Institute for Environment and Development, London.

Bahamón, Martha. (2019). Personal interview with architect at Curaduría Urbana #4, Bogota, August 2.

Borges, Jorge Luis. (1960). El hacedor, Emecé Editores, Buenos Aires.

Cosgrove, Denis. (1999). *Mappings,* Reaktion Books, London.

Creswell, John W. (2014). *Research Design: Qualitative, Quantitative, and Mixed Methods Approaches*, 4th ed., Sage, Los Angeles, CA.

Ellerman, David. (2005). "How Do We Grow? Jane Jacobs on Diversification and Specialization", *Challenge*, 48:3, pp. 50–83.

El Tiempo. (1992a). "Forero Fetecua y Vargas Lleras serían detenidos", April 16, newspaper archive: https://www.eltiempo.com/archivo/documento/MAM-101221

El Tiempo. (1992b). "A la corte, pruebas contra Forero Fetecua", April 16, newspaper archive, April 30, 1992, https://www.eltiempo.com/archivo/documento/MAM-104516

El Tiempo. (2006). "Los políticos vetados se volvieron importantes", *Revista Portafolio*, March 24, https://www.portafolio.co/economia/finanzas/politicos-vetados-volvieron-importantes-203924

Fergusson, James. (2007). "Formalities of Poverty: Thinking about Social Assistance in Neoliberal South Africa", *African Studies Review*, 50:2, pp. 71–96.

Fraser, Nancy. (2003), "Social Justice in the Age of Identity Politics: Redistribution, Recognition, and Participation", In Fraser, N. and Honneth, A. (eds) *Redistribution or Recognition? A Political-Philosophical Exchange*, Verso, New York, pp. 7–109.

Gershuny, Jonathan, Harms, Teresa, Doherty, Aiden, Thomas, Emma, Milton, Karen, Kelly, Paul, Foster, Charlie (2017). *CAPTURE24: Testing Self-report Time-use Diaries Against Objective Instruments in Real Time*, Center for Time Use Research, University of Oxford, Oxford.

Gershuny et al. (2019). "A Short History of Time Use Research; Implications for Public Health", *BMC Public Health*, 19:607, Creative Commons.

Glaw, Xante, Inder, Kerry, Kable, Ashley, and Hazelton, Michael. (2017). "Visual Methodologies in Qualitative Research: Autophotography and Photo Elicitation Applied to Mental Health Research", *International Journal of Qualitative Methods*.

GMH – Grupo de Memoria Histórica. (2016). ¡BASTA YA! Colombia: Memorias de guerra y dignidad, General Report from the Historic Memory Group, Comisión Nacional de Reparación y Reconciliación, Imprenta Nacional, Bogota.

218   *Conclusions*

Gonzalez, Olivia and Grey, Nolan. (2020). "Zoning for Opportunity: A Survey of Home-Based-Business Regulations", Center for Growth and Opportunity, Utah State University, https://www.thecgo.org/research/zoning-for-opportunity-a-survey-of-home-based-business-regulations/

Gummerus, Johanna. (2013). "Value Creation Processes and Value Outcomes in Marketing Theory: Strangers or Siblings?" *Marketing Theory*, 13:1, pp. 19–46.

Hirway, Indira. (2015). "Unpaid Work and the Economy: Linkages and their Implications", Working Paper No. 838, Levy Economics Institute of Bard College, New York.

Iser, Mattias. (2019). "Recognition", In Zalta, Edward N. (ed) *The Stanford Encyclopedia of Philosophy*, Summer 2019 Edition. https://plato.stanford.edu/entries/recognition/

Jacobs, Jane. (2003). "Unraveling the True Nature of Economics", interview with Blake Harris, Government and Technology magazine, re-published online August 17, 2009.

Kenyon, Susan. (2008). "Internet Use and Time Use: The Importance of Multitasking", *Time & Society*, 17:2–3, pp. 283–318.

León, Diana. (2019). Personal interview with officer at Secretaria de Desarrollo Económico de Bogota, August 1.

Meagher, Kate and Lindell, Ilda. (2013). "Asr Forum-Engaging with African Informal Economies: Social Inclusion or Adverse Incorporation?" *African Studies Review*, 56:3, pp. 57–76.

Merriam-Webster. (n.d.). "Requite", "Continuous". In Merriam-Webster.com dictionary. Accessed August 22, 2020.

Miller, William. (1997). *The Anatomy of Disgust*, Harvard University Press, Cambridge, MA.

Moreno, Israel. (2008). "Patrimonio Hoy: Low-income Housing that Improves Quality of Life", *Development Outreach*, 10:2, pp. 27–29.

Morgans, Julians and Rodriguez, Laura. (2020). "Three of the World's Deadliest Serial Killers Come from the Same Place: Why?", *Vice World News*, August 20, 2020.

Ostrom, Elinor. (1996). "Crossing the Great Divide: Coproduction, Synergy, and Development", *World Development*, 24:6, pp. 1073–1087.

Ostrom, Elinor, Kanbur, Ravi, and Guha-Khasnobis, Basudeb. (2006). *Linking the Formal and Informal Economy*, Oxford University Press, Oxford

Scott, James C., Boudreaux, Donald, Delong, Bradford, and Lee, T. (2010). "Seeing Like a State, A conversation with James C. Scott", September 2010, Cato Unbound, https://www.cato-unbound.org/print-issue/487

Spivak, Gayatri Chakravorty. (1988). "Can the Subaltern Speak?" *Die Philosophin*, 14:27, pp. 42–58.

Ramirez, Ricardo. (2019). Personal interview, February 12, 2019.

Razavi, Shahra. (2007). "The Political and Social Economy of Care in a Development Context Conceptual Issues, Research Questions and Policy Options", Gender and Development Program Paper Number 3, United Nations Research Institute for Social Development, Geneva.

Rodríguez, Maria Alejandra. (2012). "El que peca y reza empata: Vida y obra del urbanizador y político Rafael Forero Fetecua", *Journalism Thesis*, Pontificia Universidad Javeriana.

Rogan, Michael. (2019). "Tax Justice and the Informal Economy: A Review of the Debates", WIEGO Working Paper #41, Manchester.

The White House. (2022). "President Biden Announces New Actions to Ease the Burden of Housing Costs", May 16, 2022, Washington, https://www.whitehouse.gov/briefing-room/statements-releases/2022/05/16/president-biden-announces-new-actions-to-ease-the-burden-of-housing-costs/

Torres, Carlos A. (2019). Personal interview, July 24, 2019.

Torres, Jorge E. (2019a). Personal interview, February 12, 2019.

Index

Note: **Bold** page numbers refer to tables; *Italic* page numbers refer to figures and page numbers followed by "n" denote footnotes.

3D cadaster 79, 119

academic knowledge 83
action research, participatory 109
advanced capitalism 30
Africa: insights on formalization 178–193; urban informality in 165–166
African cities: African insights on formalization 178–193; Agnes's house in Kampala 167–169, *167–169*; dealing with informality 187–190; formalization of horizontal property and taxation 190–192; framing informality 179–186; house interviews in Kampala, Dar es Salaam, and Dakar 166–173; housing policy and housing vocabularies 186–187; Neema's house in Dar es Salaam 169–171, *169–171*; *nyumba(ni)* and *(ma)kazi* 186–187; space-use intensity findings across 173–178; space-use intensity in 164–193; Traoré's house in Dakar 171–173, *172–173*; urban formalization in 164–193; urban informality in Africa 165–166; urban services/goods/social protections 192–193
African Network of Urban Management Institutions (ANUMI) 178
agriculture: smallholder 13; urban 89, 115, 173, 177, 189
allegoric narratives 44–45
anthropology 2–3, 9, 16
architecture 2–3; abductive visual research methods 55; allegoric narratives 44–45; democratic political 11; self-built 7; space in the theories of informality 53–62

Arden, Jacinda 53
avoiders 43

Bairoch, Paul 13–14
Baziwe, Dorothy 178, 181, 187
Black Lives Matter 4n1
Bogotá: cadaster 81, 112, 120, 134, 150, 207; politics of urban formalization in 126–158; space-use intensity in 71–121; steps of formalization policy in 147; stratification maps *88*; upgrading over costs in 135n9; visual map of urban formalization policy in *140*
Bolivar, Teolinda 62
Bollrich, Elisabeth 164, 178
Bromley, Ray 27, 38
Buckley, Robert 32, 38
Building Control Act 184
Bush, George W. 35
business formalization: economical 144–145; physical 144–145

cadaster/cadastral 77, 102, 105, 107–108, 111, 134, 152, 167, 175, 190, 199–200; 3D 79, 119; Bogotá's 81, 112, 120, 134, 150, 207; conventional 199; database 114; Non-Horizontal Property (NPH) 120, 146; online geographic information system (IDECA) 90; proactive 199; use-unit 81, 89, 115
cadastral knowledge 119–120
Callon, Michel 45, 45n6
capital 25, 36; dormant 36; financial 41; human 40–42; liquid 37; political 94, 129–130
capital goods 6

222 *Index*

capitalism 39, 209; advanced 30; national 32; and self-service economy 48
Carmen 141–143
Carré, Françoise 22, 22n2
Castells, Manuel 29, 30
causal theory 44–45
Cenaprov 137–138
Chayanov, Alexander 14, 25
Chen, Martha 22, 22n2, 23
childcare 43, 49–50, 112, 116; unpaid 50
China 128, 129
CINVA (Centro Interamericano de Vivienda) 126, 127, 128, 141
Cities and the Wealth of Nations (Jacobs) 73, 73n2
code-based planning 132–136, 141, 152–153
Colombia: armed internal conflict 210n4; National Planning Department (DNP) 128n3; rise and fall of the housing movement in 137–138
Colombian Constitutional Court 127, 155
Colombian Law 1753 of 2015 106n9
Colombian National Association of Recyclers 155
commercial development 188
community groups 34
Comprehensive Employment Mission 11–13
"The Concept of Progressive Development" (Eyheralde) 128
conceptual maps 198–206
Condominium Property Act 184
consolidated informal settlement, Bogotá, Colombia 7, 82, 85–86, 101, 108–109, 116, 143, 145, 151, 166–167, 170, 175–178, 192, 197, 216
continuum 44–48, 214, 215; evidence and methods 46–47; formal-informal 202–203; informality and causal theory 44–45; limitations and critiques 47–48; policy options and interventions 45–46; recognition 197–217
co-production of urban services/goods/social protections 192–193
Cosgrove, Denis 204
cosmetic upgrading 153–154
counterproductive formalizations 45
COVID-19 pandemic 3–5, 4n1, 32n4, 165–166, 199n1, 207; *see also* pandemic
cross-sectional diagrams 89, *90*
culture: of entrepreneurialism 39; indigenous 213; of poverty 39

Currie, Lauchlin 128
Currie, Leonard 128n3

Dakar 171–173, *172–173*
Dar es Salaam 169–171, *169–171*
data analysis procedures 87–92
data collection tools: cadastre data look up 90; cross-sectional diagrams 89, *90*; day-after fieldnotes 88–89; detailed reading of photographs 90, *91*; emerging categories summary table 91–92, **92**; notebook jottings 88, *89*; photographs 88; second column reflections on fieldnotes 90; visual record of each house interview 90–91, *92*
data excavation: from conceptual maps 198–206; defined 199; from photographs 198–206
data extraction 199–201
Davidoff, Paul 127
day-after fieldnotes 88–89
The Death and Life of Great American Cities (Jacobs) 71, 73, 73n2
Delhi Group on Informal Sector Statistics 11, 16–21
Demiurge (deity) 143n12
demiurges 141–143
de-politicization of formalization policy 137–148
depth and intensity 116, 118–119
deregularization 15, 30, 32–33
development 3, 7, 9, 16, 23, 25, 27, 33, 37, 48, 143; commercial 188; economic 32n4, 181, 203; neoliberal 34; physical 147; progressive 93, 121, 127, 128, 132, 135, 207, 214; state-led 27; statistical 18; transit-oriented 74; urban 3, 6, 126–127, 139, 146, 152, 164, 177, 187, 192, 215
developmentalism 30; dualist 30; South-bound 47
development economics 9, 25, 43
diagrams, and house-stories 93–112
discrete 215; and continuous 214; events 50; intensity as count of discrete uses 112–119, *117*; mixed-use data 80; policies 201
discreteness 112–121
diversity 72–73, 82, 189; agglomerations of 206; land-use patterns of 76; mysterious vitality of 206; uses of 98, 102, 115–116
Doing Business (DB) indicator 37

dormant capital 36
Dovey, Kim 77, 78
dualism 25–29; colonializing 39n5; in development economics 25; evidence and methods 26–27; informality and causal theory 25–26; informality and poverty 25–26; judgmental 47; in labor markets 25; limitations and critiques 27–29; Lipton on 28; misplaced 28; policy options and interventions 27; relation formal-informal 26; standard 29; and trialism 180
dualist developmentalism 30
dualist policies 27
dualist predictions 32
dualists 32–33, 41–42
dualist school of thought 23–27, 43
Duarte, Janeth 154

economic 3, 9, 15, 25, 37, 148, 208; development 32n4, 181, 203; globalization 30, 138; growth 15, 27, 32, 73; home-based informal 32; intensity 8; resources 83
economists: classical 25; feminist 3; structuralist 32–33; urban development 191
economy 10, 26; formal 26, 30, 42, 43, 45, 46; informal 21, 23, 26, 30, 33, 36, 43, 44, 46, 48; modernization of 27
The Economy of Cities (Jacobs) 73
Ellerman, David 201
employment 6, 10, 18, 20, 21, 25, 41; formal 17; informal 16, 17, 18, 20, 21, 22, 41; intermittent 25; self 42
entrepreneurialism 100; culture of 39; naturalized 13; red-tape deterrents to 37
Escobar, Pablo 130n6
ethnicity 84
evaders 43
Exit and Exclusion 40
extraction 197–217

false recognition 153–154
feminist 157; economics 7, 49, 51; economists 3
fieldnotes: day-after 88–89; second column reflections on 90
financial capital 41
fiscal legibility and formalization 148–149
Floyd, George 4n1

Food and Agricultural Organization (FAO) 42
Forero Fetecua, Rafael 94, 129–130, 130n6, 131, *131*, 132, 210–211
formal 129, 132, 214; economy 24, 30, 42, 43, 45, 46; employees 20; -informal continuum 202–203; sector 20, 25, 30, 40, 43; settlements 179
formal-informal distinction 25
formality 20, 40; inclusive 180; and informality 36, 179–180; and micro-firms 41; problem as 180–181; urban 18; and voluntarism 40; and voluntarists 43
formalization(s) 148–153; actual purpose of 148–153; and code-based planning 152–153; counterproductive 45; creating fiscal legibility 148–149; of horizontal property 190–192; and informalization 191, 215; and integration 212–217; naturalizations and disincentives 149–151; practical outcomes of recognition 148–153; recognition continuum 212–216; as recognition continuum 212–217; residential to social mobility 151–152; stratification 149–151; subdivision 151–152; technical mechanics of 138–139, 141
formalization policy 138, 139; business formalization 144–145; carmen and demiurge 141–143; de-politicization and technification of 137–148; housing movement in Colombia 137–138; steps of, in Bogotá 147–148; subdivision 145–146; technical mechanics of formalization 138–139, 141
Friedman, Milton 35
Friedrich-Ebert-Stiftung (FES) 164
fundamental patrimony 6, 192

Gadamer, Hans Georg 2
gender 80, 83–84; inequality 49; thematizing 84
gender studies 44
Gershuny, J. I. 49–50
ghosts 43
Gilbert, Alan 29
globalization 34; and class-based clash 34; economic 30, 138
Global South 1
global value chains 32
Goldin, Claudia 32n4
Gold Museum 56

224 Index

goods: capital 6; people's co-production of 192–193
Google Street Maps 88
government regulations 36
Granovetter, Mark 45n6
granularity 72, 81–82, 100, 102, 112, 114–118, 119, 173–175, 177
granular knowledge 119–120
Gross Domestic Product (GDP) 17, 32, 52–53, 73, 138, 165
Guerrero Estrada, Alfredo 129

Habermas, Jurgen 2
Hart, Keith 2, 10, 16, 25, 26
Hayek, Friedrich 35
Hirschman, Albert 40
home-based enterprises 4, 27, 102–105, *103, 104, 105*
home-based firms 145
home-based informal economies 32n4
home-based workers 42, 165
homes at work: meaning of 5–6
Home-Work Convention of 1996 46
homogeneity 76, 133
horizontal mixed-use 75, *79*, 79–80
horizontal mixed-use zoning 79
horizontal property 190–192
household economics 48–50
house-stories 93–112
housing 5, 38, 43, 48, 57, 60, 72, 84, 85, 126, 136, 137, 138, 151, 166, 178, 211; acquisition for low-income ownership 86; adequate 148; affordable 151, 152; commercial 187; construction of low-income 127; defined 190; healthy 38; inadequate 23; informal 22, 48, 58, 59, 93, 120, 129, 151, 157, 165, 192, 216; low-income 127; low-rise 128; market 146; movement 137, 138, 210; national 137; network 143; policy 152, 182, 185, 186–187, 188, 216; public 27, 106, 138, 202; rental 81, 208; self-built 165; self-help 58, 94, 128, 129; social 27, 61, 106, 108, 130; specialist 56; state-led 182; stock 186; subsidies 106, 138; traditional 187; typologies 180
housing movement: in Colombia 137–138; and Organizaciones Populares de Vivienda (OPV) 137; and Political Constitution of 1991 138; unitary 137
housing vocabularies 186–187
human capital 40–42
Hussmanns, Ralf 18, 20, 46

If Women Counted: A New Feminist Economics (Waring) 51
imposed disability 209–212
"inadequate housing" 23n3
inclusive formality 180
informal 2, 11, 20, 129, 132, 214; buildings 126, 151; businesses 126; economy 21, 23, 26, 30, 33, 36, 43, 44, 46, 48; employment 16, 17, 18, 20, 21, 22, 41; food sector 42; housing 93, 192; neighborhoods 209; phenomena 126; property 148; recyclers 156; settlements 23, 126, 133, 136, 148, 151–152, 154, 155, 166, 213; workers 156
The Informal Economy Revisited 22n2
informality: alternative thinking on urban *206*; competing with 132; conceptual map of ILO's statistical definitions on *21*; continuum 44–48; dealing with 187–190; definition of 44–45; dualism 24–29; and formality 36, 179–180; framing 179–186; as "immense majority" 58; and International Labor Organization 10–23; Kenya Mission report on 12; legalism 34–39; majoritarian 43; market approaches solving 37–38; "Measuring Informality" 16; mixed with formality 179–180; place of space in theories of 53–62; rural 14; schools of thought on 23–48, *24, 48, 205*; structuralism 29–34; urban 1–3, 7, 18, 54, 58; voluntarism 39–44; when problem is not informality but formality 180–181; worldly plans and unspoken centrality of 128–129
informalization: cycles 139; and deregularization 15, 32; and formalization 191, 215; in industrialized countries 30; "informalization from above" 34; of labor 1; in the North 30; re-informalization 181
insiders 43
Institute for Liberty Democracy (ILD) 34
Institute of Human Settlements Studies (IHSS) 178
integration: and formalization 212–216; full 147; professed by formalization policy 148; vertical 34
intensity: abling 197–217; as the count of discrete uses 112, 114–116, 118–119;

economic 8; of landuses 120; of mixed-use 144; as the opposite of porosity 120–121; or depth 116, 118–119; space-use intensity 3, 7–8, 71–121, 164–193; time-use intensity 50–51; urban land-use intensity 71

International Conference of Labour Statisticians (ICLS) 16

international development organizations 10

international donor agencies 38

International Finance Corporation (IFC) 37

International Labour Organization (ILO) 9–12, 14, 16, 22, 27, 41, 46; created in 10; ILO Medium Term Plan 14; and informal economy 10–11, 27; and informal employment 17, 46, 165; and Kenya Mission 12; WIEGO network 22; *Women and Men in the Informal Economy: A statistical picture* report 22; and World Employment Program on Urban Unemployment 13–15

international organizations 9, 11

International Standard Industrial Classification of all Economic Activities 81

interviewee 50, 84, 91, 175, 178n1

interviews 84, 178; audio recordings of 88; house 82, 198; informal semi-structured 87; residents 82, 198

Jacobs, Jane 71, 72, 74, 77, 81, 201, 206

judgmental dualism 47

Juntas de Acción Comunal 130

Kamawala, Antidy 165

Kampala 167–169, *167–169*

Kampala Capital City Authority (KCCA) 183

Kapinga, Imma 165

(ma)kazi 186–187

Kenya: Comprehensive Employment Mission 11–13; employment problem 13; future wealth 13

Kenya Mission 11–12, 15, 21; *see also* Comprehensive Employment Mission

Keynes, J. M. 52

Khayangayanga, Dave 178, 183

Kiggundu, Amin Tamale 178, 181, 182, 184, 185, 188

Kikuwi, Gaston 181, 184, 189

Kisembo, Teddy 165

knowledge 4; academic 83; analytic 120; cadastral 119–120; granular 119–120; professional/technical 184; self-knowledge 156–157; surfacing 18; traditional 183; values 83

Komu, Felician 178, 191

Koolhaas, Rem 53, 54, 55, 56

Lagos: architecture 53–56; Lagos Charter 54; order in a Lagos informal market *54*; space in theories of informality 53–56

land: encroachment 109; formalization 139; invasions 95, 137; land-use mix measures 76, *76*; land-use mixture 76; land-use noncompliance 145; prices 38; public 94; social function of 152; as urban factor of production 6; -use classification by activity areas *142*; -use patterns 76

Latin American Housing Network 85, 143

Le Corbusier 56, 59, 128

Le Corbusier Museum 56

Lefebvre, Henri 4

legalism 34–39; evidence and methods 36–37; informality and causal theory 34–36; limitations and critiques 38–39; policy options and interventions 37–38; relation formal-informal 36

legalists 23, 36–38

legal pluralism 39n5

Limbumba, Tatu M. 178, 187, 191

Linking the Formal and the Informal Economy (Ostrom) 45

Lipton, M. 28

liquid capital 37

Lubell, H. 14

macroeconomics 3, 27, 30, 36

Maloney, W. F. 40, 43

maps/mapping 12, 20, *21*, 26, 43; Bogotá's stratification *88*; color-less 141; conceptual 198–206; of formalization paths for different settlements *133, 202, 203*; gymnastics 77–79; land-use 175; readability of 78–79; schematic 57; upgrading as a type of urban treatments 133, *134*; visual map of urban formalization policy in Bogotá *140, 204*

marginality 3

Martinez, Yolanda 58

226   *Index*

Mbembe, Achille 55
"Measuring Informality" manual 16
methodologies 3, 16, 26
Michelsen, Lopez *131, 132*
Migrant Workers Convention of 1975 46
Miller, G. A. 75
Miller, William 154n15
The *Minimum Rules (Normas Mínimas)*
   59–60, 132, 214
miserabilist vision of informal sector 15
misplaced dualism 28
misplaced isolation 28
Mitchell, Timothy 39
mixed-use: and Bogotá's land-use plan
   199; coding system 144; districts 72;
   horizontal 75, *79,* 79–80; intensity
   71; Jacobs' 71–74; mix-ups 74–75;
   and pandemic 199n1; praise and
   critiques of 74–75; range of 81; range
   or diversity of uses 115–116; and rising
   property values 75; streets 72; "time
   spread" 81–82; vertical 75, *79,* 79–80
mixtures 75, 179–180
modernization 15, 27
Modifiable Areal Unit Problem (MAUP)
   76
Moser, Caroline 12, 29, 33
Moses, Robert 72
Mosquera, Gilma 137
multinational corporations 34
Multinational Time-Use Survey (MTUS)
   49–50
multitasking 118, 200n2; negative 49;
   positive 49; spatial 51, 200n2; temporal
   200n2; time-use research 49–50, 80;
   time-use surveying techniques *50–52,*
   50–53
municipal governments 166, 178, 192
The Mystery of Capital (de Soto) 34, 36

Namuli, Hafisa 165
Namuwongo slum upgrading project
   (Kampala) 180
Nandudu, Sarah 179, 181, 184, 190
Naranjo, Maria Elvira 137
narratives, and house-stories 93–112
national capitalism 32
National Identification System 188
National University of Colombia 127
naturalized entrepreneurialism 13
The Nature of Economies (Jacob) 73
Navarrete, Jesus 27, 42
Ndiaye, Amadou 165
negative multitasking 49

neoliberal development 34
Newman, Oscar 72–73
New York zoning 89
Nixon, Richard 35
non-governmental organizations (NGOs)
   16, 34, 38, 83, 135, 185
Non-Horizontal Property (NPH) 120,
   145
non-standard work 17
North America 132
notebook jottings 88, *89*
Nyiti, Albert 178
nyumba(ni) 186–187

old-age security 6, 192
Oram, Nigel 128n2
Organizaciones Populares de Vivienda
   (OPV) 137, 138, 143
Organization of American States (OAS)
   127
Ostrom, Elinor 28, 45, 46, 47, 209
The Other Path (de Soto) 34
outsiders 43

Pafka, Elek 77
pandemic 3–5, 32n4, 165–166, 199n1,
   207; *see also* COVID-19 pandemic
paradox of intensification 74
Parra, Federico 155n16
participatory action research 109
Participatory Action Research framework
   127
pension 6, 41, 43, 107, 118, 131, 151, 192,
   216
Perry, G. 43
The *Phenomenology of the Spirit* (Hegel)
   156–157
photographs: as data collection tools 88;
   data excavation from 198–206; detailed
   reading of 90, *91*
physical development 147
plan-based planning: competing with
   informality 132–133; second-level
   zoning 133–136; upgrading 136; urban
   treatments 133–136
planning 3; anti-planning 184; blindness
   184–185; code-based 132–136, 141,
   152–153; ethnography land-use 184;
   inclusive 184; modern 72; partnership-
   based 152; spatial 128; transportation
   49; urban (*see* urban planning)
Plato 143n12
Polanyi, Karl 45, 45n6
political capital 94, 129–130

Popular Integration Movement (Movimiento de Integración Popular) 131
porosity 120–121, 197–217; and intensity 120–121; and value creation 206–209
Porras, Mariano 94, 129
positive multitasking 49
POT (Planes de Ordenamiento Territorial) 136
poverty 26, 37, 47; culture of 39
pre-industrial economy 5
private entrepreneurs 38
professional/technical knowledge 184
progressive development 93, 121, 127, 128, 132, 135, 207, 214
psychoanalysis 2
public health 4, 49, 74
public housing 27, 106, 138, 202
public policy 136, 210

qualitative methodological approach 206

race 83–84
recognition 197–217; cosmetic upgrading and false 153–154; formalization 212–216; philosophy of 156–158; policies designed as 215; practical outcomes of 148–153; real 206; remuneration and redistribution 154–156; true recognition 154–156; two-sidedness of 215; and urban formalization 216
recycling 81, 89, 115, 154, 155n16, 155, 165, *172*, 173, 176–177, 197–198, 209
redistribution 45n6, 154–156
remuneration 154–156
rentier capitalists 39, 151
research 6, 153, 201, 206; action 109; qualitative methods 198; quantitative methods 198; space-use 80; time-use 49–50, 80; visual 6, 198–206
residential mobility 151–152
re-zoning 188
rhizomes 44
Rodríguez, Daniel A. 76
Rodríguez Orejuela, Gilberto 130n6
Romer, Paul 37
Roosevelt, Franklin D. 128n3
Roy, Ananya 34

Samper, German 56–61
Sassen, Saskia 4, 5, 29, 30
Scott, James C. 74, 200
second-level zoning 133–136
Seeing Like a State (Scott) 74

self-built architecture 7
self-employment 42, 53
self-fulfilling prophecy 13
self-knowledge 156–157
self-service economy 48
Sepúlveda, Saturnino 129
Sert, Jose Luis 128
severance 6, 43, 192
Severe Acute Respiratory Syndrome (SARS-CoV-2) 4n1; *see also* COVID-19 pandemic
sites and services programs 7, 84, 86, 93, 116, 127, 133, 141, 182
slums 23, 23n3, 29, 137, 15, 154, 165, 183, 188; upgrading 127, 137–138
smallholder agriculture 13
small-scale enterprises 29
social mobility 151–152
social protection 4, 6–7, 31, 33, 40, 121, 151–152, 166, 178, 197, 208, 212; and informal housing arrangements 192; packages 42; people's co-production of 192–193; policies 27, 152
Social Protection Minimum Standards Convention of 1952 46
social security programs 43
Song, Yan 76
de Soto, Hernando 34, 36–39, 46, 143
South Africa 32
South/Southern 8, 48, 56, 57, 128; -bound developmentalism 47; formalization 126–132; ideas 57; John Turner 127–128; knowledge-production 179; pirate urbanizers as champions of gray 129–132; realities 56; self-help 127–128; shelved worldly plans 128–129; students 56; unspoken centrality of informality 128–129; urbanism 56; urban planning 185
space 53–62; learning from lagos 53–56; Samper's doctrine 56–62; standardization for desegregation 56–62; in the theories of informality 53–62; wealth of the poor 56–62
space theory 72
space-use intensity 3, 7–8, 71–121, 164–193; in African cities 164–193; African insights on formalization 178–179; cadastral knowledge 119–120; components of 81–82; co-production of urban services/goods/social protections 192–193; cross-sectional diagrams 88; data analysis procedures 87–92; data collection tools

87–92; day-after fieldnotes 88–89; dealing with informality 187–188; defining 71–82; detailed reading of photographs 90; discreteness and non-porousness 112; documenting 82–112; findings across African cities 173, 175–178; five house-stories 93–112; formalization of horizontal property 190–192; framing informality 179–186; granularity 112, 114–115; horizontal and vertical mixed-use 79–80; intensity as count of discrete uses 112, 114–116, 118–119; intensity as opposite of porosity 120–121; intensity or depth 116, 118–119; Jacobs' mixed-use 71–74; mapping gymnastics 77–79; mixed-use mix-ups 74–80; notebook jottings 88; origin of 80–81; photographs 88; range or diversity of uses 115–116; second column reflections on fieldnotes 90; unit of analysis and boundary problems 76; urban informality in Africa 165–166; visual record of house interviews 90–91

space-use research 80

spatial multitasking 51, 200n2

standard dualism 29

state-led development 27

Statistical Commission of United Nations Statistics Division (UNSD) 16

statistical developments 18

statistics: informal sector 16–21; labor 16; labor surveys or employment 32; of space-use intensity variables **114**; traditional housing 187

structuralism 29–34; definition of informality and causal theory 29–31; evidence and methods 32–33; limitations and critiques 33–34; policy options and interventions 33; relation formal-informal 31–32

structuralists 23, 29, 30, 32–34, 47

subsidies: governmental 106n9; housing 106, 138; "subsidies to the demand" 106, 138; utility 151

surfacing knowledge 18

survey/surveying 49–53, *50–52*

Sustainable Development Goals 23, 46

Tanzania 180, 192

tax/taxation 187, 190–192

technical mechanics of formalization 138–139, 141

technification of formalization policy 137–148

temporal multitasking 200n2

Thatcher, Margaret 35

Theory of the Peasant Economy (Chayanov) 14

Third World 30, 38–39

Timaeus (Plato) 143n12

time spread, and mixed-use 81–82

time-use 48–53; and household economics 48–50; intensity 50–51; research 49–50, 80; surveying techniques *50–52,* 50–53

titling 36–38, 141, 147, 148

transit-oriented development 74

trialism 180

true recognition 154–156

Tufte, Edward 3

Turner, John 62, 127, 128

Ugandan Bureau of Statistics 183

unemployment 6, 151; disguised 25; urban 14

UN Habitat 23n3

Unión Patriótica (UP) 137

United Nations (UN) 11, 22, 23, 46; System of National Accounts (SNA) 16

United Nations Development Program (UNDP) 12

United Nations Human Settlements Program 22

United Nations System of National Accounts (UNSNA) 52–53

Universal Declaration of Human Rights 46

unpaid childcare 50

upgrading: defined 139; formalization policy in Bogotá 147–148; HabitArte upgrading program in Usaquén *153*; informal settlements 127n1; as leaky bucket 136; mapping *134*; physical 180–188; policies 7, 74, 127; slum 127, 137–138; structural 143; upgrading over costs in Bogotá 135n9

urban: histology 57; informality 1–2, 18, 54, 58; informal sector 14; mixtures 75; planning 129; qualities 134; services 137, 192–193; unemployment 13, 14; volumetric 143

urban agriculture 89, 115, 173, 177, 189

urban development 3, 6, 126–127, 139, 146, 152, 164, 177, 187, 192, 215

urban formality 18

urban formalization 164–193; in African cities 164–193; African insights on formalization 178–179; dealing with informality 187–190; formalization of horizontal property 190–192; framing informality 179–186; and recognition continuum 216; space-use intensity 173, 175–178; urban informality 165–166; urban services/goods/social protections 192–193

urban formalization in Bogotá 126–158; actual purpose 148–153; code-based planning 132–136; de-politicization of formalization policy 137–148; origins in the South 126–132; plan-based planning 132–136; practical outcomes of recognition 148–153; recognition 153–158; technification of formalization policy 137–148

urban informality 9–62; in Africa 165–166; Comprehensive Employment Mission 11–13; Delhi Group on Informal sector statistics 16–22; evidence and methods 26–27; informality and causal theory 25–26; and International Labor Organization 10–11; limitations and critiques 27–29; mainstream theories and visible alternatives 9–62; policy options and interventions 27; relation formal-informal 26; schools of thought on informality 23–24; women/men in informal economy 22–23; World Employment Program 13–16

urbanization 1, 15, 38; formal 59; formal but unplanned 179; incomplete 132; informal 57–58, 94; legal 120; Patio Bonito 95; progressive 58–59

urban land-use intensity 71

urban planning 34, 43, 71–72, 74–76, 132, 185–188, 192; mixed-use in 76; modernist 71; Southern 185; strategic 120

urban redevelopment 146

urban treatments 202, 203

use-unit, cadaster 81, 89, 112, 114–115

Vanek, Joan 22, 49
vertical mixed-use 75, 79, 79–80
vertical mixed-use zoning 79
Vikundi vya Biashara Ndogo (VIBINDO) Association 189

violence 126, 210, 211; covert 211; deadly tide of 53; discussion on 209; epistemic 212; inflicting 211; physical 209; of remaining stratified and unrequited 209–212; veiled 211

visualization 18, 20, 21, 112, 139, 202; capabilities 79; conceptual 201; formalization 205

visual research 198–206; conceptual maps, data excavation from 198–206; photographs, data excavation from 198–206

voice and exit theory 40

voluntarism 39–44; evidence and methods 41–42; informality and causal theory 39–40; limitations and critiques 43–44; policy options and interventions 42–43; relation formal-informal 40–41

voluntarist 23, 43

Waring, Marylin 51, 52
waste management 154
The Wealth of Nations (Smith) 49
WhatsApp messages 90
Why Planning Does Not Work (Nnkya) 184
WIEGO (Women in Informal Employment: Globalizing and Organizing) network 22, 23
Wiener, Paul Lester 128
Women and Men in the Informal Economy: A statistical picture report 17, 22
work at home 5
Worker's Bank (Banco de los Trabajadores) 130n6
working homes 3–5
World Bank 37, 41, 143, 152, 153, 169, 183
world economy 30, 32
World Employment Program 11, 13, 14, 15
World Employment Program on Urban Unemployment 13–15
World Health Organization 4
World War I 10
World War II 128n3

zoning: CIAM monofunctional zoning principles 144; horizontal mixed-use 79; New York 89; regulations 74, 78; re-zoning 188; second-level 133–136; vertical mixed-use 79